THE A-Z MEDICAL HANDBOOK

THE A-Z

MEDICAL HANDBOOK

YOUR GUIDE TO DIAGNOSES AND TREATMENTS

FROM ACNE TO INFLUENZA, MIGRAINE TO WHOOPING COUGH

BLITZ EDITIONS

Published in this edition 1992 by Blitz Editions
an imprint of Bookmart Ltd
Registered Number 2372865
Trading as Bookmart Limited
Desford Road, Enderby, Leicester LE9 5AD

Reprinted 1993

Printed in the Slovak Republic
50 946/02

ISBN I-85605-086-6

The material in the A-Z Medical Handbook has already appeared in partwork form as The Encyclopedia of Health.

Dr Steve Carroll, consultant on this book, obtained his medical qualifications at King's College Hospital, London. He retired from full-time general practice six years ago to become a medical journalist and writer. Dr Carroll has written many articles in both lay and medical publications, and his first book on health and fitness was published in February 1992.

a

ACNE

Acne is a common skin complaint in which spots, blackheads and pimples appear on the face, neck and body. It is most common in the teenage years, with over 50 per cent of teenagers suffering from it at some time.

CAUSES: At the root of the problem are the sebaceous glands, which secrete an oily fluid known as sebum. During adolescence, the hormonal changes taking place stimulate these glands into producing greater quantities of sebum than before, so making the skin greasier. The problems start if the exit to the gland (in the hair follicle) becomes blocked. The sebum begins to 'back-up' in the gland, causing it to swell slightly, and this 'plug' at the exit may turn black on contact with the air, so causing a blackhead. This isn't due to dirt but to a chemical process known as oxidation. If bacteria and sebum are trapped inside the gland by the plug, the tissues become inflamed and form a pimple.

TREATMENT: Always see your doctor if you have bad acne, particularly if it seems to be developing into painful boils or abscesses. The doctor may prescribe antibiotics. Adolescents usually grow out of acne without any further complications or any long-term scarring. Spots that turn into boils or abscesses can leave scars. Sometimes the skin looks pitted, at other times a 'bridge' of puckered or furrowed skin develops over a sunken scar. Cosmetic surgery may help, but this will have to wait until after you have 'grown out' of the acne. Severe cases may be treated with a drug derived from vitamin A.

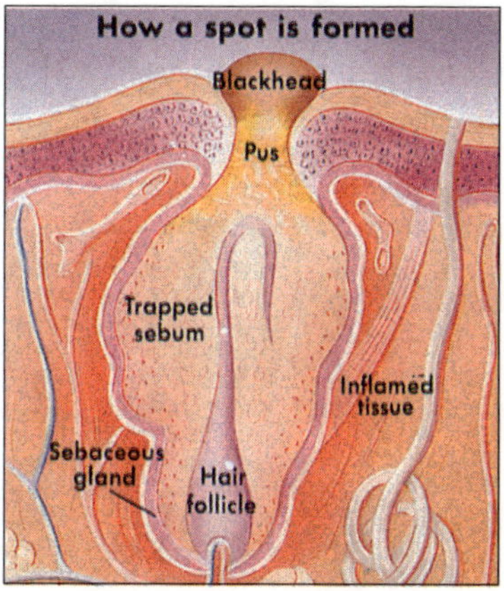

ADDICTION

see ALCOHOLISM, DRUG ADDICTION

ADDISON'S DISEASE

Addison's disease causes a decrease in the production of steroid hormones by the adrenal glands. The lack of hydrocortisone causes an abnormally low energy level. It is a rare disease, affecting mainly people between the ages of 30 and 50. In extreme cases, and if the disease is not treated, you run the risk of developing acute adrenal failure.

CAUSES: Addison's disease is caused when the body's immune system attacks its own tissues – in this case the adrenal glands.

SYMPTOMS AND SIGNS: The onset of symptoms is gradual and includes weight loss, poor appetite, fatigue, weakness and anaemia. You may also sufffer from digestive troubles, with diarrhoea or constipation, nausea or vomiting. Your skin may appear to be permanently suntanned.

TREATMENT: You will be prescribed hydrocortisone tablets. If you suffer from any illness or infection, your doctor may want to increase your dose of hydrocortisone.

ADENOIDS

Adenoids are fleshy pieces of tissue just above the opening from the back of the nose into the back of the throat. They are part of the body's defence system, helping to prevent germs from the nose reaching the throat.

CAUSES: When children have a lot of catarrh, their adenoids often become enlarged. It used to be thought that enlarged adenoids were the cause of the constantly

Self **Help**

ACNE

- Wash regularly with soap and water, drying vigorously each time.
- Try a special 'oily skin' cleansing cream and allow it to be wiped away, but always rinse afterwards.
- Wash greasy hair frequently and keep it off the face.
- Change towels and pillowcases frequently to prevent acne spreading.
- If you feel you must squeeze your spots, use a special comedone (blackhead) extractor and confine your attention to blackheads and whiteheads that are not inflamed. Once you have squeezed, leave well alone and don't use an antiseptic cream; the skin will heal better on its own.
- Try one of the special skin 'peeling' products, containing either benzoylperoxide, sulphur, resorcinol, salicylic acid or phenol. You may feel a mildly burning sensation on first application and a moderate reddening and peeling of the skin over the next few days. Don't apply too vigorously or too often.

Self Help

ADENOIDS

It is important to try to find out what the child is allergic to, and, if possible, to remove it, or to give medicines or special nose sprays to quieten the allergic response.

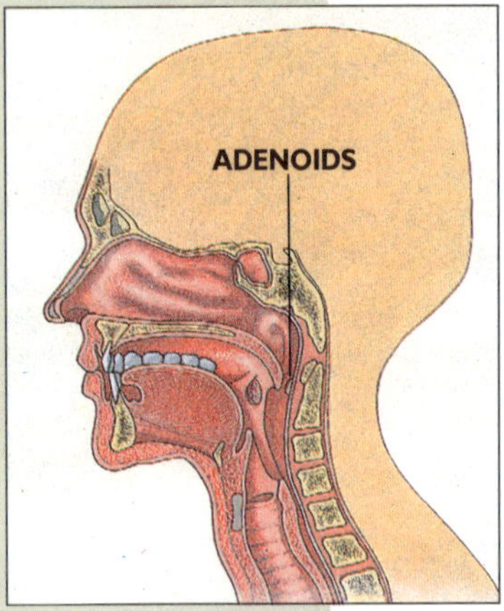

Useful Addresses

AIDS

The Terrence Higgins Trust
52-54 Gray's Inn Road
London
WC1X 8JU
Tel: 071 831 0330

Helpline: 071 242 1010

National AIDS Helpline
0800 567123
(free calls from anywhere in mainland Britain, 24 hours a day)

blocked nose that many children between the ages of three and eight seem to have, but it now seems far more likely that enlarged adenoids are the result of the catarrh, and not the cause of it. Most children previously referred to as 'adenoidal' are more likely to be diagnosed as suffering from a nasal allergy.

Symptoms and signs: Symptoms of swollen adenoids include hearing difficulties, loss of smell, taste and appetite, and dry gums. The affected child also tends to be listless.

Treatment: Nowadays adenoids are rarely removed simply because of nasal catarrh, and even if they are, they may re-grow again in a few months. Occasionally, however, enlargement of the adenoids interferes with the passage of air up the Eustachian tube into the middle ear. If a child has recurrent problems with deafness caused by mucus collecting in the ear, the adenoids may have to be removed. This is probably now the main reason for removing a child's adenoids. By the time the child is seven or eight, his/her catarrh will probably have disappeared altogether.

See also CATARRH.

AIDS

AIDS stands for Acquired Immune Deficiency Syndrome. 'Acquired' refers to any condition that is not present at birth. 'Immune Deficiency' means that the body's immune system, which fights off illnesses, is not working efficiently. And 'syndrome' refers to the fact that it includes a range, or group, of symptoms and signs. This immune deficiency is a late consequence of infection by the Human Immunodeficiency Virus (HIV). The great majority of people known to be infected with

ASK THE DOCTOR

Q Does everyone who has HIV infection go on to develop AIDS?

A Yes. Some drugs, such as AZT may be helpful for some HIV+ people in slowing down the onset of AIDS but, at the moment, there is no cure. Because more people are being tested for HIV earlier, the average length of time between a positive test result and people developing AIDS is increasing.

Q Is the AIDS epidemic increasing in the UK?

A Yes. The scale of the AIDS epidemic is daunting and it is increasing in the UK, though the exact size of the problem in five or ten years' time has not been estimated with confidence.

Q I'm thinking of having an HIV test. If the result is positive, whom do I have to tell?

A You don't have to tell anyone. Before you have a test, you should consider many factors. Some employers and insurers discriminate against people with HIV or AIDS. A test at a GU (genito-urinary) clinic means confidentiality is legally guaranteed. If you do tell your GP, the fact that you've had the test will be noted on your medical records and if you consent to your doctor giving a medical report on you, your doctor will be able to disclose information that would otherwise be confidential. Whether you tell your lover or not about your test or result is a personal decision. Safer sex (using condoms or alternatives to unprotected penetrative sex) is always an option, whether HIV+ or not.

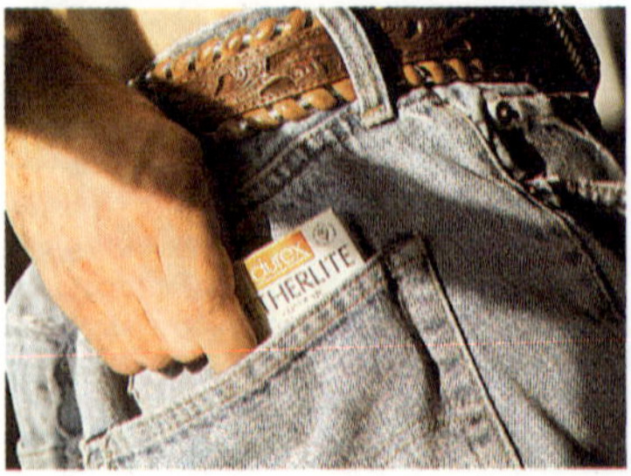

Using condoms can give some protection against contracting HIV.

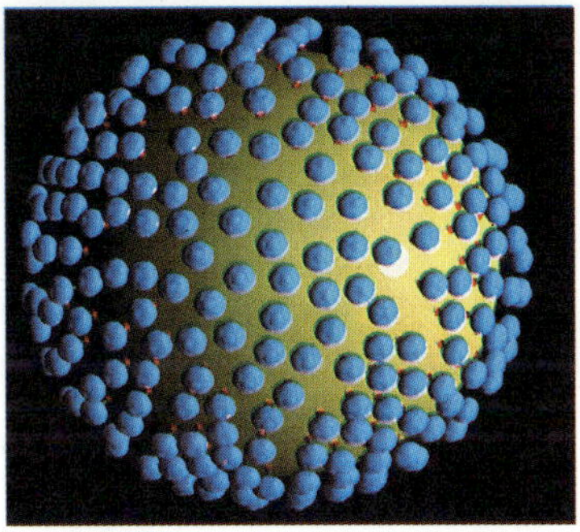

Computer graphic representation of the external structure of the AIDS virus.

HIV in the UK are homosexual and bisexual men, who have contracted the virus through homosexual intercourse, and haemophiliacs, who were infected before 1985, when the contamination of donated blood was controlled. However, this trend is changing. Injecting drug users and heterosexual men and women now represent an increasing percentage of those with HIV infection.

Causes: High-risk activities that are able to transmit HIV from one person to another include sexual contact – especially unprotected vaginal and anal intercourse – and shared use of needles and syringes. HIV is not transmitted by insect bites, nor through kissing, coughing, sneezing, or sharing a toilet.

Symptoms and signs: There are many 'opportunistic' infections and two types of cancer that may be caused by AIDS. Because of the number of different ways in which AIDS can manifest itself, symptoms and signs are varied and numerous. They include fevers, sweats, an irritating cough, diarrhoea, herpes infections, shingles, and dry itchy skin.

Treatment: People with AIDS or HIV infection can expect progress in the therapy available, but it is not yet possible to expect any treatment to eliminate HIV from the body and anti-viral therapies may have to be taken for long periods.

ALCOHOLISM

Alcoholism is excessive and compulsive drinking resulting in physical dependency on (addiction to) alcohol. It is a chronic disease. Many people can drink alcohol without becoming addicted to it but alcoholics reach a point where they cannot stop drinking of their own free will. Alcoholism is alarmingly common – up to 10 per cent of the population is likely to suffer from it to some degree. How much someone has to drink before they have an alcohol-related problem depends on many factors, including his/her sex, size and emotional well-being. The recommended safe level of alcohol consumption is 14 units per week for women and 21 units per week for men. A unit is half a pint of normal strength beer or lager, or a standard pub measure of spirits, wine or sherry.

Causes: Addiction can result from purely social drinking or from abuse of alcohol to cope with the stresses of life. There is no evidence to prove that there is a particular type of person who is likely to become 'hooked' on booze. It can happen to anyone, in any social class or walk of life.

Symptoms and signs: At first, drinking will be no more than a very strong habit. Gradually the amount of alcohol needed to produce the desired effect increases and the drinker feels unable to live daily life without it and s/he may consume dangerous amounts of alcohol without seeming drunk. Alcoholics frequently lie to themselves and to other people, even hiding bottles, in order to deny addiction. Violent outbursts, especially towards partners and families, alternating with deep remorse, can be common.

If alcohol is not available, the alcoholic suffers withdrawal symptoms and feels ill. Nausea and delirium tremens (DTs) – tremors and hallucinations – can follow. The alcoholic thinks that only another drink can alleviate the symptoms. Alcoholism seriously damages the body. Among the complaints it causes are: brain damage, cirrhosis of the liver, stomach irritation, nausea, vomiting and pain, anaemia and general weakness due to a multiple vitamin deficiency.

Treatment: The most important steps in the treatment of alcoholism are for the alco-

ASK THE DOCTOR

ALCOHOLISM

Q I used to be an alcoholic but I haven't had a drink for 10 years. Does this mean I can have the occasional alcoholic drink again?

A Unfortunately not. The only way you can be sure to stay out of danger is never to drink alcohol again.

Useful Addresses

ALCOHOLISM

Accept
724 Fulham Road
London SW6 5SE
071 371 7477

Alcohol Concern
305 Gray's Inn Road
LONDON WC1X 8QF
Tel: 071 833 3471

Alcoholics Anonymous,
PO Box 1
Stonebow House
Stonebow
YORK YO1 2NJ
0904 644026

Alcohol is a drug and has a noticeable effect on the body even when it is drunk in small quantities.

holic to accept his/her addiction, to understand what it is doing to them and, above all, to want to stop drinking. Treatments are rarely successful without these steps. Some alcoholics are most successfully treated in hospitals or clinics, while others respond well to self-help organisations such as Alcoholics Anonymous. Some doctors prescribe tranquillisers during the initial period of withdrawal, and vitamin supplements, especially vitamin B complex, are often given. Eating a good, balanced diet is also essential to recovery.

The alcoholic's only chance of complete recovery, once s/he has stopped drinking, is never to drink alcohol again. If this is achieved, the liver will regenerate and mind and body can return to normal.

ALZHEIMER'S DISEASE

Alzheimer's disease is the failure of the brain, or dementia. It is one of the most underdiagnosed conditions among elderly people today. It is estimated that, in Britain, one person in 10 over the age of 65 has the condition, and as many as one in five over the age of 80. More rarely, it can also affect people in their fifties or even forties. It is incurable and progressive, though rates of progression vary from person to person.

CAUSES: Not known. Aluminium has been implicated but there is no firm evidence.

SYMPTOMS AND SIGNS: The earliest symptom is usually a gradual loss of memory. Short-term memory is particularly affected, while long-term memory may still be good. There may also be a reduction in powers of reasoning and comprehension, together with a loss of interest in formerly habitual pursuits. In the later stages of the disease, there may be signs of emotional instability, with mood swings, aggressiveness and anti-social behaviour.

TREATMENT: No medical cure is available at the moment. Anyone suffering from Alzheimer's disease may eventually require round-the-clock care, which is only available in hospitals or homes. If your doctor recommends this course of action, you would probably be well advised to take it.

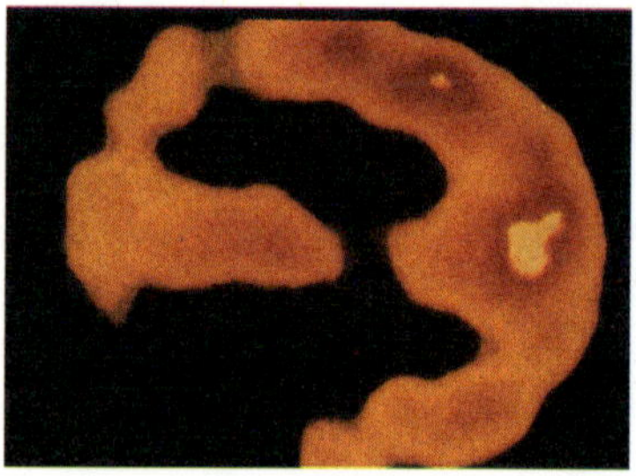

A scan of the human brain showing evidence of Alzheimer's disease.

AMOEBIC DYSENTERY

see DYSENTERY

AMENORRHOEA

In itself amenorrhoea – loss of periods – can't do any harm. It may even happen naturally, after pregnancy for example, because the hormones controlling menstruation are temporarily disrupted but it may in rare cases be a symptom of some more serious disorder.

CAUSES: When, for some reason, the balance of hormones that control the menstrual cycle is upset, the system breaks down and amenorrhoea can occur.

ASK THE DOCTOR

ALZHEIMER'S DISEASE

Q My mother is 64. She is becoming very scatty and often forgets things. Does this mean she's got Alzheimer's disease?

A No. Loss of memory is common in old age and does not necessarily mean dementia. But keep an eye on how she progresses, just in case.

Useful Addresses

ALZHEIMER'S DISEASE

Alzheimer's Disease Society
158-160 Balham High Road
LONDON SW12 9BN
081 675 6557

Help the Aged
16-18 St James Walk
LONDON EC1R 0BE
071 253 0253

Natural causes are pregnancy, post pregnancy, breastfeeding and age. Some diseases can produce loss of periods: tuberculosis, anaemia, thyroid disease, anorexia nervosa. Drugs may also provoke this: for example, the Pill, some tranquillisers and anti-depressive drugs, as well as drugs used to control blood pressure. Stress can cause periods to stop or be delayed. Occasionally, there's a physical abnormality or a glandular disorder responsible which will need investigating.

Symptoms and signs: Loss of periods.

Treatment: Amenorrhoea in itself causes no problems except that it means a woman cannot get pregnant while it lasts. If there is some underlying disorder that needs to be treated, periods will usually return with restored health. If there is no ill health and periods have not returned after four to six months, consult your doctor.

ANAEMIA

Strictly speaking, the word anaemic means 'without blood', but it is usually used to describe people who don't have enough healthy red blood cells in their bloodstream. The most common type of anaemia is the result of iron deficiency and affects two or three people in every 100.

Causes: Bleeding, such as heavy periods in women, is a common cause of anaemia. The condition may also be due to the excessive destruction of red blood cells so that the bone marrow cannot produce enough to replace those that are lost. Alternatively, anaemia can be the result of the insufficient production of red blood cells. This may be due to a number of factors. Iron-deficiency anaemia is caused by a shortage of iron, which is vital for the body to produce healthy red blood cells. Vitamin deficiency anaemia and pernicious anaemia are both forms of anaemia in which there is an inadequate supply of vitamin B12 and folic acid. As B12 is in most dairy produce and meat, vegans are the only people likely to suffer from these forms of anaemia. However, B12 deficiency can arise in a few people who are not able to absorb the vitamin properly.

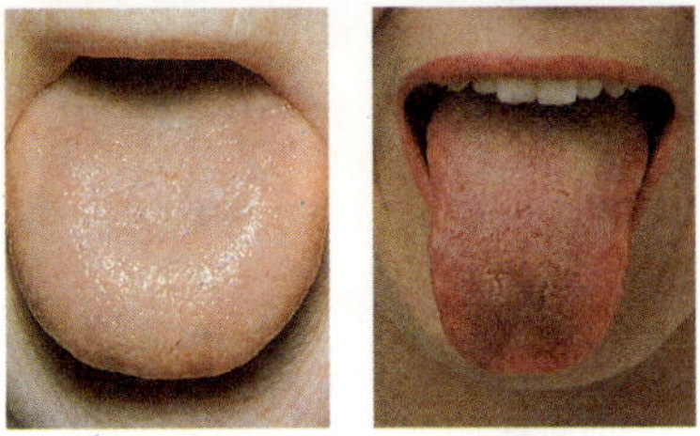

The tongue on the left is pale, showing anaemia. On the right, a normal, healthy, pink tongue.

Symptoms and signs: Anaemics feel particularly tired and listless because the body is not getting enough oxygen for its needs. Their skin tends to lose its healthy bloom, and a face that's paler than usual is one sign. If the condition becomes severe, the patient will also be short of breath, and the ankles may swell.

Treatment: Curing iron deficiency may just mean adjusting your diet and eating more meat (especially offal), eggs and cereals, all of which are rich in iron. You can also suffer from an iron deficiency even if your diet supplies plenty of iron as some people cannot absorb it properly. Sometimes this is caused by an inflammation of the bowels, sometimes it is due to an allergy, which can be corrected. If, however, you suspect that you are anaemic, it's advisable to see a doctor. Vitamin-deficiency anaemia and pernicious anaemia can be cured very simply by injections of vitamin B12. Folic acid deficiency, on the other hand, is a problem of diet. Sufferers should try to eat the foods that are good sources – particularly green, leafy vegetables and liver.

ANEURYSM

An aneurysm is a swelling on the wall of an artery. It is permanent and can form anywhere but causes most trouble when it forms in arteries in the head or aorta. An aneurysm may press on and damage nerves, organs or blood vessels. They can interfere with the blood flow causing blood clots to form and can burst and cause internal bleeding.

Self **Help**

ANAEMIA

Eat a nutritious and well-balanced diet. Meat–especially kidney and liver–and all dairy produce, are rich in iron and vitamin B12; folic acid is found in green vegetables, but be careful not to overcook them because this can destroy the vitamin content. If you have any 'high risk factor'(heavy periods, for example, or a strict vegetarian diet), be especially careful to ensure that you get enough of the right kinds of food.

ASK THE DOCTOR

ANAEMIA

Q My daughter, who is 24, is terribly pale. Could she be anaemic?

A It's possible, though if she doesn't also have other symptoms, such as listlessness, it's not very likely. If you're worried, talk to her and suggest she sees a doctor.

ASK THE DOCTOR

ANGINA PECTORIS

Q If I have angina am I likely to have a heart attack?

A Angina does not mean a heart attack is inevitable. With care, and a reasonable amount of exercise under a doctor's supervision, many people find that their angina improves.

Useful Addresses

ANOREXIA NERVOSA

Anorexia & Bulimia Nervosa Association.
Tottenham Women & Health Centre Annex
Tottenham
LONDON N15 4RX
081 885 3936

Eating Disorders Association.
Sackville Place
44 Magdalen St
NORWICH NR3 1JE
0603 621414

CAUSES: There may be a congenital weakness of the artery wall, which then swells up under pressure from a normal flow of blood. Inflammation of the artery wall also causes aneurysm, as does atherosclerosis – a build-up of fatty deposits on the artery wall – and high blood pressure.
SYMPTOMS AND SIGNS: Aneurysms in the head usually show no symptoms until they burst, when a severe headache is likely to be followed by unconsciousness. If the aneurysm is in the section of the aorta that passes through the chest, you develop a cough, chest pain and hoarseness. If it is in the abdomen it can be seen as a throbbing lump. A burst aneurysm in the aorta can be fatal .
TREATMENT: Surgery is the usual treatment. You can help to lessen the risks of aneurysm if you keep cholesterol and blood pressure levels low.

ANGINA

see ANGINA PECTORIS

ANGINA PECTORIS

Angina is a warning symptom of coronary heart disease. The blood supply to the heart muscle has become so diminished that when the heart is called upon to work hard, it does not get enough oxygen and so suffers from 'cramp'.
CAUSES: Unhealthy coronary arteries that have lost their elasticity are the main cause of angina. These seem to be a result of the modern western way of life.
SYMPTOMS AND SIGNS: Angina causes an intense pain in the chest – often centrally, but sometimes moving to the jaw or upper arms (particularly the left arm). This pain typically comes on with exercise, such as walking up stairs or up a hill, but it always goes away within a few minutes of resting. The pain is suffocating – some people say it is like having their chest crushed in a vice.

If you regularly have pain in the chest during exercise it is worth checking with your doctor. It could be due to angina but the pains can sometimes be confused with indigestion or pains from the lungs or ribs. An electrocardiogram (ECG) test may help the doctor diagnose it.
TREATMENT: The doctor will check your weight and blood pressure. If you are overweight, s/he will suggest that you slim to the correct weight for your height, and if your blood pressure is high, s/he may prescribe drugs. If you smoke, you will be told to stop.

There are certain drugs that can help angina. Glyceryl trinitrate – tablets that dissolve under the tongue – are often used to relieve pain, but the doctor may also prescribe other tablets to be taken regularly which prevent the heart over-working when you take exercise.

A few people with severe angina can be helped by balloon angioplasty or bypass surgery, which enables blood to flow more easily to the heart muscle. The symptoms of angina improve and the eventual risk of developing a heart attack diminishes.
See also HEART DISEASE.

ANOREXIA NERVOSA

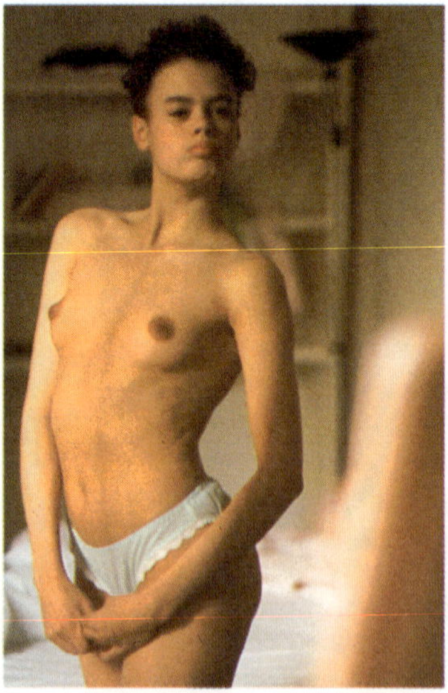

Even if an 'ideal' weight, an anorexic will see herself as several sizes larger.

Anorexia nervosa, also known as 'slimmer's disease', occurs when an individual diets to an irrational degree. Sufferers claim they need to lose weight, usually with absolutely no justification. Classically, anorexia starts in young females between 12 and 18 who are usually intelligent, often very ambitious academically and frequently physically attractive. It's also possible, however, for males to suffer from the condition, too.

CAUSES: For an adolescent feeling the pressures to do well and at the same time having to come to terms with the adult world, slimming can provide a refuge. Although a 'trigger' tends to spark off the condition, this is often the 'last straw' in a complex tangle of unconscious motives and emotions.

SYMPTOMS AND SIGNS: Although an anorexic diets to the point of becoming too thin, she staunchly maintains that she is still fat and is terrified of putting on weight. She may take up frantic exercise in order to keep her weight down. Anorexics have an obsessive interest in food and love cooking meals for other people, although, paradoxically, they will often refuse to eat with other members of the family. Eventually, as an anorexic becomes increasingly emaciated, her periods will stop.

TREATMENT: An anorexic first has to recognise that she has a problem; until then she remains both physically and mentally immature. It requires medical attention if her weight falls below 80 per cent of her 'ideal' weight. If the loss is greater or the condition goes on for longer that six months, specialist treatment should be sought.

See also BULIMIA NERVOSA.

APPENDICITIS

Appendicitis is infection and inflammation of the appendix. In acute appendicitis, the pain is usually severe and gets progressively worse. This is dangerous because the appendix might burst causing peritonitis, which is a potentially fatal condition. Acute appendicitis almost always entails an emergency operation.

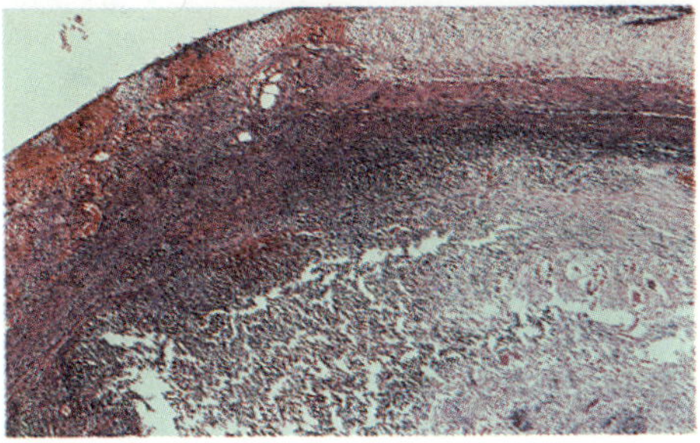

A section through the human appendix showing gangrenous appendicitis.

CAUSES: Appendicitis occurs when the narrow canal of the appendix gets blocked. Mucus collects behind the blockage and is turned to pus by the bacteria that are always present in the appendix. The appendix begins to swell up like a small bag, causing pain and sometimes resulting in dangerous complications.

SYMPTOMS AND SIGNS: Acute appendicitis comes on suddenly, without any previous signs of illness, though you may have suffered from constipation or diarrhoea for a day or two before. In a typical case, the first signs of the illness are mild, sometimes cramp-like pains, spread throughout the centre of the abdomen. After a few hours, the pain becomes more troublesome and typically moves to a definite spot over the appendix – that is, on the right side between the hipbone and the navel. After the stomach pains have started, nausea is common and you may vomit.

These symptoms occur in about 50 per cent of patients with acute appendicitis, but many people have different symptoms. The pain, for example, may be more severe from the outset, and may not settle in one particular spot but continue to be generalised. Depending on how the appendix is lying within the abdomen, the pain may be felt down one leg or in the patient's back or, in a pregnant woman, the pain may be higher.

TREATMENT: The patient needs immediate medical attention. S/he should be sent to hos-

ASK THE DOCTOR

ANOREXIA NERVOSA

Q Is it true that anorexics often have very dominant parents?

A Not necessarily. Though relationships within the family certainly have a lot to do with the development of anorexia, no one pattern emerges. If a mother is dominant, the struggle at mealtimes may reflect the girl's attempts to break away and assert her independence. In other cases, a father may be jealously over-protective of his daughter and her refusal to eat may be both a protest against this and an encouragement to be still more protective.

ASK THE DOCTOR

APPENDICITIS

Q Is it true that appendicitis is a modern disease?

A Relatively speaking yes. Appendicitis was rare until the end of the last century and even today is uncommon in Asia and Africa. In modern industrialised countries, one person in 15 develops appendicitis at some time. The reason for this isn't clear, though lack of dietary fibre may be a factor.

ASK THE DOCTOR

ARTERIOSCLEROSIS

Q What can I do to decrease the risk of developing arteriosclerosis?

A Avoid smoking and keep your weight down to a reasonable level. Cutting down on saturated fats will help prevent the blood cholesterol level rising. Keeping your salt intake down may reduce any tendency towards high blood pressure. A moderate amount of dry white wine or dry sherry helps circulation and may reduce the level of harmful cholesterol in the blood.
Since stress at work may be a contributary factor, it may be worth changing to a less stressful job, or considering early retirement.

ASK THE DOCTOR

ASTHMA

Q As an asthmatic, do I have to give up sport?

A No, as long as you are sensible. Doctors now realise that many asthma sufferers are helped by developing their fitness in this way - a number have become world class athletes. Some asthmatics may need medication to take part in sports without wheezing but, in time, exercise develops the lungs.

pital for an operation to remove the appendix. See also PERITONITIS

ARTERIOSCLEROSIS

Arteriosclerosis is commonly called hardening of the arteries. The most usual form is a condition known as atherosclerosis, when fatty deposits (cholesterol) and minerals collect in the walls of the arteries and make them less elastic and narrower. The condition may reduce the flow of blood and eventually cut off the supply of blood to the heart, brain, muscles or kidneys. It is a common disease in western society, although women under 40 rarely suffer from it.

CAUSES: Overeating, especially if the diet is high in animal fats and refined sugar, can lead to hardening of the arteries, as can lack of exercise and high cholesterol levels in the bloodstream. Cigarette smoking makes the artery walls more permeable so that they are more likely to 'soak up' cholesterol and fatty deposits. High blood pressure, including that caused by constant emotional stress, is also thought to be a cause. The general ageing process also contributes to atherosclerosis.

SYMPTOMS AND SIGNS: If the narrowing of the arteries reduces blood supply to the heart, brain, kidneys, muscles etc, they will not function properly, causing angina, high blood pressure, leg cramps and other diseases. Narrow arteries may also cause blood to stick to the artery wall and clot there. If the thrombosis (clot) is in the heart circulation, it can cause a coronary thrombosis (heart attack), if it is in the brain circulation it can cause a stroke. Pains in the legs, abdomen or back may also be symptoms.

TREATMENT: Once arteriosclerosis is suspected, the diagnosis can be confirmed by further investigations in hospital. There are drugs that can reduce the amount of cholesterol in the bloodstream and anti-coagulants that reduce the risk of blood clots. Experiments show that one aspirin tablet each day can help to keep the blood thin for up to 48 hours, and aspirin is being increasingly prescribed by doctors for vascular diseases. Surgery is successful in replacing or repairing severely affected sections of arteries, but prevention is certainly better than treatment.
See also ANGINA, HEART ATTACK, STROKE, THROMBOSIS.

THE UNSEEN KILLER

Atherosclerosis causes more deaths than any other condition in the UK. One-third of all deaths are caused by atherosclerosis heart disease involving the coronary arteries. Because atherosclerosis reduces the blood flow in major arteries to the kidneys, legs and intestine, it also causes a number of other illnesses. Coronary artery disease kills six times as many men as women between the ages of 35 and 40.

ARTHRITIS

see RHEUMATOID ARTHRITIS

ASTHMA

Asthma is a condition in which the patient has recurrent attacks of wheezing. Usually each attack clears up completely with medical treatment. Attacks produce a variety of disability from mild distress to severe incapacity. Asthma can develop at any time in life but most often starts in childhood.

CAUSES: In asthmatics, the bronchial tube muscles which take air into the airspaces in the lungs become irritated by one or more 'trigger'. The muscles contract, causing the tubes themselves to narrow so that air can't move freely in or out of the lungs. The tubes also produce more mucus than usual, which reduces the air flow still further. Asthmatics tend to have more trouble getting air out of, rather than into, the lungs.

There are many possible asthmatic 'triggers'. The first attack of asthma is often set off by a lung infection. Subsequent attacks may be brought on by a similar infection or even an ordinary cold. Allergies can also trigger attacks. Some drugs may provoke a wheezing attack if the asthmatic has become allergic to them. Exercise can also bring on

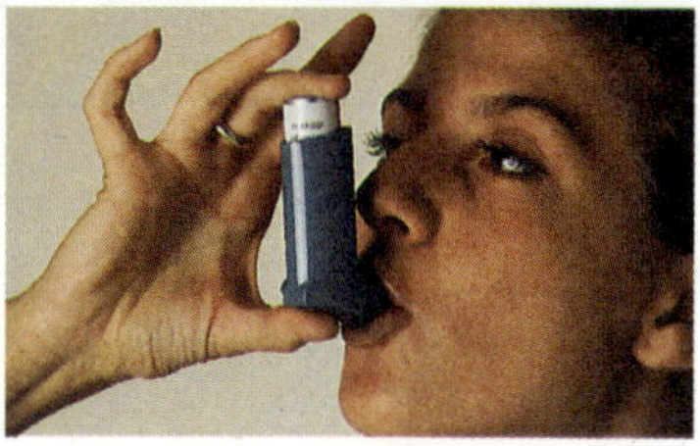

The inhaler is a convenient way for many asthmatics to take vital drugs.

an attack, as can emotional upsets and even sudden changes in the weather and temperature.

Symptoms and signs: Wheezing is a characteristic symptom of asthma, sometimes accompanied by a cough. The pulse rate rises and often sufferers can't speak because they are so short of breath.

Treatment: An attack can be treated using drugs that widen the contracted bronchial tubes - these are often taken via an inhaler. Steroids may also be prescribed and antibiotics may be taken in cases where the attack was triggered by a bacterial infection.

If the attack is particularly severe or normal medication doesn't help, call a doctor immediately.

ATHEROSCLEROSIS

see ARTERIOSCLEROSIS

ATHLETE'S FOOT

Athlete's foot is a fungus infection (ringworm) of the feet.

Causes: It is a common infection which spreads readily from one person to another, often via swimming pools or communal showers in schools and sports centres. It can be transmitted from damp floors or wooden boards in showers and changing rooms. All fungal infections tend to thrive in moist conditions, so avoid shoes and socks that make your feet sweat.

Symptoms and signs: Skin between the toes blisters, scales and splits. The feet may also start to smell.

Treatment: Wash the feet carefully twice a day, then dry them thoroughly, especially between the toes. Dust your feet with a medicated powder containing an antifungal agent, such as tolnaftate or undecenoic acid, or paint with a proprietary brand of anti-fungal paint, available without prescription. Athlete's foot is easily treatable, especially if caught in the early stages, but if it persists see your doctor as you may need antifungal tablets.

Self **Help**

ATHLETE'S FOOT

Wear cotton socks to absorb the perspiration from the feet, and avoid wearing shoes that make your feet sweat.

b

BACK PAIN

Back pain is one of the most common complaints. Many back pains have no immediately obvious cause. They are often the result of strained ligaments or painful muscle spasm and inflammation brought on by bad posture, general tension, lifting incorrectly or sudden strain through twisting or reaching awkwardly. They can also be caused by an inadequate environment such as poorly designed seating or work surfaces, or too soft a bed. The facet joints linking one vertebra to the next can also be damaged or strained. Other back pains include lumbago – a pain in the lower or lumbar region of the back and fibrositis or trigger point phenomenon – inflammation of the muscles supporting the back.

Muscular tension can cause pain in the neck, shoulders or upper back. If you are under stress or have bad posture, the muscles in the back can become very tense and sore. The muscles bunch into hard nodules at recognised trigger points in the neck and shoulders. The nodules can easily be felt and may twitch and feel very painful if pressure is applied to them.

See also FACET JOINT STRAIN, FIBROSITIS, LUMBAGO, PROLAPSED DISC (SLIPPED DISC), SCIATICA, SPINAL CORD INJURY, SPONDYLITIS, SPONDYLOSIS.

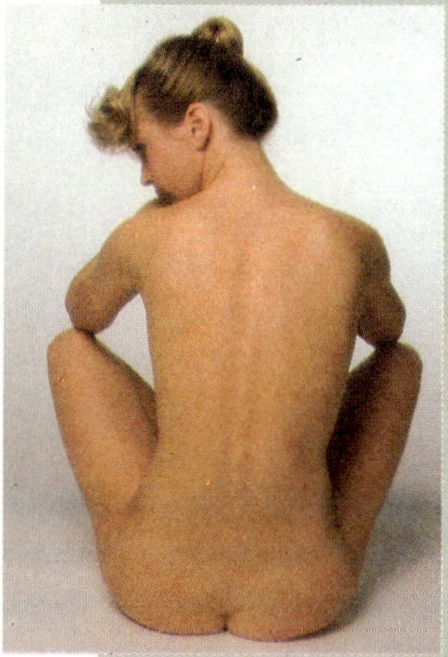

More working days are lost through back pain than any other illness and it affects around one person in 50.

Self **Help**

BARTHOLIN'S CYST

A comfortably hot bath can be soothing.

ASK THE DOCTOR

BIRTHMARK

Q My daughter has a port-wine birthmark on her face and wants to use make-up to disguise it. Where can she learn camouflage techniques?

A The Disfigurement Guidance Centre (see Useful Addresses) hold skin camouflage clinics. They are based in Fife, Scotland, but if this is too far for you to travel, they may be able to tell you of a clinic nearer your home.

Useful Addresses

BIRTHMARK

Disfigurement Guidance Centre
PO Box 7
Cupar
FIFE KY15 3AS
0333 312350

Naevus Support Group
58 Necton Road
Wheathamstead
St Albans
HERTS ALS 8AU
058283 2853

BAD BREATH

see HALITOSIS

If a Bartholin's gland becomes infected, which is known as bartholinitis, it may produce an abscess. This may have to be removed surgically.

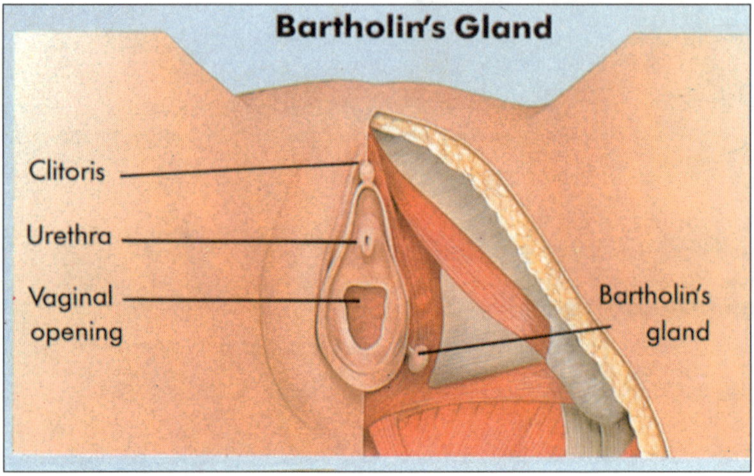

BARTHOLIN'S CYST

There are two small glands, called Bartholin's glands, on either side of the entrance to the vagina, whose function it is to produce sufficient mucus to lubricate the vagina during sexual arousal.

Causes: If one of the ducts of the glands becomes blocked, a cyst may form, which can become infected.

Symptoms and signs: Swelling and pain to one side of the vagina.

Treatment: Antibiotic treatment is usually necessary. Do not use antiseptic lotions or creams. If an abscess forms, surgical drainage may be required.

BIRTHMARK

A birthmark is an area of discoloured skin which is present from birth or appears soon after. Some, such as the common strawberry mark, are only temporary. Others, including port-wine stains, are permanent.

Causes: Some birthmarks are caused by tiny abnormal blood vessels under the skin, while others are the result of abnormal development of the cells that produce skin pigment. Both types are quite harmless.

Symptoms and signs: Discoloured skin.

Treatment: Most birthmarks don't need treatment, and unless there are very good cosmetic reasons, they should be left alone. If a birthmark is extremely unsightly, laser techniques can remove or lighten them. It is often preferable, however, to use camouflage make-up. It is better to try to come to terms with having a birthmark than it is to treat one. Sometimes, removal of a port-wine stain can leave an equally unsightly scar.

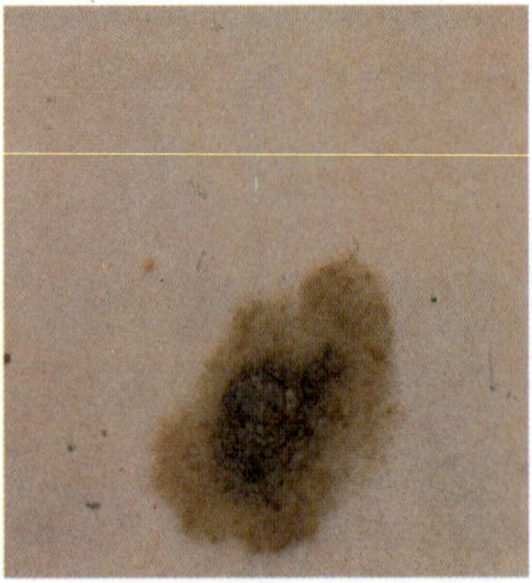

Unsightly birthmarks can be removed surgically, but it is usually better to leave them alone.

BITES

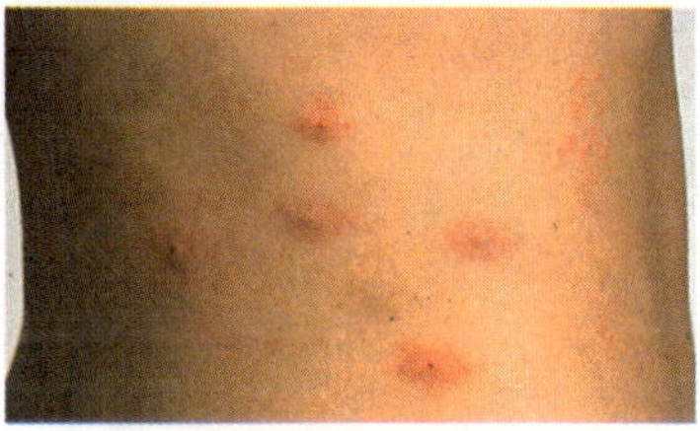

Insect bites are primarily an allergic reaction. Most insects attack after dark.

Although insect and animal bites are unpleasant, most are not serious conditions. However, there is a risk of rabies with animal bites outside the UK.

CAUSES: Some people are highly allergic to the toxins in insect bites or to the poison in a snake's venom. In severe cases, they may suffer an intense allergic reaction. Most of the time, however, a few simple measures will prevent infection.

SYMPTOMS AND SIGNS: If a wound is infected, it will appear swollen, red and develop pus. All animal bites, including human bites and non-poisonous snake bites, should be treated immediately, irrespective of whether they are already infected.

TREATMENT: Wash the bite with antiseptic and apply antihistamine cream to insect bites to relieve itching. Cover animal bites with a clean, dry dressing, preferably sterile, and bandage in place. For animal bites, if you have had a tetanus booster recently, wash several times in the next 48 hours and keep the wound covered. If you have not had a tetanus injection for over five years, see your doctor as soon as possible. Never scratch the affected area.

See also RABIES.

BLACK EYE

see BRUISES

BLACK OUT

see FAINTING

BLADDER STONES

A bladder stone may be a kidney stone that has been passed through the ureter, but most bladder stones are formed in the bladder itself, as a result of stagnant urine, for example, in those who have an enlarged prostate gland.

CAUSES: The stones are thought to be caused by an over-concentration of calcium in the urine and they are particularly common in warm climates where people lose so much body water in sweat that they tend to produce less urine. It is known that stones run in families and that men are more prone than women, as are people over 30. Children may develop a rare type of stone caused by an inherited chemical abnormality in the blood.

SYMPTOMS AND SIGNS: Symptoms include an over-frequent urge to pass urine, pain on passing urine and blood in urine, especially in the last few drops.

TREATMENT: If a stone is too big to pass out naturally, it must be removed. This is usually done using a cystoscope, which is inserted up the urethra under general anaesthetic. An instrument is passed up through the cystoscope to either draw out the stones or crush them into small pieces which can then be washed out. Ultrasound may be used to bombard the stones with high-frequency waves, which will shatter the stone so that

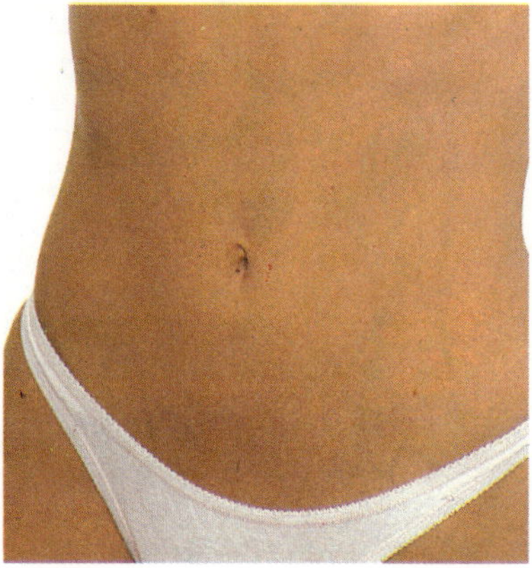

The bladder is located in the pelvis, behind the pubic bones.

ASK THE DOCTOR

BITES

Q I have an ants' nest in my garden and have frequently been bitten. Is there anything I can do to help ease the pain?

A Ant bites are acid so applying a paste of sodium bicarbonate should neutralise them and help relieve the pain.

Self **Help**

BITES

To soothe a painful bite, bathe it in cold water and use antiseptic cream to stop infection. If the pain is bad, apply some calamine lotion or an antihistamine cream.

Self **Help**
BLEPHARITIS

Wash the skin around the eyes morning and night with a cotton-tipped bud soaked in warm salt water or a warm solution of sodium bicarbonate. Keep the area clean and wash your hair with anti-dandruff shampoo.

Self **Help**
BOILS

To ease the pain and help bring the boil to a head, you can apply a warm kaolin poultice or even a face flannel wrung out in hot water.

ASK THE DOCTOR
BOILS

Q How infectious are boils?

A The bacteria that cause boils are particularly virulent and it is possible for them to spread from the boil to warm food where they may produce toxins that cause food poisoning. So don't handle food if you are suffering from boils. [See FOOD POISONING].

they can be flushed out more easily. Another alternative is a minor operation that involves making an incision in the bladder wall in order to reach the stone.

BLADDER TUMOURS

Tumours of the bladder can be benign or malignant. While they can usually be treated effectively, prompt action is needed to prevent damage to the kidneys due to obstruction of urine flow and, in the cases of malignancy, to other parts of the body.
CAUSES: Tumours of the bladder are fairly rare and are most common in men over the age of 50. The incidence is higher among workers in the dye and rubber industries and is thought to be caused by exposure to certain chemicals. Smoking appears to increase the chances of getting bladder cancer.
SYMPTOMS AND SIGNS: Blood in the urine is usually the first sign, though this may be due to other causes such as cystitis. There may be a slight burning sensation when urinating and an increase in frequency.
TREATMENT: If a tumour is found, it will be removed. Small benign tumours are usually burned away, other tumours may be surgically removed. If the tumour is cancerous, the whole bladder may have to be removed.

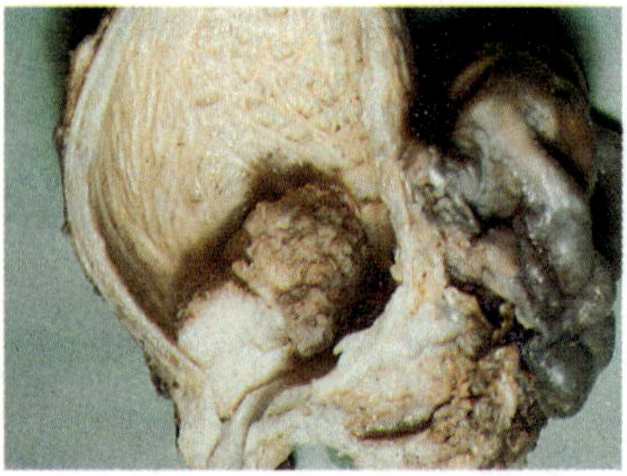

Those who smoke and who work in the rubber or dye industries are more likely to get bladder cancer.

BLEPHARITIS

Blepharitis is an inflammmation of the eyelid margins, which causes redness and makes the skin area around the eyes flaky.

Extreme cases of blepharitis may lead to corneal ulcers, though this is rare.

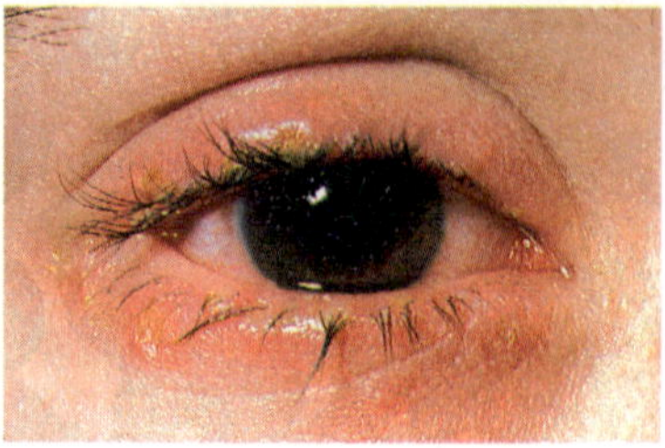

CAUSES: The cause is not known exactly, but it is linked with dandruff and seborrhoeic eczema. If bacteria invades the area the infection may get worse.
SYMPTOMS AND SIGNS: Your skin looks red and flaky and your eyes feel gritty and irritated. In bad cases, small ulcers may develop on your lid margins and your eyelashes may fall out. Flakes of skin sometimes make their way into the eye and cause conjunctivitis.
TREATMENT: Try to treat the problem yourself (see SELF HELP). If the redness and irritation last longer than a couple of days, consult your doctor, who will be able to prescribe an antibiotic and steroid preparation. Blepharitis often recurs and needs repeated treatment.

BLOOD POISONING

see SEPTICAEMIA

BLOOD PRESSURE

see HYPERTENSION, HYPOTENSION

BOILS

Boils are painful, red, pus-filled swellings that can form in the skin on almost any part of the body. They are caused by a type of bacterium that lives quite harmlessly on the surface of the skin, but which causes infection beneath the skin's surface. People who suffer from eczema, or any complaint that effects the structure of the skin's surface, are more susceptible to boils or carbuncles. Carbuncles

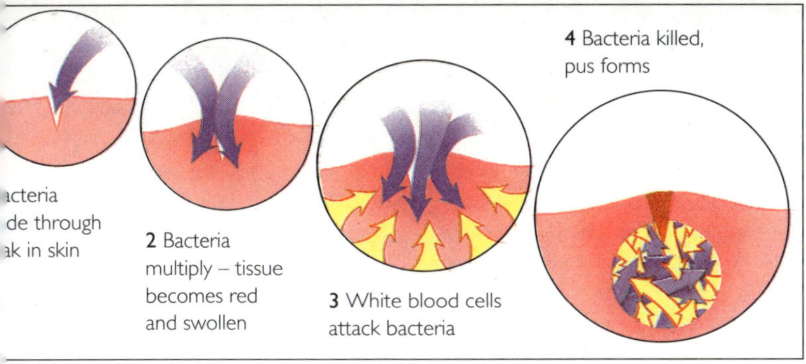

Don't be tempted to squeeze or lance a boil yourself – this could easily lead to infection.

are simply large boils or a collection of boils joined together.

Causes: The boil first appears when the bacteria start to multiply under the skin and produce toxic chemicals which inflame the surrounding area. In an attempt to combat the chemicals, more and more white blood cells rush to the area of infection until a pocket of pus is formed in the skin. This becomes the centre of the boil. Pus is a mixture of cell debris, white blood cells and bacteria.

Symptoms and signs: Boils usually develop on the legs, arms and trunk. The first symptom is a small, red, painful area of skin, which may be slightly swollen. As the pus starts to form, the centre becomes yellow and the pain and swelling increase.

Treatment: If you suspect that you are developing a large boil, it is worth consulting your doctor right away because he may be able to prescribe an antibiotic to deal with the infection before it gains a foothold. If the boil is about to burst, your doctor may lance it to allow the pus to drain away. Larger boils will need a general anaesthetic. If the boil is recurrent, your doctor may prescribe an antiseptic or antibiotics.

BOTULISM

Botulism is a serious but extremely rare kind of food poisoning. It attacks the nervous system rather than the intestines.

Causes: It is caused by the bacterium Clostridium botulinum.

Symptoms and signs: Symptoms develop within two hours of eating the contaminated food. The patient usually feels dizzy, has double vision, headaches and progressive paralysis. There may also be accompanying nausea, vomiting and diarrhoea.

Treatment: Hospital treatment and careful nursing are required.

BOWEL CANCER

Bowel cancer is the third most common cancer in Britain.

Causes: As with most cancers, it is difficult to know for certain what causes bowel cancer. People over the age of 40 are more susceptible, and the risks increase with age. Also more at risk are people with ulcerative colitis and a history of rectal polyps. Diet may well hold a clue to the development of this disease as the incidence is far higher in countries where highly refined, low-fibre foods are eaten regularly.

Symptoms and signs: The most common symptom is a persistent change in bowel movements – either increased constipation or persistent diarrhoea. Go to your doctor if these continue for more than ten days. Other symptoms include blood mixed in the faeces, a tender spot in the abdomen or a lump in the abdomen.

Treatment: The doctor will examine your abdomen. You may then be referred to a specialist who will look at the bowel wall internally with an instrument called a sigmoidoscope. If cancer is suspected, the next step is an X-ray

ASK THE DOCTOR

BOTULISM

Q I've heard that botulism is caused, in the main, by canned foods. Is this still the case?

A No, the canning industry takes strict precautions against any possibility of botulism, which is largely why it is now such a rare disease.

Q Can botulism be fatal?

A Yes. Once paralysis sets in and the patient loses the ability to breathe, death is certain without artificial respiration.

Q Am I putting my family at risk of botulism when I make home-made jam?

A The acid in fruits used in jams usually destroys the botulism poison. However, other foods may still be a problem and you need to take great care with home canning.

ASK THE DOCTOR

BRAIN TUMOUR

Q My mother died of a brain tumour last year. Does this mean I'm likely to develop one too?

A There is little known about what causes brain tumours, but there seems little evidence to suggest that the condition runs in families.

ASK THE DOCTOR

BREAST CANCER

Q At what age am I most at risk from breast cancer?

A Breast cancer kills more women between the ages of 35-54 than any other disease. A breast X-ray (mammography) is usually recommended for women over the age of 40, who come from a family where there is a history of breast cancer.

Q Is it possible to reconstruct the breast after masectomy?

A Yes. It may be possible to insert a plastic or silicon implant under the surface layer of skin, although this may not be suitable for everyone. Your doctor should be able to advise you.

and stool investigations. The usual treatment for bowel cancer is surgery. If the cancer is large or if the rectum is involved, the whole colon and rectum need to be removed. The surgeon then constructs a colostomy – an artificial opening on the surface of the abdomen – so that a bag can be attached to collect excreted waste. If the cancer is confined to a small area and is not too near the rectum, it is often possible to cut out a small section of the bowel. The ends are then stitched together and the bowel functions as before.

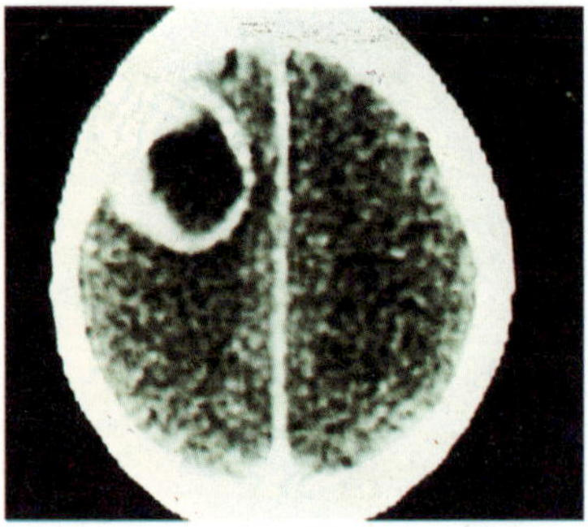

The dark area in the top left hand corner indicates the size of the brain tumour.

BRAIN TUMOURS

Brain tumours are lumps or growths that develop in or near the brain. Like tumours which occur in the lungs and elsewhere in the body, these growths are made up of groups of cells that have somehow escaped the body's usual control mechanisms. The result is that they reproduce more rapidly than healthy cells, often damaging nearby organs and interfering with their normal functions. Most brain tumours are benign but cause problems because of a build-up of pressure. A primary cancer in the brain is rare.

CAUSES: Doctors know very little about how brain tumours develop. Malignant tumours in the brain have usually spread from cancer somewhere else in the body.

SYMPTOMS AND SIGNS: Distortion and displacement of the soft brain tissue cause a gradual increase in the pressure within the skull, resulting in severe headaches, nausea or vomiting. Continued pressure may damage the optic nerve, causing blindness, and can progress to cause a loss of consciousness or even death. Any tumour that puts pressure on the brain can change the electrical activity in its immediate vicinity, which may result in epileptic fits. Brain tumour symptoms usually develop over a period varying from days to months. Contrary to popular belief, persistent headaches alone are very rarely indicators of a brain tumour.

TREATMENT: Some tumours can be removed by surgery, although this may be very difficult as there is a risk of damage to the surrounding brain. Radiotherapy or chemotherapy can help shrink the tumour. Above all, early diagnosis is very important.

BREAST CANCER

As the commonest form of cancer among women living in Western countries, breast cancer strikes one woman in every 14.

CAUSES: It is thought that environment and lifestyle are important factors in how likely a woman is to develop breast cancer.

Some doctors believe that there may be a link between diet and the occurrence of breast cancer. Heredity seems to play a strong part. Any woman with a close relative who's suffered from breast cancer has a much higher risk. Prolonged use of the Pill and HRT (hormone replacement therapy used to treat 'change of life' symptoms) have also been blamed.

Having a child at an early age appears to give a woman a certain amount of protection against developing breast cancer later on in life.

SYMPTOMS AND SIGNS: One of the earliest signs of breast cancer is the presence of a hard, rather ill-defined lump in one of the breasts. The lump is nearly always painless and may occur anywhere in the breast. To begin with, it moves freely.

As the tumour gets larger, it pulls in the skin over it to produce a characteristic 'dimple' and may also affect the milk ducts, causing these to shrink and the nipple to become inverted.

If the tumour continues to spread, it may attach itself to the overlying skin, sometimes causing skin inflammation. It may also invade the tissue beneath, becoming fixed to the underlying muscles. The cancer may spread into the lymphatic glands under the arms. Early diagnosis is most important. The danger lies in the fact that it has the capacity to spread all over the body.

TREATMENT: Having found a lump, find out if it is malignant – fortunately most are not. If breast cancer is diagnosed early on, while the tumour is still small, surgery can often effect a cure. The surgeon usually does a lumpectomy, where just the growth is removed. Occasionally partial or complete masectomy (breast removal) will be carried out. Surgery is often followed by a course of chemotherapy and/or radiotherapy. Post-menopausal women may be given a course of anti-oestrogen treatment. After the initial treatment, doctors follow up their breast cancer patients indefinitely so that if the disease recurs it can be detected as soon as possible.

SELF-EXAMINATION OF THE BREASTS

The best time to examine your breasts is just after your period. Always examine yourself at the same time each month. Don't worry if they feel lumpy – what matters more is that they should feel the same.

If you think you have found something during the course of an examination, feel the same part of the other breast, just to make sure it's not just the way both breasts are made. If there is something unusual, don't panic, but do not hesitate to check with your doctor.

1 Stand in front of a mirror with your arms at your sides and look for anything unusual in the size or appearance of the breasts. Look for puckering or dimpling of the skin or changes in outline.

2 Raise your arms above your head and look at yourself from varying angles, by turning from side to side, to see if there have been any changes. Make sure there's no discharge from the nipple.

3 Lie down on a bed with your head on a pillow; place a pillow or folded towel under your left shoulder. Put your left hand under your head and use the right to examine your left breast. With fingers together, use the flat of your fingers to gently, but firmly, feel the breast. Think of the breast as being divided into four quarters of a circle, and begin by examining the upper, inner quarter.

4 In the same way, examine the lower, inner quarter, and the area all round the nipple, as shown.

5 Move your left arm down to your side and start examining the lower, outer quarter.

6 In exactly the same way, examine the final quarter and feel in the armpit itself, looking for any lumps. Repeat the whole process for the right breast, but using your left hand of course.

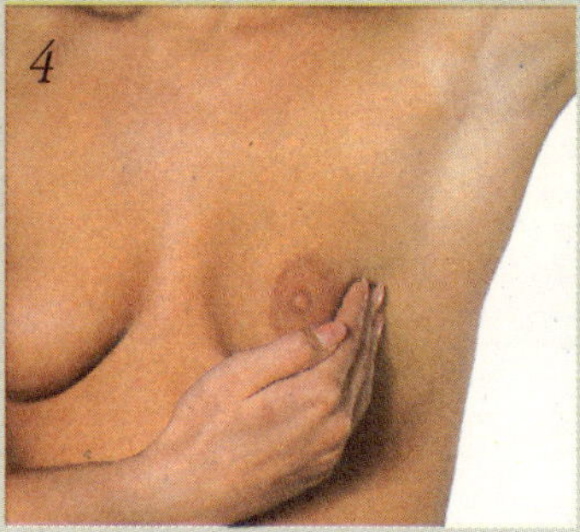

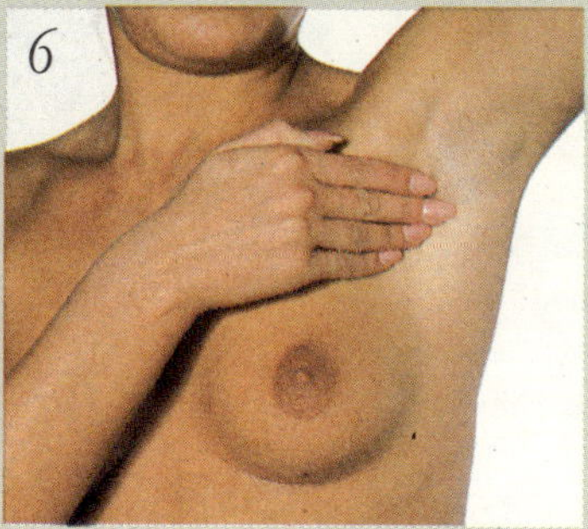

Useful Addresses

BREAST CANCER

Women's National Cancer
Central Campaign
Suna House
128-130 Curtain Road
LONDON EC2A 3AR
071 729 4688

Breast Care & Mastectomy
Association
15-19 Britten Street
LONDON SW3 3TZ
071 867 8275

ASK THE DOCTOR

BREAST CYSTS

Q Does needle aspiration of a breast cyst hurt?

A No, it is a virtually painless procedure, though you will feel a slight prick when the needle is inserted.

ASK THE DOCTOR

BRONCHITIS

Q I have chronic bronchitis. Does this lead to heart disease?

A The two diseases, chronic bronchitis and heart disease, are not linked, however, the main cause of both is smoking, so if you are a smoker you stand a greater risk of getting both diseases.

BREAST CYST

A breast cyst is a fluid-filled sac that forms in one of the sebaceous glands or milk ducts around the nipple.

CAUSES: A cyst forms if the duct to one of these glands becomes blocked.

SYMPTOMS AND SIGNS: A lump in the breast.

TREATMENT: The doctor will perform a needle aspiration, to draw off fluid from the cyst with a thin needle attached to a syringe, both as a means of confirming it as a harmless lump and to cause it to disappear.

See also BREAST CANCER.

BRONCHIAL CARCINOMA

see LUNG CANCER

BRONCHITIS

Bronchitis is an inflammation of the larger air passages, or bronchi, leading to the lungs. There are two different types of bronchitis: acute and chronic. Acute bronchitis can affect anyone and usually clears up after a few days. Chronic bronchitis is usually recurrent and leads to a deterioration of lung function.

ACUTE BRONCHITIS

CAUSES: Acute bronchitis is caused by viruses or bacteria which invade the lining of the tubes leading to the lungs. The lining begins to swell, the tubes narrow and excess mucus is secreted causing irritation, which brings on a productive cough.

SYMPTOMS AND SIGNS: Breathing may become wheezy and you'll be dogged by a persistent cough that produces a greeny-yellow phlegm. Generally you'll feel feverish, lose your appetite and feel unwell. The illness lasts for 7-21 days and, in normal healthy adults, the condition is nothing to worry about. However, in babies and the elderly complications are more likely to arise.

TREATMENT: If you smoke – stop, at least for a while. Stay at home and take plenty of hot drinks and painkillers as directed on the packet. If the illness becomes severe, breathing is impaired or you have a pain in your chest, consult your doctor, who may prescribe antibiotics if there is a risk of further infection. If you use a cough mixture, you should use an expectorant.

CHRONIC BRONCHITIS

Chronic bronchitis is a dangerous disease,

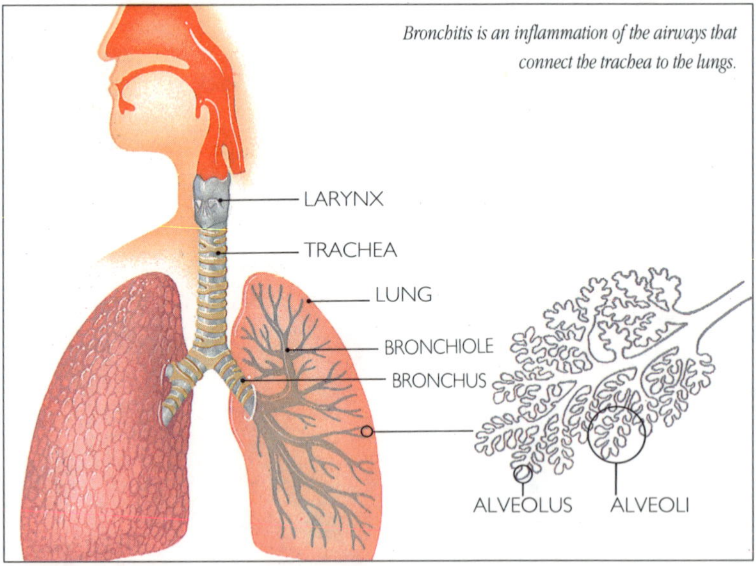

Bronchitis is an inflammation of the airways that connect the trachea to the lungs.

which largely affects smokers. Repeated infection of the airways makes them thickened and obstructed. Because of this deterioration, any cold or bout of flu is more likely to cause severe problems to the sufferer.

CAUSES: Smoking is the most common cause of chronic bronchitis and even the children of heavy smokers are at risk. The disease is also more common in industrialised areas.

SYMPTOMS AND SIGNS: The first symptom is often a heavy morning cough that produces sputum or phlegm. Many smokers don't think twice about what they regard as a 'normal' cough, until they become increasingly breathless and wheezy.

As the condition worsens, the patient is susceptible to emphysema, even heart failure. Some sufferers literally become blue in the face as a result of lack of oxygen.

TREATMENT: Stop smoking! Your doctor will determine how advanced the disease is and may prescribe an inhaler to relax the walls of the internal airways, or suggest a course of antibiotics.

BRUISES

Blood from an injury that has damaged blood vessels under the skin collects in surrounding tissues to form a bruise.

A large collection of blood beneath the surface of the skin is known technically as a haematoma.

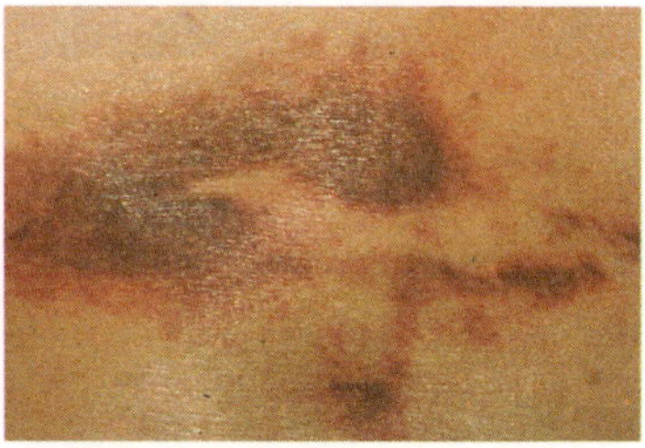

CAUSES: Bruises usually occur as the result of a fall or blow. Some people bruise more easily than others.

SYMPTOMS AND SIGNS: A bruise goes through a spectrum of colours before it disappears after about a week. Usually blue, purple, or black at first, it gradually fades to yellow. The bruise turns yellow as a result of the breakdown of haemoglobin released from red blood cells.

TREATMENT: Do not rub or massage it, but apply an ice pack for about 10 minutes immediately after the injury to reduce the area of bruising and swelling by narrowing damaged blood vessels. If a leg is bruised, rest it with your feet propped up. The skin around the eyes is particularly sensitive and so it bruises very easily, causing a black eye.

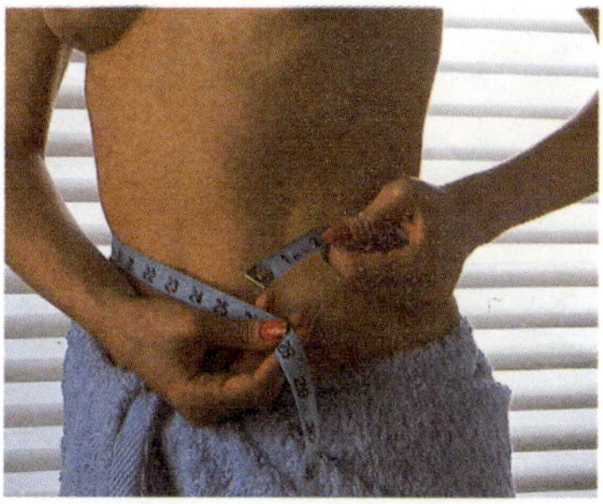

Bulimia sufferers are not necessarily very thin, some are normal weight.

BULIMIA NERVOSA

Bulimia nervosa is an eating disorder related to anorexia nervosa, which mostly affects young females.

CAUSES: Like anorexics, bulimics have a profound fear of becoming fat. Bulimia is a common condition in people who have suffered from anorexia in the past.

SYMPTOMS AND SIGNS: Bulimics binge on enormous feasts of 'forbidden' foods and then control their weight by self-induced vomiting or by taking huge quantities of laxatives. A sufferer's teeth may become damaged by the acid from the stomach brought into the mouth by frequent vomiting.

TREATMENT: Bulimics primarily need to acknowledge that they have a problem with their self-image and how they relate to food. This may involve a course of psychotherapy.

See also ANOREXIA NERVOSA.

Self **Help**

BRONCHITIS

Avoid smoke-filled rooms and anyone who is likely to pass on a cold. Many people find that they have to give up their job if it is in a polluted area or even move to a warmer climate.

Useful Addresses

BULIMIA NERVOSA

Eating Disorders Association
Sackville Place
44 Magdalen Street
NORWICH
Norfolk NR3 1JE
0603 621414

ASK THE DOCTOR

BULIMIA NERVOSA

Q My sister has been treated for bulimia. She seems to be OK now. Might she have a relapse?

A It's quite possible and you're right to be prepared for this. It's not unusual for bulimia to recur months – or even weeks – after treatment.

ASK THE DOCTOR

BUNIONS

Q How can I persuade my daughter not to wear the silly shoes she so often seems to set her heart on? I have bunions – I know how painful they are – and I would hate her to get them too.

A The sight of your bunions should be enough to put her off! Tell her that she probably has an inherited predisposition to bunions and that she should therefore be especially careful to wear sensible shoes. Sensible shoes used to mean dreadful Granny styles but they're actually much more stylish nowadays, so this shouldn't be a problem.

ASK THE DOCTOR

BURNS

Q How can you tell a burn's severity and whether it requires medical attention?

A Seek medical attention if the burn is larger then 2.5cm (1 inch) square; if it's wet and oozing; if the pain continues after administering first aid; if the burn was caused by a corrosive chemical or by electrical contact; or if the victim is either very young or very old.

BUNION

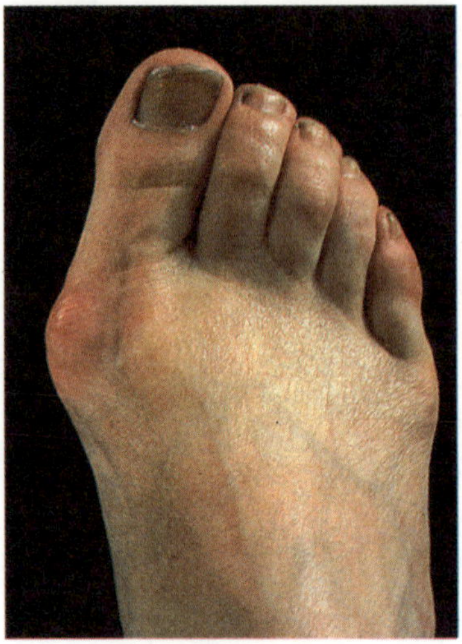

High-heeled shoes can cause bunions, but often there is a hereditary disposition.

Bunions occur as the result of the displacment of the joint of a toe – usually the big toe. It doesn't happen suddenly but is caused by pressure on the foot, which slowly forces the toe into the wrong position over a matter of months or even years. Instead of lying straight, the toe moves inwards and forms an angle. To protect this bony protruberance from friction, a protective layer of tissue forms a cushion over it, but, unfortunately, this itself often becomes inflamed and painful.

CAUSES: The problem is partly the result of ill-fitting shoes, but some people are more prone to developing bunions than others. The trouble is aggravated by arthritis, especially in elderly people.

TREATMENT: Often all the chiropodist can do about a bunion is to try to relieve discomfort by removing calluses and keeping pressure off the toes with specially designed appliances and pads. In extreme cases, surgical shoes may be the only answer. Occasionally an operation may be considered to remove part of the bone or bones in the toe. The operation isn't always successful and may create its own problems.

BURNS

Burns cause serious injury and death every day. Burns are classified as first, second or third degree, according to the depth of skin affected. First-degree burns, which are the most superficial, destroy only the skin's epidermis (outer layer), though the dermis (thicker underlying tissue) may also be affected. Second- and third-degree burns are more serious and destroy more of the layers of skin.

CAUSES: A burn can be caused not only by fire but also by scalding, strong friction, corrosive chemicals and electricity.

SYMPTOMS AND SIGNS

A minor burn causes painful reddening and perhaps blistering. A severe burn leaves a painless white or charred area.

TREATMENT: The affected area should be placed immediately under a steady flow of cold water for at least 10 minutes, or until the pain stops. If a blister forms, do not prick it as it will leave the raw skin underneath open to infection, as well as increasing pain. Do not put any cream, ointment or grease on a burn. If you need to protect it, use a clean dry dressing – do not use an adhesive dressing.

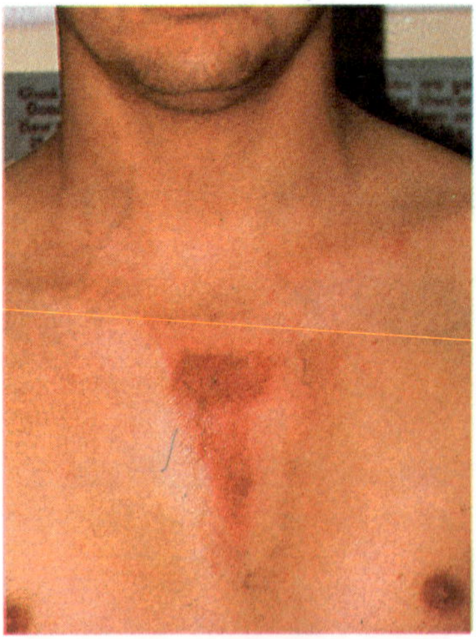

This triangular-shaped burn was caused by a welding accident. The scar will be lifelong.

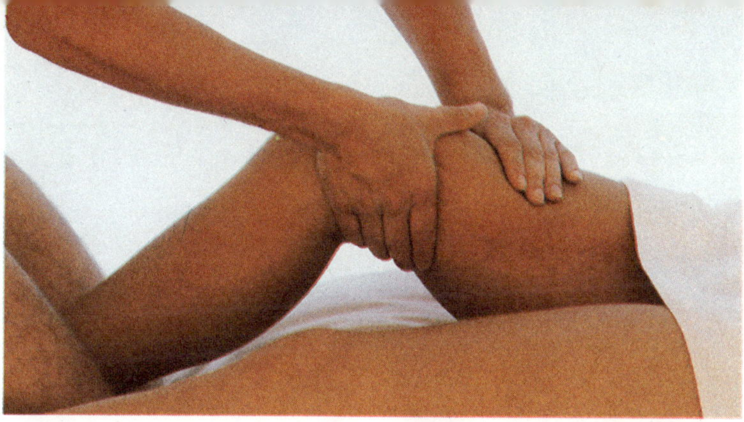

The joint most commonly affected by bursitis is the knee.

BURSITIS

A bursa is a soft fluid-filled sac which acts as a pressure pad to protect a bone or joint. Bursitis is the inflammation of a bursa.

CAUSES: Bursitis is caused by continual pressure over a bursa. Joints that are particularly susceptible to bursitis include the knee (housemaid's knee), elbow, shoulder, heel, and the base of the big toe.

SYMPTOMS AND SIGNS: A painful swollen area over a joint or bone, which may redden and feel hot.

TREATMENT: Bursitis usually clears up within a week or two, especially if pressure on that particular bone or joint is eased. If symptoms persist, see your doctor, who may draw off fluid with a syringe. If you have recurrent bursitis, your doctor may suggest you have the offending bursa injected with an anti-inflammatory steriod or that you have it removed.

C

CALLUS

see CORN

CANCER

One in four people in Britain will develop cancer at some time in their lives. It's the second most common cause of death (after heart disease).

CAUSES: All forms of cancer have a common cause: cells which change their nature and start multiplying when they don't need to. The organs of the body are made up of millions of tiny cells, which are specialised to perform different functions. When required, these cells divide to replace those which are worn out. Each healthy cell has a built-in mechanism, which regulates how quickly it must divide to keep pace with the loss of the cell it is replacing. But sometimes a cell starts multiplying when it doesn't need to, producing abnormal cells which spread haphazardly in all directions. These displace the normal cells and form the malignant tumour or cancer. In time, the cancer tends to spread from the original organ and may be carried to other parts of the body or blood. The original cancer is known as primary cancer. When carried to other sites, the cancer is referred to as secondary (matastasis). Many factors, including ageing, heredity, viral infection and the sun, can influence the behaviour of cells. For causes and symptoms of different cancers, see individual entries.

CANDIDA ALBICANS

see THRUSH

CARBUNCLES

see BOILS

ASK THE DOCTOR

BURSITIS

Q My son is a builder and has had bursitis diagnosed several times now in his shoulder. Is it serious?

A No. Bursitis is not a serious disorder, though it can be painful. Your son should work out what it is that's causing it – it's probably something he does in the course of his work – and either change the way he does it or wear some sort of protective pad to cushion the affected area.

Useful Addresses

CANCER

British Association of Cancer United Patients (BACUP) and their Families
121-123 Charterhouse Street
LONDON EC1M 6AA
071 608 1785

Cancerlink
17 Britannia Street
LONDON WCIX 9JN
071 831 2451

Cancer Research Society Campaign
2 Carlton House Terrace
LONDON SW17 5AR
071 930 8972

ASK THE DOCTOR

CATARACT

Q Do cataracts inevitably get worse and cause blindness?

A No, many just stay as they are – though doctors can't always predict whether they will get worse or stay the same.

Q How successful is surgery for removing cataracts?

A It is one of the most successful and safest of modern medical practices. The patient can be up the day after the operation, and out of hospital four days later.

Useful Addresses

CATARACT

Partially Sighted Society
Queens Road,
DONCASTER
South Yorks DN1 2NX
0302 323132
0302 368998

Self Help

CATARRH

There are several inhalation decongestants available at chemists. Most of them contain menthol and can be dissolved in a bowl of boiling water. Nasal decongestants are very effective, but should not be used for long periods.

CATARACT

A cataract is an imperfection in the clarity of the lens of the eye, which reduces the definition of the image that reaches the retina. It affects sight to different degrees, according to how far developed it is.

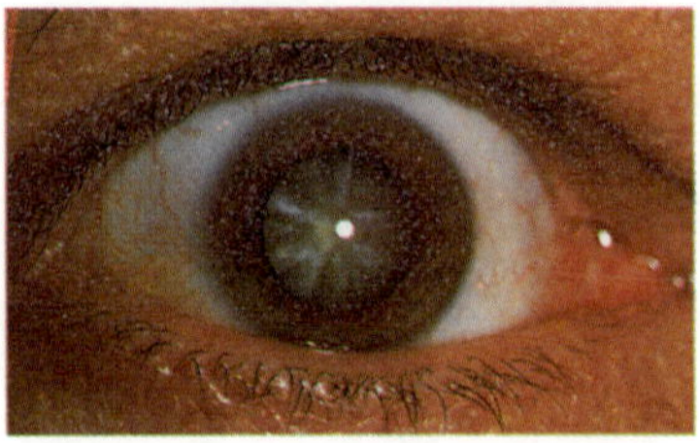

A cataract doesn't hurt and causes only visual symptoms, which are generally slowly progresssive.

CAUSES: A senile cataract is the most common form of cataract and is caused simply by the ageing of the eye's lens. As people grow older, their lenses usually become less transparent, though the rate of change varies from one person to another. Secondary cataracts are those that are caused by factors not related to ageing, such as eye infections, injury to the lens, or metabolic disorders like diabetes. High-voltage electrical shocks, some types of radiation and the use of certain drugs have also been known to cause secondary cataracts.

SYMPTOMS AND SIGNS: The effects of a cataract can be compared with a normally sighted person seeing through a mist or through a fog, depending on the severity of the condition.

TREATMENT: The only treatment for a cataract is surgery, though many people with this condition do not undergo surgery because their cataracts are so small – like a speck of dust on the lens. Even if the cataract covers a wider area, the deterioration in a person's sight may not be enough to justify surgery.

CATARRH

Catarrh is a widely used general term referring to the discharge of mucus, usually from the nasal sinuses and the air passages in the nose and throat. A runny nose, referred to by doctors as nasal catarrh, is a very common problem.

CAUSES: Catarrh may have a number of different causes, among which the three most common ones are colds and flu, nasal allergies, such as hay fever, and irritation of the lining of the nose. Catarrh may be brought on by irritation from gas or oil fires or airborne chemicals. Certain drugs may also stimulate the nose to produce a discharge. Conditions such as allergic rhinitis, nasal polyps and any distortion of the nasal passage may also bring it on.

SYMPTOMS AND SIGNS: The fluid that is discharged may be thin and clear but is more usually thick and opaque. There is some discomfort and breathing is often impaired, particularly when lying down.

TREATMENT: If you have a stuffy nose and live in a hot, dry, centrally heated house, try turning down the thermostat and using a humidifier. If smoke is the problem, avoid any kind of smoky atmosphere, and if you're a smoker, cut down or, better still, give up altogether. If working in a dusty environment, make sure you wear the appropriate mask.

CEREBRAL PALSY

Cerebral palsy occurs only in young children. There are many types and these vary a great deal in their severity. The condition is sometimes so mild that it can only be recognised by an expert, or it may be so severe that the child needs to be constantly in a wheelchair.

CAUSES: Cerebral palsy can only develop before a child's brain has stopped growing, at the age of about six or seven. It is caused by damage to areas of the brain, making normal control of movements impossible. In most cases, damage occurred either before or during birth. It can also result from meningitis, from an accidental injury to the head, from self-poisoning from drugs found in the home, or from lead poisoning from chewing lead-painted toys or furniture. Many cases of cere-

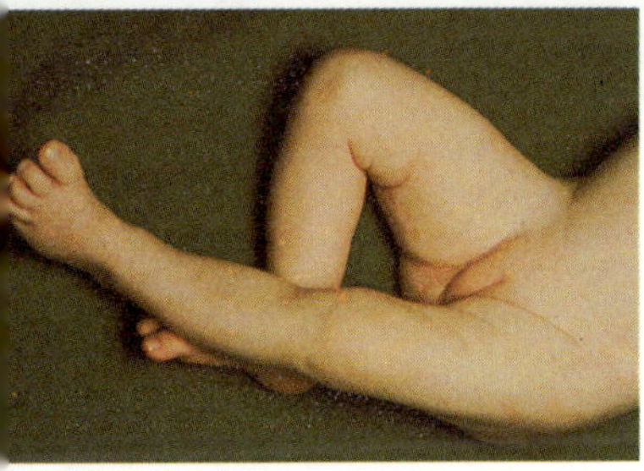

In over 90 per cent of cases of cerebral palsy, the damage occurs before or during birth.

bral palsy cannot, however, be explained.

SYMPTOMS AND SIGNS: Groups of muscles become stiff and immobile. Walking may be unsteady, or the child may have difficulty moving one or both arms. Movements may be irregular and uncontrolled. Associated problems include mental handicap, poor eyesight, hearing loss, difficulty speaking and a tendency to epileptic seizures.

TREATMENT: Although the brain abnormality that causes cerebral palsy is permanent, a lot can now be done to help children who suffer from this disorder. Treatment is usually based on physiotherapy by means of manipulation and exercises.

CEREBRAL THROMBOSIS

see STROKE

CERVICAL CANCER

The cervix is the narrow canal connecting the vagina with the main part of the womb. If detected early, cancer in this area stands a very good chance of being cured completely.

CAUSES: It is not known for certain what causes cervical cancer, but sexual intercourse seems to play a part. The tumours occur mainly in 35-50 year old women who have had children and is very rarely found in virgins. The risk of developing cancer of the cervix seems to be increased if you start having sexual intercourse at an early age and also if you have had a large number of sexual partners. The papilloma virus, which is transmitted by sexual intercourse and is the cause of vaginal warts, may also be a cause of cervical cancer. It may be that a long and varied sex life increases your risk of exposure to this virus.

SYMPTOMS AND SIGNS: The most common symptom is a watery, bloody discharge, which may have an offensive smell. The discharge is likely to be brought on or increased either by sexual intercourse or vaginal douching. Bleeding after intercourse, bleeding between periods and bleeding after the menopause are other possible symptoms which should be promptly investigated.

TREATMENT: The doctor will perform a smear test (below) and an internal vaginal examination. If the cancer is in its early stages, the patient will probably be treated in outpatients, using laserbeam treatment or freezing to destroy the cancerous cells. If the cancer is more extensive, a cone biopsy is usually performed under general anaesthetic. This is a very minor operation, which involves the removal of a cone-shaped piece of tissue from around the part of the cervix that protrudes into the vagina. More advanced cases will require a hysterectomy or radiotherapy.

CERVICAL SMEAR TEST

Women who have been sexually active are advised to have smear tests every three years up to the age of 60. Women who have, or who have had, vaginal warts are advised to have a smear test every year. Your own doctor can perform this simple test, or you can have it done as part of your regular check-up at a family planning clinic. A

A cervical smear test is quite painless and offers a 95 per cent chance of detecting abnormal cells.

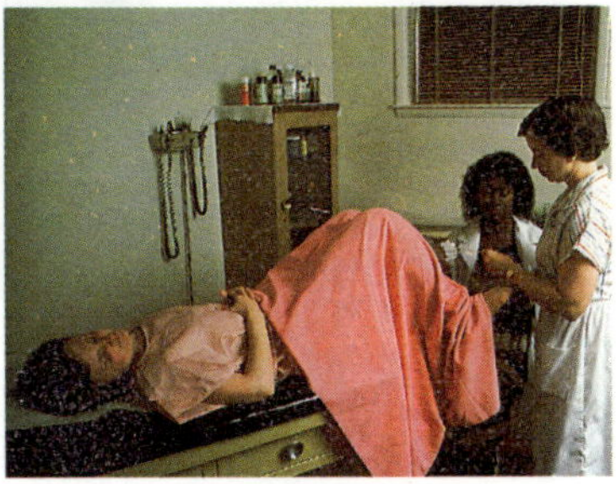

ASK THE DOCTOR

CEREBRAL PALSY

Q Is cerebral palsy hereditary?

A No, though if a mother has already had one child with the disease, she is marginally more likely to produce another with the same disorder. First children are slightly more prone to cerebral palsy than second and subsequent ones.

Q How common is cerebral palsy?

A Throughout the world, about one child in 300 is affected. In Britain, the figure is about one in 500. It is slightly more common in babies who are premature or very small at birth, and more boys than girls are affected.

Useful Addresses

CEREBRAL PALSY

The Spastics Society
12 Park Crescent
LONDON W1N 4EQ
071 436 2601

wooden spatula is rubbed across the neck of the womb to remove some of the surface cells. These cells are then placed on a microscope slide and sent to a laboratory to be analysed. By showing the existence of precancerous cells, the test can predict the possibility of cancer developing so that treatment can be given long before a tumour develops.

CHICKENPOX

Chickenpox is usually a childhood disease, characterised by an itchy rash and a slight fever. It can be worse in adults.

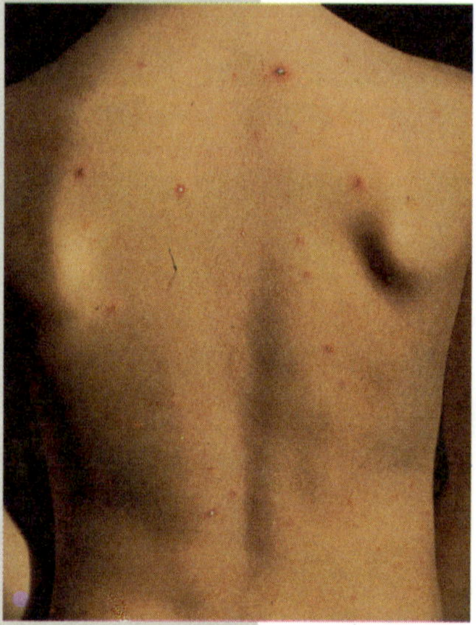

Chickenpox is a common contagious disease which three out of four people catch as children. Once someone has had chickenpox, s/he won't catch it again, but the virus can lie dormant and cause shingles in later life.

CAUSES: Chickenpox is caused by a virus which mainly affects the skin and the lining of the throat and mouth. The incubation period is between 12 and 21 days.

SYMPTOMS AND SIGNS: The first symptom is an itchy rash. This starts as tiny flat spots but these soon become filled with clear fluid. After a few days, these blisters burst and crust over. The spots tend to come out in crops and are accompanied by a raised temperature. Symptoms may be more severe in adults than in children.

TREATMENT: There is no cure for chickenpox, but fortunately it is not a serious condition. Drink lots of liquids to make up for losses due to feverishness. Apply calamine lotion or antihistamine cream to the skin to ease the itching.

See also SHINGLES

Self **Help**

CHICKENPOX

Add a cupful of bicarbonate of soda to your bath water to help relieve the itching. Do not scratch spots, as this can lead to scarring.

CHILBLAIN

Prolonged exposure to low temperatures will eventually turn skin a very pale colour, as the blood vessels constrict in order to conserve heat. A chilblain occurs when this normal reaction is taken to extremes.

SYMPTOMS AND SIGNS: Chilblains are painful, itchy and irregular patches on the feet. Usually varying in colour from dull blue to dusky red, they can turn a purplish brown-black in advanced cases and, if neglected, the intense cycles of itching/scratching can make the whole area raw and ulcerated.

CAUSES: Although they are a reaction to cold and damp, the real cause is lack of an adequate blood supply. A fault in the nervous system, which hampers the body's inner 'thermostat', means that the blood supply is not properly regulated.

Anybody who works in extreme heat or cold or in damp conditions is more likely to develop chilblains, and the elderly, too, are especially vulnerable, not only because of poor circulation but also because they may not eat properly. With any of these predisposing factors, tight-fitting shoes or socks or spending too long on your feet can be enough to set off the problem.

TREATMENT: It is possible to buy special chilblain creams from the chemist, and a doctor may prescribe drugs to relieve them.

Chilblains are more common in the young, and the elderly, and women are more prone to them than men.

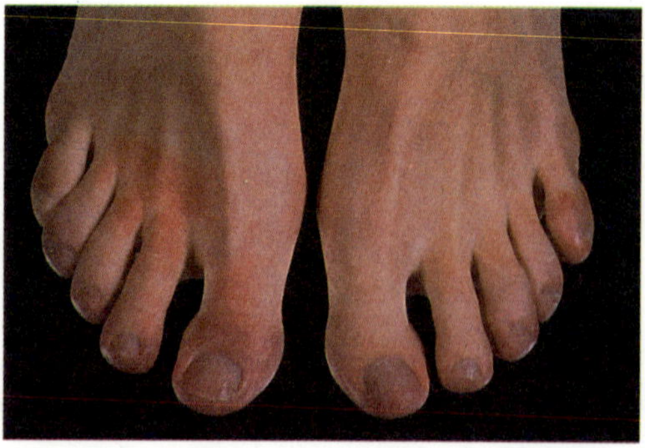

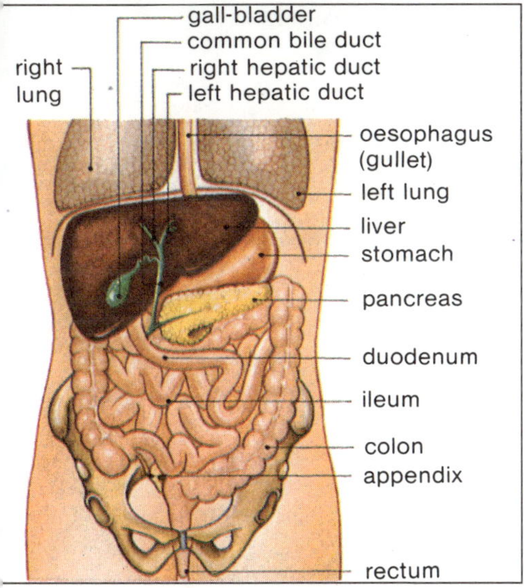

CHLAMYDIA INFECTIONS

Chlamydia are small bacteria responsible for a number of infections. Diseases caused by chlamydia include salpingitis, infant pneumonia, and NSU (non-specific urethritis). The causes, symptoms and treatment depend on which particular infection is present.
See also NSU, SALPINGITIS.

CIRRHOSIS

Cirrhosis of the liver occurs when healthy liver cells are replaced by fibrous scar tissue preventing the liver from working efficiently. Once damage has occurred it is irrevocable.

CAUSES: Alcohol is the cause of cirrhosis in the majority of cases, but not all. It can also aggravate existing conditions. Cirrhosis also occurs as a result of chemical abuse, for example cleaning fluids as well as some anaesthetics and drugs, including overdoses of paracetamol. People who have hepatitis B or glandular fever are more likely to get cirrhosis, as are those who have suffered a heart attack.

SYMPTOMS AND SIGNS: There are usually no symptoms in the early stages of cirrhosis. In more advanced cases there may be a loss of sexual appetite, a tingling sensation in the hands and feet and weight loss. In men breasts may swell and your testicles may shrink. Your abdomen will swell and fine red vein lines appear on the surface of your skin.

There are around 4,000 cases of cirrhosis of the liver reported in the UK each year.

TREATMENT: Your doctor will take blood tests to discover the extent of the damage and find out the cause of the disease. Once the cause is discovered, you will be referred to the appropriate physician, psychiatrist or help-group and advised to take an alcohol-free diet and rest.

Light micrograph of the human liver suffering from cirrhosis.

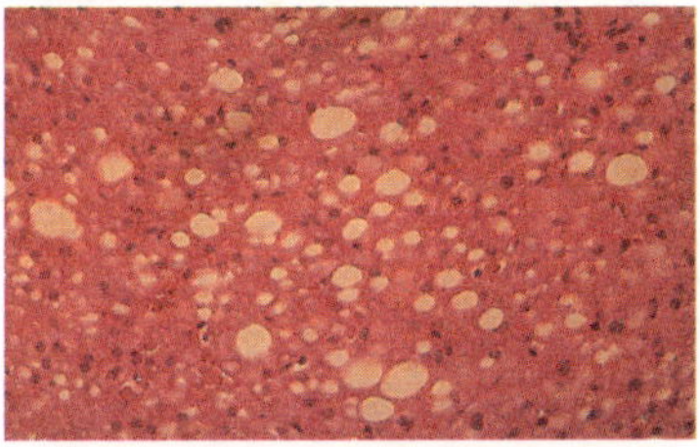

COELIAC DISEASE

Coeliac disease is an allergy of the small intestine to gluten, a protein present in most grains, which makes it less able to absorb nutrients. Coeliac disease is rare and is nearly always discovered in childhood.

CAUSES: None known.

SYMPTOMS AND SIGNS: These usually start soon after cereals have been introduced into the baby's diet, and include poor weight gain, or even weight loss, frequent loose, pale, smelly faeces, a lot of wind, and a general inability to thrive.

TREATMENT: The only possible treatment is to exclude all grain gluten from the diet,

Self **Help**

CHILBLAIN

If you are prone to chilblains, keep your feet warm. Try to slip out of cold or damp footwear as soon as possible, and avoid sudden changes in temperature. Warm feet slowly and indirectly. Potential chilblain sufferers should keep their feet warm all the time by wearing woollen hosiery and trousers and snuggling into boots, rather than by roasting their feet in front of a fire or on top of a hot-water bottle.

ASK THE DOCTOR

CIRRHOSIS

Q Just over a year ago I had cirrhosis. I am now fully recovered. Does this mean that I can start drinking again?

A If the root of the disease was alcohol abuse, the answer is no. However, if hepatitis or glandular fever brought on the disease you are now free to start drinking again. To be on the safe side, check with your doctor.

Useful Addresses

COELIAC DISEASE

Coeliac Society of the UK
PO Box 220
HIGH WYCOMBE
Buckinghamshire
HP11 2HY
0494 437278

Self **Help**

COLD SORES

- At first sign of a cold sore, try dabbing the area with lemon juice.
- At first sign, try applying ice cubes to area.
- Try dabbing on plain yoghurt, which can be soothing.

Useful Addresses

COLD SORES

The Herpes Association
41 North Road
LONDON N7 9DP
071 609 9061 (Helpline)
071 607 9661 (Office)

including wheat and rye. Other than dietary restrictions of this kind, which will probably be lifelong, the patient can lead a perfectly normal life.

COLD SORES

A cold sore is a blister which forms around the mouth or inside the nose. Cold sores can be irritating and unsightly, and cause a lot of local discomfort, but they are not dangerous. They are produced by a strain of the herpes simplex virus, to which most people have been exposed by the time they are five years old. Most people, however, build up a natural immunity, which is so effective that they never suffer from cold sores. Unfortunately, for the minority who do suffer from them, they are a real and painful nuisance.

Causes: Once the herpes virus has infected the skin, it remains hidden there, lying dormant between attacks. The body produces a partial immunity, which controls the virus for most of the time until a certain 'trigger' causes it to flare up. This can be a cold, a bout of flu, a chest infection, or a sore throat. Exposure to sunlight or harsh winds can also act as a trigger. Some women have a tendency to cold sores during menstruation.

Symptoms and signs: People who suffer recurring attacks of cold sores soon learn to tell when one is starting. There is a sudden itchy tingling in the skin in the affected area, which can begin up to two days before the cold sore erupts. When this happens, an inflamed cluster of tiny blisters develops. These fill with a yellowish-white fluid and feel itchy and hot – a sensation which is soon followed by tenderness and pain. Occasionally, these inflamed blisters burst within two to four days of appearing, but in all cases they start to heal by drying up. During this process, if the sore is left alone, a crust forms, which will eventually fall off.

Treatment: Anti-viral lotion is available from the chemist or doctors and you need to start applying it as soon as symptoms begin.

ASK THE DOCTOR

COLD SORES

Q When I get anxious I often develop a cold sore. Is there any connection?

A Yes. Stress can act as a trigger. You should learn to cope through relaxation techniques.

Q Do cold sores have a tendency to run in families?

A Yes. It has not been proved that this is so, though it is possible that the inability to develop a sufficient immunity to the virus that causes it is hereditary.

Q My mother suffers from cold sores and she insists on kissing my baby whether she has them or not. Can they be passed on in this way?

A The cold sore virus can probably be passed on to very young children like this. So, you should tactfully persuade her not to kiss your baby when she has a cold sore.

Cold sores tend to occur in a cluster around the mouth. The first sign of an outbreak is a tingling sensation.

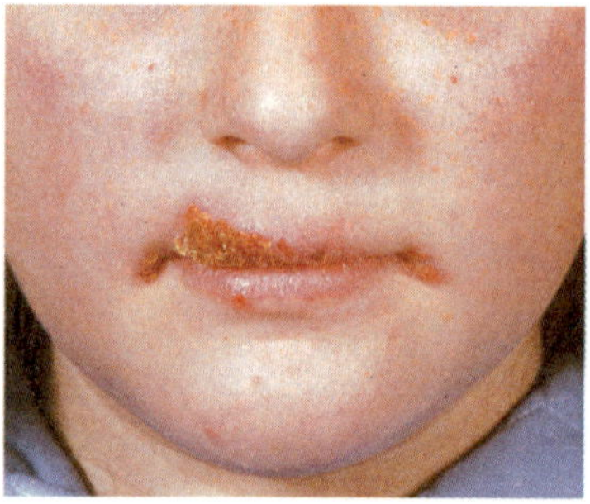

COMMON COLD

The disease that we call the common cold is, in fact, caused by any one of more than 200 viruses. It is normally confined to the nose and throat, although the viruses can infect the larynx and the lungs.

Causes: We all get colds – we are likely to have our first before we are one year old. As we get older we become immune to certain viruses. Viruses are passed on in droplets when we cough or sneeze.

There are nearly 200 different viruses that can cause the common cold.

SYMPTOMS AND SIGNS: To some extent, symptoms depend on the virus responsible for the cold. You can expect sneezing, watery eyes, a sore throat, coughing, hoarseness and a runny nose. You may also get an unpleasant nasal discharge, a headache and a slight temperature.

TREATMENT: Adults can take paracetamol or aspirin to help them sleep. Drink plenty of fluids (preferably water and fruit juices) and, above all, take plenty of rest. Keep warm and – if possible – try not to infect other people. Most colds clear up on their own after three or four days; if the infection spreads to the sinuses, ears, larynx or lungs and you start running a high temperature, consult your doctor.

CONJUNCTIVITIS

The sclera or 'white' of the eye is covered by a translucent membrane called the conjunctiva, which easily becomes inflamed if exposed to irritation or infection. This inflammation, known as conjunctivitis, or 'pink eye', makes the normally white part of the eyeball appear pinkish or reddish in colour.

CAUSES: Conjunctivitis is often caused by an allergy – to pollen, house dust or make-up – when it's known as allergic conjunctivitis, or by reaction to some kind of environmental pollution, such as factory fumes, tobacco smoke or too much chlorine in a swimming pool, when it's known as chemical conjunctivitis. Neither allergic nor chemical conjunctivitis is contagious. Conjunctivitis may also, however, result from a bacterial or viral infection, in which case it can spread rapidly from one person to another, especially if strict rules of hygiene aren't observed. This is known as infectious conjunctivitis.

SYMPTOMS AND SIGNS: These include red, itchy, burning eyes, which water a good deal. With infectious conjunctivitis, the inner eyelids are often inflamed and there may also be a discharge from the eyes, which tends to gum the lids together overnight. If bacteria are the cause of the conjunctivitis, the discharge tends to be pus-like; if it is due to a virus, the discharge will be thinner and more watery.

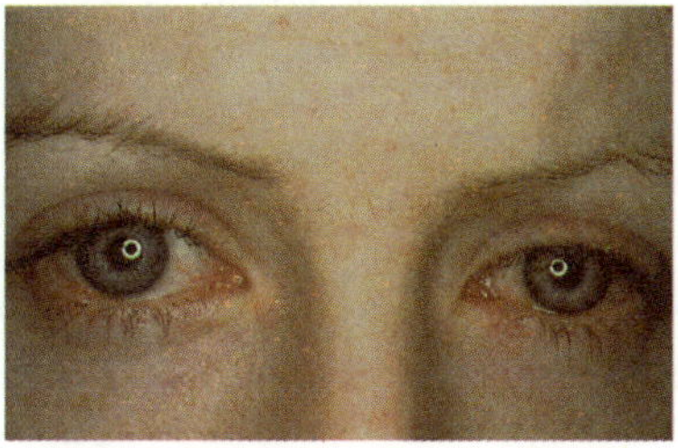

If you have conjunctivitis, do not cover your eye with a patch as this will only aggravate the problem.

TREATMENT: Conjunctivitis is not a serious condition but, if left untreated, it can occasionally develop into a more serious disorder, such as an ulcerated cornea. It is therefore important to see your doctor, who will diagnose the cause and prescribe the appropriate medication. With allergic and chemical conjunctivitis, the best treatment is to identify and remove the cause of the irritation, but if this is not possible, the doctor will prescribe some drops to soothe and lubricate the eyes. These may contain either a mild local anaesthetic to alleviate the soreness or a corticosteroid such as cortisone to deal with the inflammation. Infectious conjunctivitis is usually treated with antibiotic drops or ointment.

see also CORNEAL ULCER.

Self **Help**
COMMON COLD

Commercial 'cold cures' and nasal sprays may help but don't overdo them. Steam inhalations can help clear your head. Dissolve the preparation in hot water, cover your head with a towel and inhale. A commercial humidifier may help – they are available from your chemist.

Self **Help**
CONJUNCTIVITIS

- Non-prescription eye drops containing a mild antiseptic for cleansing the eyes are sometimes helpful.
- Dark glasses may help.
- If highly chlorinated water is a problem, wear goggles to protect the eyes while swimming.
- If you have infectious conjunctivitis, do not touch your eyes unnecessarily, do not share face cloths or towels with anyone else, and wash your hands thoroughly after applying your eye medication.

Self **Help**
CONSTIPATION

If you have become constipated through an unavoidable change in diet, add two or three tablespoons of bran to your usual breakfast cereal. Prunes and figs are also traditional and effective remedies. Many different kinds of laxatives are available from your chemist, but you shouldn't take any of them regularly except on the advice of your doctor. Avoid 'lubricant' laxatives like liquid paraffin because they can cause serious damage to the lining of the bowel.

Self **Help**
CORN

If you are particularly prone to corns, it may be worth investing in a corn file to cut through the upper layers and ease discomfort. It is often easiest to rub away the hard skin with a pumice stone while you're in the bath. However, if you're diabetic or have a circulation problem, your feet should only be treated by a professional.

CONSTIPATION

Constipation is a condition in which the passing of faeces is infrequent or difficult. It is not usually a problem in itself, but it may be a symptom of a more serious disorder.

CAUSES: The most common causes of constipation are sudden changes in the kind of meals you eat, not drinking enough fluid, bad eating habits or not enough exercise. If you find you are having to eat food that is quite different from the type you're used to, perhaps when you go on holiday, you may find that you become constipated for a time. Long-term constipation usually results from not eating enough foods that are rich in fibre.

SYMPTOMS AND SIGNS: The most obvious symptom of constipation is passing a bowel motion very infrequently. However, what is 'normal' varies enormously from one person to another. If you are constipated, the motion tends to be hard, often formed into pellets joined together, and you have to strain to pass it. You may feel some discomfort in your stomach from time to time – often a gripping pain, which may be central or low down in the abdomen.

TREATMENT: Constipation usually can be relieved by eating foods that are high in fibre, such as wholemeal bread, root vegetables, fruit and breakfast cereals enriched with bran. You should also drink at least three pints of water a day. Walking and other gentle regular exercise can help.

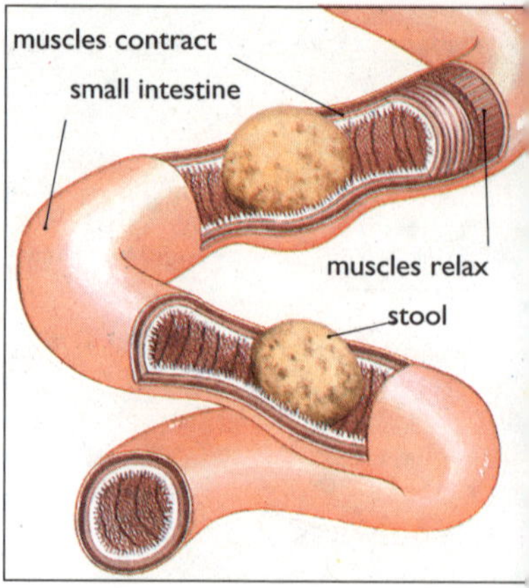

Constipation may be particularly bad during pregnancy and may be made worse by piles.

CORN

Corns and calluses are areas of skin that have thickened because of constant pressure. Corns are small and develop on the toes; calluses are larger and commonly develop on the soles of the feet.

CAUSES: Most people suffer from corns at some point, often because they wear ill-fitting or worn-out shoes. As a result, they develop patches of thickened, hardened skin at the various points where skin meets shoe with too much friction or pressure. Corns and calluses are especially likely to occur over any unusual prominence such as a hammer toe.

SYMPTOMS AND SIGNS: A corn – which looks like a hardened yellowish mass – may or may not be painful, but there's always a danger that it may become a problem at a later stage.

TREATMENT: Chiropodists gently plane away the callus and may recommend regular applications of dichloroacetic acid to prevent it from re-forming. They may advise the temporary or permanent use of an insole or a replaceable pad to wear inside a shoe – to relieve excess pressure on the foot.

People who have high arches are especially prone to corns, because the arch increases pressure on the toes.

CORNEAL ULCER

Because of its position over the front of the eye, the cornea is the part most susceptible to infection and injury. In nearly all cases, only one eye is affected. Corneal ulcers are not common and affect mainly people whose work puts them at risk of foreign bodies entering the eye.

CAUSES: A corneal ulcer may result from a severe, untreated corneal infection, the most common being conjunctivitis. Infection can also be caused by damage to the surface of the cornea – by a scratch or burn. If the cornea is accidentally injured in some way, a secondary infection may develop. Corneal infections can be caused by either bacteria or viruses. Occasionally, chronic inflammation of the cornea may occur as the result of a disease or infection elsewhere in the body, in which case the disorder itself needs treating as well as the localized inflammation. Whatever the cause of the infection, if it is severe and left untreated, it can result in a corneal ulcer.

SYMPTOMS AND SIGNS: You may feel discomfort or pain in the eye, vision may be impaired, and the white of the eye may become pink or red. You may be able to see the ulcer as a whitish patch.

TREATMENT: Your doctor may stain the surface of your eye with a yellow dye to show up an invisible ulcer. If an ulcer is caused by injury or infection of the cornea, treatment is usually given as antibiotic drops, ointment, tablets, or injections near the eye. In severe cases, you may need surgery – either to seal off a perforated cornea or to deal with scars that have drastically reduced vision. These are matters for an eye specialist to deal with.

CORONARY HEART DISEASE

see HEART DISEASE.

CORONARY THROMBOSIS

see HEART ATTACK.

COUGHS

The cough is a simple reflex. You take a breath, the vocal cords in the larynx close up, blocking the windpipe, the chest contracts and pressure builds up in the air passages. When the cords open, this pressure is suddenly and violently released and anything clogging the air passages – dust, germs, mucus – is shifted towards the throat.

CAUSES: Coughing can be due to any number of conditions – from minor ailments like colds and flu to more serious conditions like chronic bronchitis, asthma and whooping cough.

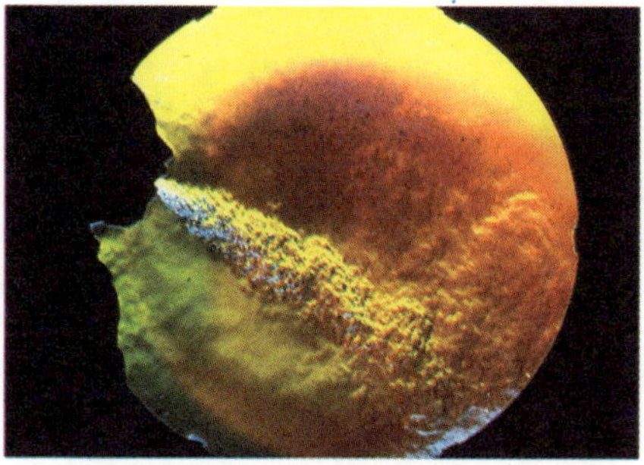

When you cough, the stream of air expelled from the lungs reaches a considerable distance.

SYMPTOMS AND SIGNS: Coughs are often worse in the morning. You may find that you are bringing up thick yellow or green phlegm. Sometimes a minor irritation may start the cough reflex even though there is not enough material to clear from the lungs – this is known as a dry cough. If you cough up blood or have severe pains as you cough, you should see a doctor immediately.

TREATMENT: Although traditionally prescribed for coughs, most proprietary cough medicines are of limited value; since most coughs are 'good' for the lungs it makes sense to allow the cough to run its course. Do not use cough suppressants for a productive cough. If the cough is due to bacterial bronchitis, a course of antibiotics should cure it. The more serious conditions require expert medical attention.

ASK THE DOCTOR

CORNEAL ULCER

Q Can a corneal ulcer be caused by infection from a cold sore?

A Yes – which is why it is so important not to touch your eyes after touching your mouth when you have a cold sore . A corneal ulcer caused by the cold sore – or herpes simplex virus – is usually invisible (see also COLD SORES)

Self **Help**

COUGHS

The best way to relieve most minor coughs is to use a steam inhalation. If it is due to a cold or flu, a drink of hot lemon and honey or medicated lozenges should help. If you smoke, give it up.

ASK THE DOCTOR

COUGHS

Q My daughter gets croup whenever she has a cold. What should I do?

A You will know she has croup because she will have a coarse cough and make a rasping noise while breathing. Run a very hot bath to saturate the bathroom with steam. Sit your daughter in the room and if that doesn't help, call the doctor.

CRAMP

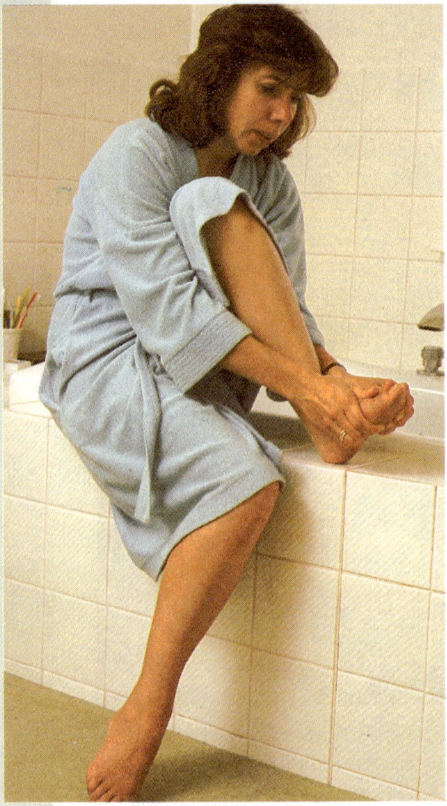

Night cramps are particularly common in elderly people and pregnant women.

Cramp is a painful spasm in the muscles.

CAUSES: There are several causes of cramp. The most common are a build up of lactic acid during vigorous exercise or a spasm from a trapped nerve in the lower back. Salt deficiency is a rare cause of cramp.

SYMPTOMS AND SIGNS: A sudden pain in the leg suggests that certain groups of muscles are in spasm.

TREATMENT: The simple way of relieving cramp is to rest and if there is a pain in the affected limb, stretch the affected muscle.

CYST

see BARTHOLIN'S CYST, BREAST CYST, EYE CYST, MIDDLE EAR CYST, OVARIAN CYST, SEBACEOUS CYST.

CYSTIC FIBROSIS

Cystic fibrosis is a disease that affects the pancreas and other mucus-secreting glands, such as those located in the lungs and the lining of the intestine.

CAUSES: It is an inherited disease and its cause is unknown. There is a one in four chance of having it if both parents are carriers.

SYMPTOMS AND SIGNS: The disease is sometimes obvious soon after birth. Newborn babies normally pass a thick greenish substance, known as meconium. If this mucus is absent, the meconium remains very thick and cannot be passed, forming an obstruction which may need to be removed surgically. More usually, the condition becomes obvious between the ages of three and 18 months, when the baby will develop diarrhoea and fail to gain weight in the normal way. Children with cystic fibrosis also tend to suffer from chest infections.

TREATMENT: If cystic fibrosis is suspected, your doctor will arrange for a special test to be carried out to confirm the diagnosis. S/he will recommend a special diet and other treatments. Unfortunately, there is no cure for the condition, although if the diagnosis is made early much can be done to help the child. First a special diet high in carbohydrate and fat is prescribed and your child takes an enzyme preparation with every meal to help him/her digest food. Regular doses of antibiotics will prevent chest infections. Parents are taught how to give a child physiotherapy to keep his/her chest clear. Many children with

Cystic fibrosis is characterised by a tendency to chronic lung infections.

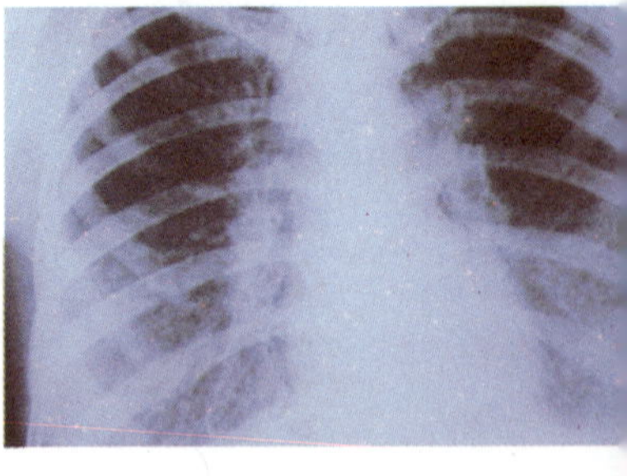

Useful Addresses

CYSTIC FIBROSIS

Cystic Fibrosis Research Trust
5 Blyth Rd
BROMLEY
KENT BR1 3RS
081 464 7211

cystic fibrosis will survive into adulthood, although there is always the danger that they may contract a serious infection resulting in severe permanent damage to the lungs. Tragically, a few of the more severely affected children die even before reaching their teens.

CYSTITIS

Cystitis is an inflammation of the bladder, most commonly suffered by women, although men and young children can also be affected.

CAUSES: Cystitis occurs when bacteria that live in and around the rectum, which normally cause no problems, find their way to the opening of the urinary tract. This can happen when you wipe your bottom from 'back to front' instead of the other way round, or if you have not washed in the correct way after a bowel movement (see SELF HELP).

Bacteria can also be introduced into the urethra during vaginal intercourse. Over-enthusiastic sexual intercourse may cause additional inflammation around the urethra.

During pregnancy, women often find that emptying the bladder becomes more difficult because of the pressure on the neck of the bladder.

SYMPTOMS AND SIGNS: Wanting to pass urine very frequently and, when you do, suffering a scalding sensation, which can be mild or intense. The urine often smells unpleasant and there may be blood in it. With a severe attack, you may also run a temperature, get low abdominal pain or backache, and feel generally unwell.

TREATMENT: The moment you recognise the symptoms of cystitis, put a urine sample into a clean, screw-top jar for your doctor. Drink 600ml (1 pint) of water to dilute the urine and a further 300 ml ($^1/_2$ pint) every 20 minutes for three hours. Because the bacteria thrive in an acid environment, you should also take an alkaline substance, such as bicarbonate of soda – dissolve one teaspoonful in water every hour for each of the three hours (though not if you have heart trouble or kidney stones). Avoid all drinks and foods that contain acid or produce it in the body, like coffee, tea, carbonated soft drinks, oranges, grapefruits and highly spiced dishes such as curry. Also avoid tobacco and alcohol. If the pain persists, take some strong painkillers and go to your doctor with your urine sample and discuss possible causes for the attack. If the doctor suspects infection, s/he may prescribe a course of antibiotics. It is important to complete the course even if your symptoms disappear.

Cystitis is more common in women because of their shorter urethra.

Self **Help**

CYSTITIS

To make passing water less painful during an attack, hold a towel-wrapped hot-water bottle high up between your legs for a little while first.

To prevent further attacks, avoid everything acidic or highly spiced and drink plenty of water each day; restrict intake of tobacco and alcohol; avoid tight jeans or trousers; wear cotton rather than nylon briefs, and stockings or open-crotch tights rather than ordinary tights. Don't use soap around the vaginal area: wash before and after making love, and use a water-based lubricant during actual intercourse. Afterwards, pass water as soon as possible to flush out any bacteria. After a bowel movement, always wipe from front to back and, if possible, wash while you are sitting on the toilet by soaping the back passage and pouring a bottle of warm water past the vaginal area towards the back.

Useful Addresses

CYSTITIS

Angela Kilmartin
75 Mortimer Road
LONDON N1 5AR
Tel: 071 249 8664

d

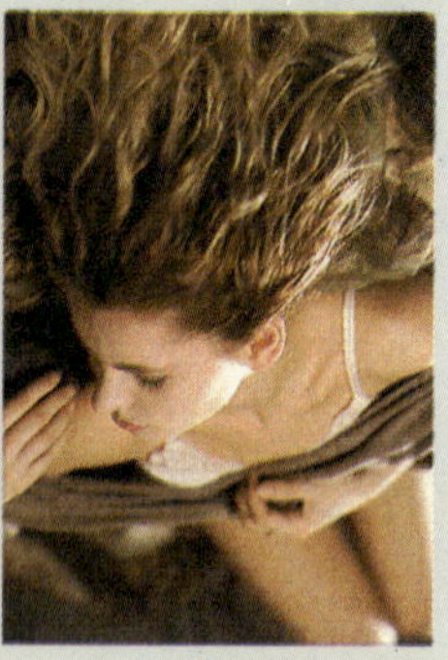

Don't wash your hair too often. An over-dry scalp can be as bad as a greasy one.

DANDRUFF

Dandruff is a harmless condition in which the scalp starts to flake. These flakes appear in the hair and fall on to the shoulders. It is most common among people in their late teens and early twenties.

CAUSES: The actual cause of dandruff is not clear but it is known that it is a result of the speeding up of a natural process. Sometimes there is an underlying fungal infection of the scalp. Dandruff appears when the skin on the scalp sheds its dead cells rather more quickly and profusely than usual. It is usually worst on greasy skins.

SYMPTOMS AND SIGNS: Dry white scales are shed on to clothes. Occasionally, dandruff can develop into a more severe seborrhoeic dermatitis, the signs of which are a reddened, greasy and very itchy scalp with brownish scales in the hair.

TREATMENT: Wash the hair two or three times a week with a mildly medicated shampoo. If symptoms persist, try a stronger shampoo containing cetrimide, zinc pyrithione or selenium sulphide. Don't use these shampoos for long periods of time. If the condition persists, it may need antifungal shampoo.

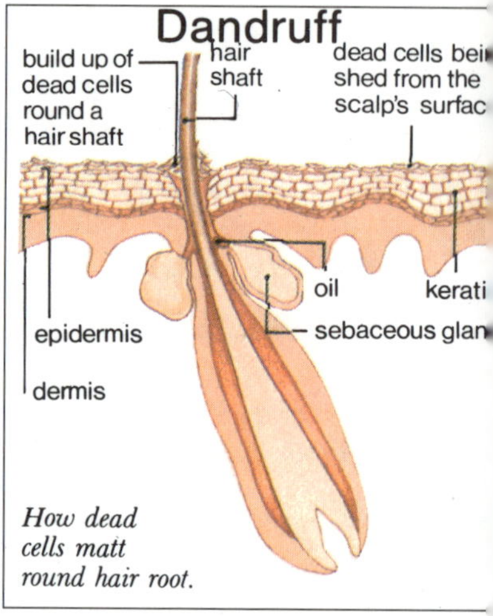

Dead cells are shed from the scalp's surface and matt around the hair root causing dandruff.

DEEP-VEIN THROMBOSIS

Deep-vein thrombosis is the formation of a blood clot in the deep veins of the body. It is most likely to occur in the legs, though it can occur anywhere. Occasionally, deep-vein blood clots can break off to form an embolus, which can travel up to the lungs and block the pulmonary trunk. This can be fatal.

CAUSES: If the lining of a vein is damaged in any way, the blood is more likely to clot and cause a blockage. Deep-vein thrombosis is

A large clot – up to 1.3cm / ½ inch across and several centimetres long – may need surgical removal.

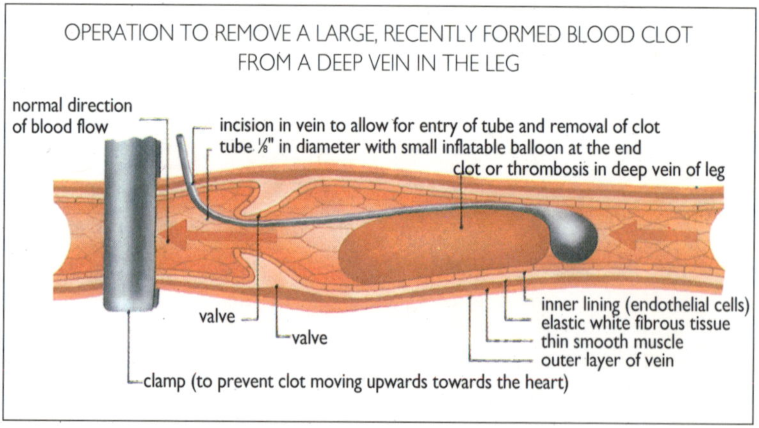

ASK THE DOCTOR

DANDRUFF

Q My brother has dandruff, can I catch it from him?

A No, dandruff is not infectious. It can't be passed on to other people by, for instance, using the same hairbrush or comb. However, it's not a good idea to share brushes or combs in case of fungal infection.

most often seen in people who are immobile – especially after having had an operation – overweight, or taking oestrogen, either in the form of the Pill or as hormonal replacement therapy at menopause.

Symptoms and signs: There may be no visible symptoms, but deep-vein thrombosis can cause painful swelling, especially around the ankle and calf. This swelling will remain indented after it has been pressed.

Treatment: Your doctor may prescribe drugs to stop the blood clotting. Try to keep your leg – or the affected area – raised whenever you lie down. Exercise, however gentle, should help the condition. Keep your weight down and if you smoke, give up. Occasionally, the clot may need to be removed by surgery.

DEHYDRATION

This is simply a shortage of water in the body.

Causes: Dehydration is the result of either insufficient intake of liquid or a dramatic loss of liquid as a result of diarrhoea, sunstroke or vomiting.

Symptoms and signs: As well as a furious thirst, you will also experience dizziness, nausea and extreme exhaustion. The skin often loses its spongy texture and looks more wrinkled than usual.

Treatment: In mild cases, the cure is simple – replace lost fluids by drinking non- alcoholic drinks. In serious cases, an intravenous drip may be necessary. Prevent dehydration in the first place by taking plenty of liquids, especially when it's hot or you are exerting yourself. If you have diarrhoea or vomiting, take a rehydrating preparation recommended by your chemist. This will contain all the salts and minerals that your body needs. Dehydration is much more serious in children.

See also DIARRHOEA, SUNSTROKE AND VOMITING.

DELIRIUM TREMENS

See ALCOHOLISM

DEMENTIA

See ALZHEIMER'S DISEASE

DENTAL ABSCESS

A pus-filled hole in the tissue around the tooth root, which is embedded in the jawbone.

Causes: Receding gums, severe tooth decay or dead pulp are the main causes of dental

Even healthy activities such as taking a sauna can cause mild dehydration. Take plenty of fluids.

ASK THE DOCTOR

DEEP-VEIN THROMBOSIS

Q I suffer from varicose veins. Does this mean I'm likely to develop thrombosis?

A Sometimes blood clots do form in varicose veins, just under the skin close to the surface of the leg. These clots develop into obvious painful lumps, but they are superficial thromboses and usually settle down quite quickly with rest. See also Thrombosis and Heart attack.

Q A few months ago I had a deep-vein thrombosis as a complication of my hysterectomy and I still get a swollen leg from time to time. Is this a problem?

A This is likely to happen. Avoid long periods of standing up, try wearing support tights or stockings, and make sure you take regular exercise.

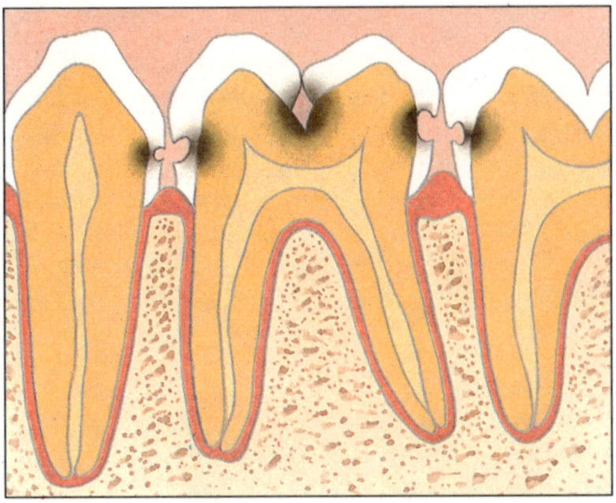

Left: Abscesses are likely to form beneath teeth already attacked by decay. The dark sections on the diagram show points that have been attacked as a result of a lack of essential minerals in the saliva.

Below: The effects of sugar on tooth decay. One sweet held in the mouth for three minutes produces over 11 minutes of decay. If you chain-suck sweets, the effects last even longer.

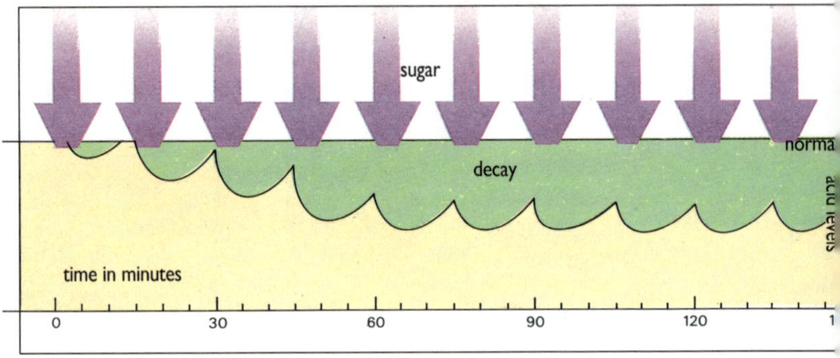

Self **Help**

DENTAL ABSCESS

Relieve the pain by taking a couple of aspirins (or you may need stronger painkillers containing codeine, available from your chemist). Rinse your mouth thoroughly every hour with salt water, to encourage the abscess to burst and so release the pus. Make an appointment to see your dentist as soon as possible.

Self **Help**

DEPRESSION

Mild cases of depression can be alleviated by a special treat, but true depressive illness will not respond to this treatment. Regular exercise may help to combat depression.

abscesses. The dead pulp gives off harmful products as well as bacteria and can easily spread to infect the whole jawbone. If the abscess is untreated, it can eat into the bone creating a small canal, just before it emerges through the gum. This is called a 'gumboil'.

Symptoms and signs: An abscess will be extremely painful, especially when you chew your food. If the gumboil bursts you will be able to taste a revolting pus, although this may relieve the pain slightly. The abscess may affect the glands around the neck and your face will probably appear slightly swollen. You're likely to have a high temperature and feel generally unwell.

Treatment: Your dentist may try to save the tooth. Firstly, a tiny hole may be drilled through the crown to release the pus. In this case, the root canal and pus chamber will be cleaned out and disinfected before a temporary filling is put in place. Your dentist will prescribe a course of antibiotics and give you a permanent filling at a later date and the tooth may need to be crowned.

DEPRESSION

Depression is a mental illness and people who suffer from it are unable to lift themselves out of their misery. Their gloomy outlook gradually worsens and they eventually become unable to lead a normal life.

Causes: Basically, there are two different kinds of depression. 'Reactive' depression is an extreme reaction to a trauma or emotional blow. 'Endogenous' depression is brought on by some internal cause, such as a viral infection like glandular fever. A tendency to endogenous depression is thought to run in families.

Symptoms and signs: Depression is usually accompanied by some physical loss of

There is a marked contrast between 'feeling low' and a case of genuine clinical depression.

energy, constipation, headaches and a lack of appetite. Sufferers generally feel persecuted, and in extreme cases find it impossible to lead a normal life.

TREATMENT: Approach your doctor if you believe that your unhappiness is more than a passing mood. Your doctor may refer you to a specialist and you will probably be prescribed anti-depressants and psychotherapy.

DERMATITIS

This is the general term used to describe a number of types of skin inflammation (often used synonymously with the term eczema). There are two different types of dermatitis. One is due to external causes, such as allergies to cleaning fluids or chemicals, while the second is due to internal causes, brought on by metabolic disorders or hereditary conditions.

See also ECZEMA

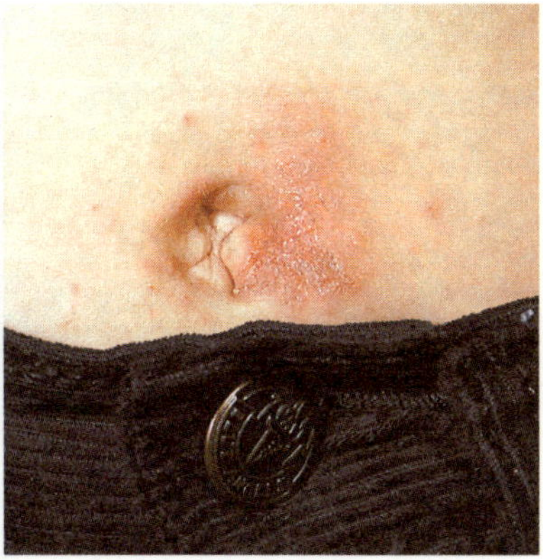

Allergy caused by skin contact with a nickel-plated stud on a pair of jeans.

DETACHED RETINA

See RETINAL DETACHMENT

DIABETES MELLITUS

Diabetes affects one in 70 people in the UK. In most cases, there is no cure for this serious condition, but modern medicine has it well under control.

CAUSES: Diabetes is caused by a lack of the hormone insulin, which controls the way the body uses sugar. When we eat bread, cakes and other foods containing sugar and starch, the digestive processes in the bowel break down the sugar and starch into glucose, which is absorbed into the bloodstream. Insulin, which is produced in the pancreas (a small organ located just below the stomach), helps the body process the glucose in the blood, so that it can be used to fuel muscle activity and other body functions. After processing, any excess can be stored in the liver as glycogen (starch) to be converted later into energy or fat. In a diabetic, the pancreas doesn't produce enough insulin to allow the glucose in the blood to be used. In some cases, no insulin at all is produced.

Heredity plays an important part in this disease – nearly one-third of diabetics have a family history of insulin deficiency. Age can also cause the pancreas to become inefficient. Many who develop the disease in later life are overweight, so it may be that the pancreas is failing to keep pace with the body's demands for insulin to deal with the increased volume of body tissues.

ASK THE DOCTOR

DIABETES

Q I have recently been diagnosed as diabetic. Can you tell me if it will affect my hormones or change my behaviour at all?

A Discovering that you have diabetes, or any other condition, can be traumatic and you're likely to be under more strain than usual, but your basic temperament shouldn't change.

Sufficient insulin from the pancreas is required to process the glucose found in our daily diet.

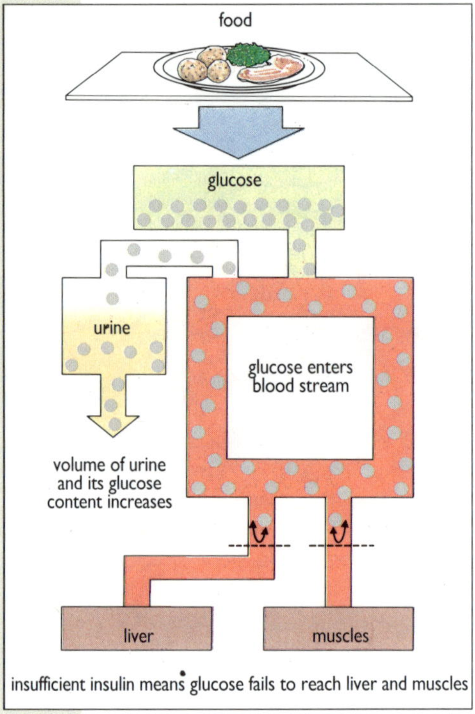

Symptoms and signs: There are two main types of diabetes: insulin dependent diabetes and non-insulin dependent diabetes. **Insulin dependent diabetes** occurs when the body produces virtually no insulin. This form usually develops in the early teens – though it can appear later. It usually develops very quickly, often over a few days. The child or young adult feels increasingly weak, becomes intensely thirsty, passes large quantities of urine. S/he may lose weight rapidly because, unable to use or store its glucose, the body draws on its stores of fat for energy. There may also be confusion and sleepiness. Without prompt treatment, the condition can worsen to such an extent that the diabetic may lose consciousness and pass into a coma. The breath may smell of dry-cleaning fluid or alcohol.

Diabetics are more likely to suffer from certain types of infection than other people because sugar encourages the growth of bacteria, fungi and viruses. Common problems include recurrent boils and carbuncles; thrush and itching in the genital regions because of the high blood sugar level in the urine; and the failure of cuts and other injuries to heal.

Non-insulin dependent diabetes is a milder form which results when the body produces some insulin but not enough for its requirements. Most people in this group are over 40 and overweight. The initial symptoms of thirst and excessive urine usually come on over a period of months. Tiredness, pins and needles, blurred vision may all be symptoms, but it is very rare for the older diabetic to go into a coma.

Treatment: Treatment will depend on the type of diabetes.

Insulin dependent diabetics need regular treatment with insulin injections. Once the correct dose of insulin has been established, the symptoms disappear and the urine no longer contains large amounts of sugar.

Once on insulin, diabetics must be careful about food. Regular meals throughout the day are a must. If they have an insulin injection and don't eat, the level of glucose in the bloodstream will fall dramatically, and they can pass out – this is called a hypoglycaemic attack.

As well as having regular meals, insulin dependent diabetics need to be particularly careful about the quantity of sugar and starch that they eat. They need some, but not too much. So diabetic diets are prescribed to

Inside a human kidney. The pale area shows the glomeruli (filters) undermined by diabetes.

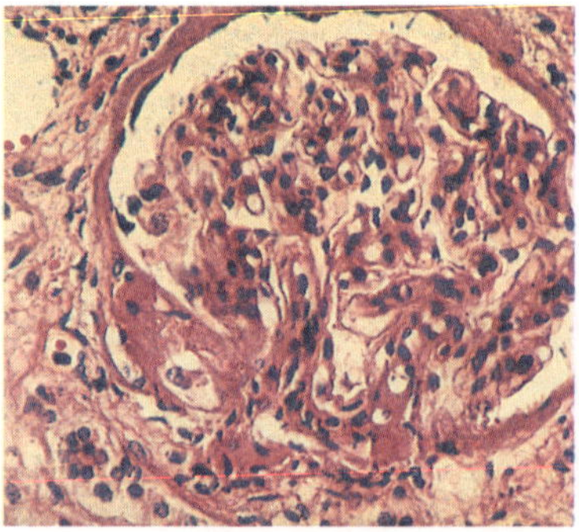

Useful Addresses

DIABETES

British Diabetic Society
10 Queen Anne Street
LONDON W1M OBD
071 323 1531

Irish Diabetic Association
82-83 Lower Gardiner St
DUBLIN 7
Republic of Ireland
(Dublin) 363022

contain specified amounts of sugar.

Diabetics are provided with simple kits for testing the level of sugar in their urine and sometimes their blood. This way they can keep their own check and get treatment quickly if the sugar content suddenly goes up.

Non-insulin dependent diabetics usually improve with a carefully controlled diet to rid them of any excess weight and to reduce their sugar and starch intake. A regular check will be kept on the blood sugar level, and if it settles, no further treatment is needed.

If diet alone is not sufficient, tablets may be prescribed. These will either stimulate the pancreas to produce more insulin, or will help the insulin already available to work harder. Occasionally, insulin injections become necessary if the condition worsens.

DIARRHOEA

Diarrhoea is the frequent passing of soft or watery faeces. It is not a disease in itself, so much as a sign of illness.

CAUSES: The most common cause of diarrhoea is infection, whether it is bacterial or viral. Changes in diet, gastric flu, inflammation of the intestine and food poisoning are also common causes. Drugs, especially antibiotics, can result in diarrhoea as they tend to alter the levels of harmless bacteria in the bowel and so allow more sinister bacteria to take hold.

SYMPTOMS AND SIGNS: As well as frequent passing of watery faeces, you are also likely to experience stomach cramps. Extreme cases may lead to persistent blood or mucus in your stools.

TREATMENT: If you have an attack of diarrhoea, start drinking extra quantities of clear fluid. It is a good idea to try to replace some of the salts that are lost from the body as well, so clear chicken soup or even a stock cube in water is good. It is better not to eat anything solid at all – apart perhaps from jelly – for twenty-four hours.

Chemists sell various preparations to make the motion more solid but it is still important to drink plenty of liquids.

Usually diarrhoea will settle within a day or two. If it does not, or if the diarrhoea has blood in it, then you should see your doctor.

If a child has diarrhoea and is drinking very little, take him to see your doctor if this lasts for more than twelve hours, or immediately

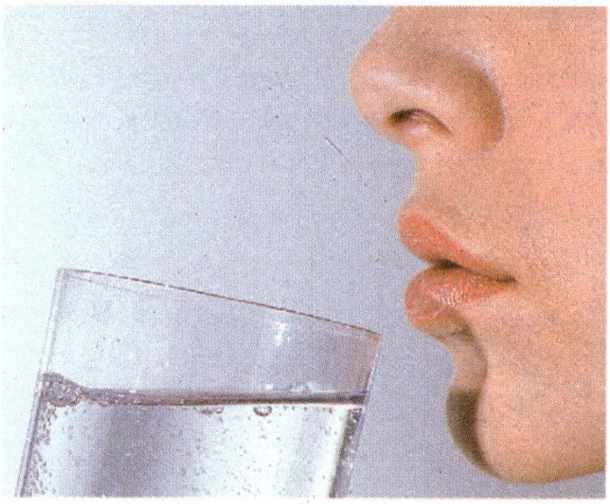

After an attack of diarrhoea, it is important to replace not only lost fluids but lost salts as well.

if the child shows unusual loss of energy or drowsiness. The doctor may prescribe a salt/sugar preparation to replace lost salts and provide energy. If dehydration becomes a serious problem, the doctor will usually advise admission to hospital. Dehydration can then be corrected by means of a 'drip' feed, containing salts, sugar and fluid, directly into a vein.

DIARRHOEA ABROAD

Everybody dreads getting diarrhoea on holiday. Gippy tummy', 'Spanish tummy', 'Montezuma's revenge' – whatever you call it, traveller's tummy can spoil a holiday. Simple, basic food hygiene is important. Be particularly wary of shellfish, salads (which should be washed well) and ice-cream.

If you are travelling in rural areas in underdeveloped parts of Europe, Africa or Asia, it is better not to drink tap water unless it is sterilised first with special tablets obtainable from a chemist. Otherwise you should stick to bottled mineral water, and avoid ice in drinks if worried about hygiene.

See also Dehydration and Dysentery.

DIPHTHERIA

Diphtheria is a highly infectious, often fatal, disease which, thanks to routine immunization, has been almost eliminated in the developed world. It has not, however, been completely eradicated; those most at risk are children between six months to 10 years who have not been immunized.

CAUSES: Diphtheria is caused by a bacterium known as *Corynebacterium diphtheriae*, which usually infects the nose and throat, although it may grow on the skin, resulting in the formation of ulcers. It occasionally infects the mucous membranes of the vagina and anus.

People can catch diphtheria through inhal-

Self **Help**

DIVERTICULITIS

Once an attack of diverticulitis is over, you can help to prevent the illness recurring by including plenty of fibre in your diet. This will discourage further diverticula from forming, and guard against infection developing in the existing pouches.

A dislocated knee. Do not attempt to rectify dislocations yourself.

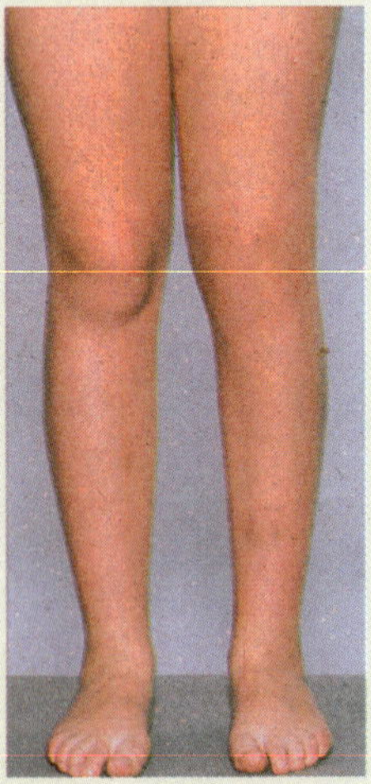

ing droplets containing the bacilli, which are spread through the air every time an infected person talks, coughs or sneezes. You can also get the disease by touching any items that s/he has used or been in contact with.

SYMPTOMS AND SIGNS: The incubation period for diphtheria is between two and six days. The patient starts by being generally off-colour, with a slight temperature, sore throat, stiff neck and swollen glands. In the most common form of the disease – throat or tonsillar diphtheria – a thick, greyish yellow membrane grows over the tonsils; this may extend into the mouth or down the back of the throat and may cause problems with swallowing and breathing.

By this stage, the patient is gravely ill, with a husky voice and a high-pitched cough. The temperature may rise to about 38.9°C (102°F).

TREATMENT: Early diagnosis is important. If the doctor suspects diphtheria, the patient will be admitted to a hospital for infectious diseases. Treatment includes anti-toxin and antibiotic injections.

Once treatment starts, the patient usually starts to recover within two or three days and can expect to be out of hospital in seven to 10 days. During the next three weeks, it's important for the patient to take life easy and to get plenty of rest.

DISLOCATION

Dislocation is a term used to describe the displacement of a joint from its usual position. It is usually as a result of a fall or injury. Occasionally it occurs during a violent seizure.

CAUSES: If you have dislocated a joint you will not be able to move it properly. The two joints that are most likely to become dislocated are the shoulder and the jaw. The shoulder socket is particularly shallow, which allows the upper arm a wide range of manoeuvrability. Dislocation can occur when the arms are flung above the head in self defence, and is particularly common with horse riders if they fall on to outstretched hands. Some babies are born with a dislocated hip, but early treatment will rectify this.

SYMPTOMS AND SIGNS: The joint will swell up very quickly, and look out of shape, it will be difficult to move and extremely painful.

TREATMENT: Never try to manipulate a dislocated joint back into position – you should seek professional help. You may need a general anaesthetic, but a local anaesthetic may suffice. Occasionally the joint will go back on its own, but you still need to see a doctor. Some people suffer from repeated dislocation, either because of a congenital abnormality or because the tough capsule that surrounds the joint has been damaged in a previous injury.

DIVERTICULITIS

Diverticulitis is the inflammation of the pouches, or diverticula, which form in the wall of the colon as a result of a condition called diverticulosis, a complaint that mainly affects the elderly.

CAUSES: Diverticula form primarily as a result of a low-roughage western diet, but they are not a problem in most cases, some people who have diverticula may simply suffer from wind or a feeling of distension, or show no symptoms at all. However, because the bowel contains vast numbers of bacteria, infection can develop in these diverticula. In addition, spasm in the bowel can cut off blood supply to some of the diverticula. Diverticulitis occurs when these small bulges become infected and inflamed.

SYMPTOMS AND SIGNS: In severe cases of diverticulitis, there is aching in the lower abdomen, there may also be diarrhoea or constipation, and pus or blood may be passed with faeces – sometimes heavily.

TREATMENT: Occasionally, your doctor may prescribe a course of antibiotics. It usually clears up after a few days, but if it doesn't an operation may be necessary.

DIVERTICULOSIS

see DIVERTICULITIS

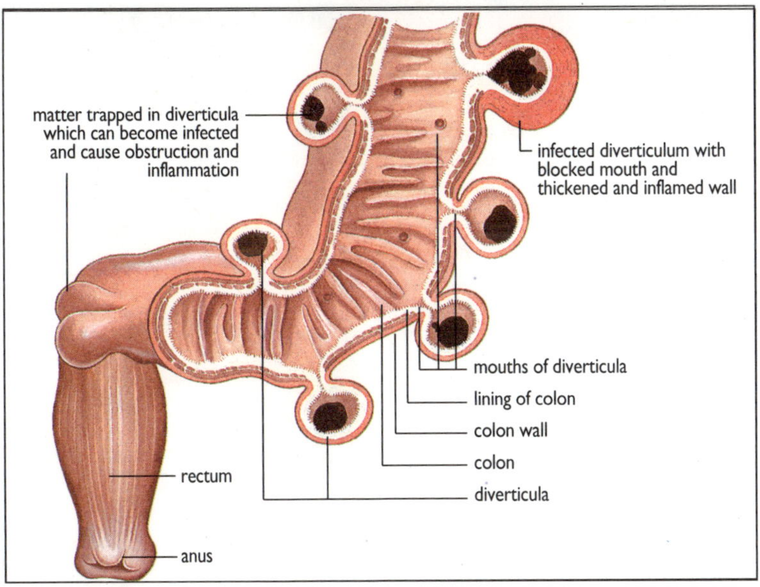

The colon shown in section, with its walls severely inflamed by diverticulitis.

DRUG ADDICTION

The term 'drug' includes a substance taken for medicinal reasons, but it also more loosely means a habit-forming substance. Addiction, or dependence, is an illness that is brought on by taking repeated doses of certain drugs.

CAUSES: People either become addicted to a drug when they are prescribed it for a long time, or because they choose to take the drug for its pleasurable effects, and then find it hard to stop.

Drugs that are commonly abused are divided into two categories: 'soft' and 'hard'. So-called soft drugs include things like cannabis, which is mainly a sedative, but it can also produce hallucinations. It is the 'hard' drugs, such as heroin, that can lead to severe addiction. Prescription drugs can also lead to dependence, for example, benzodazepine tranquillisers and sleeping tablets, which are effective for a short time, but dependence can easily occur. Sniffing glue or cleaning solutions can easily lead to addiction as well as physical and mental breakdown.

SYMPTOMS AND SIGNS: The symptoms of withdrawal of drug abuse vary according to the type of drug, but they can vary from shakes to seizures, anxiety to psychosis.

TREATMENT: Drug addiction can be very difficult to treat for several reasons. If the addiction involves a prescribed drug, your doctor should find an alternative. Often the addiction involves an illegal substance and the addict may be reluctant to seek help. It may take a friend or relative to recognise the problem. Addiction, however, is not always obvious. Medical or psychiatric advice should be sought as soon as possible.

See also ALCOHOLISM.

DUODENAL ULCER

see PEPTIC ULCER

Useful Addresses

DRUG ADDICTION

RELEASE
388 Old Street
LONDON EC1V 9LT
071 729 9904 (Mon-Fri 10-6pm)
071 603 8654

After coming off hard drugs the patient may be prescribed 'soft' medication such as anti-depressants.

ASK THE DOCTOR

DYSENTERY

Q I'm going to West Africa in a few months time. Are there any precautions I can take against dysentery?

A Prevention is by far the best course of action. Avoid any raw salad ingredients, peel fruit, avoid ice-cream and ice, and drink only bottled or tinned beverages.

Q Can one die of dysentery?

A It can be fatal in the very young, the very old, and the very sick – as, for example, where people have been severely weakened by malnutrition. It's only really likely to happen where medical facilities are inadequate.

Useful Addresses

DYSLEXIA

British Dyslexia Association
98 London Road
READING RG1 5AU
0734 668271/2

Dyslexia Institute
133 Gresham Road
STAINES
Middlesex TW18 2AJ
0784 463851

DYSENTERY

Dysentery is a severe form of diarrhoea, often with bloody faeces. It is rare in developed countries but a real risk to travellers in tropical and subtropical parts of the world.

CAUSES: There are two forms of dysentery: amoebic dysentery, which is caused by a microscopic amoeba; and bacillary dysentery, which is caused by the shigella bacillus. Both types are spread by poor hygiene and infected foods and water.

SYMPTOMS AND SIGNS: Bad diarrhoea, often streaked with blood and pus. There are, usually, also violent stomach cramps, vomiting and wind.

TREATMENT: As with any diarrhoea, you need to take plenty of fluids and stop eating until the condition clears.

Bacillary dysentery usually gets better with no specific treatment.

Amoebic dysentery is more difficult to cure and needs medical treatment. Antibiotics will probably be prescribed and the stools checked at regular intervals until they are clear of the amoeba.

See also DIARRHOEA.

DYSLEXIA

The dictionary defines dyslexia as 'word blindness' or 'great difficulty in learning to read or spell'. But, of course, thousands of children have difficulty with these skills without being dyslexic.

CAUSES: About four per cent of children in the UK are thought to suffer from dyslexia. It appears in children of all intellectual abilities but no one knows for sure what causes the problem. It may be that a part of the brain is not fully 'mature', or that there is a problem with the mechanisms that connect one part of the brain to another. There are often other people in the family with this problem.

SYMPTOMS AND SIGNS: A dyslexic child is usually clumsy, restless, and may have difficulty in learning to talk. The reading and spelling problems come later. These include confusing words and letters with their mirror opposites ('b' for 'd', 'was' for 'saw'), bizarre spelling, and great difficulty in distinguishing left from right.

Only around 10 per cent of people who suffer from dyslexia are women.

TREATMENT: Children with dyslexia need specialised help and tuition. Discuss the problem with your child's teachers. If your child is severely handicapped, a dyslexic school may be the answer.

DYSMENORRHOEA

Dysmenorrhoea means very painful periods.

CAUSES: The muscles of the uterus go into spasm under the influence of hormones released from the lining. The higher the levels of these hormones, the more forcibly the walls of the uterus contract.

SYMPTOMS AND SIGNS: Strong pains may begin a few hours before the actual bleeding starts, often accompanied by backache and a feeling of pressure in the pelvis.

TREATMENT: Some women find that exercise helps. Acupuncture, meditation, evening primrose oil, even a change of diet to include less meat and more vegetables have their enthusiastic exponents. So long as it's taken in good time, simple aspirin is one of the most effective painkillers. If none of these remedies helps, consult your doctor.

See also ENDOMETRIOSIS.

DYSPAREUNIA

Dyspareunia is the technical term given to painful sexual intercourse.

Causes: Some women who find attempts at intercourse difficult and painful tell their doctor that they think they are 'too small'. Occasionally this can be due to a tough hymen with a small opening, but generally the reason is tension, apprehension and some underlying fear of penetration.

Intercourse can sometimes be painful if the man penetrates the woman too quickly, without any preliminary caressing; she may still be quite unaroused, perhaps tense and certainly dry because the natural lubrication is only secreted in the vagina when she feels sexually excited.

For some, deep penetration can cause pain. This may be due to an ovarian cyst or endometriosis and needs specific treatment. Temporary discomfort, itching and some pain can be caused by the dryness that often accompanies vaginal infections, particularly the fungal yeast infection known as thrush.

Symptoms and signs: Most women experience temporary discomfort at some time, while others have more serious difficulties, often after childbirth or during the menopause. The tensing of the whole vagina and a spasm of the muscles around the entrance is a condition called vaginismus and may be due to fear of sex.

Treatment: Consult your doctor, he will be able to advise you and may show you how to use lubricating jelly and how gradually to stretch the opening of the vagina by inserting one, then two or even three fingers. If the hymen is particularly thick, it could be stretched and incised by a gynaecologist in a simple operation under general anaesthetic.

Your doctor may also be able to advise on different positions for lovemaking and give you the opportunity to talk about your inner feelings and anxieties.

See also ENDOMETRIOSIS, THRUSH, VAGINISMUS.

DYSPEPSIA

see INDIGESTION

e

ECZEMA

Eczema is an inflammation of the skin; the itching may be accompanied by redness, flaking and tiny blisters. Doctors seem unable to agree whether to use the term eczema or dermatitis.

Causes: There are many different types of ezcema – it is particularly common in children. Causes vary – it may be due to an allergic reaction, it may be inherited, or it is sometimes due to stress. The three most common types are listed below.

Symptoms and signs: Infant eczema. A child may show signs of eczema at just a few months old. A rash starts on the face and may spread to the rest of the body. The irritation can be intense and it can be hard to prevent him/her scratching.

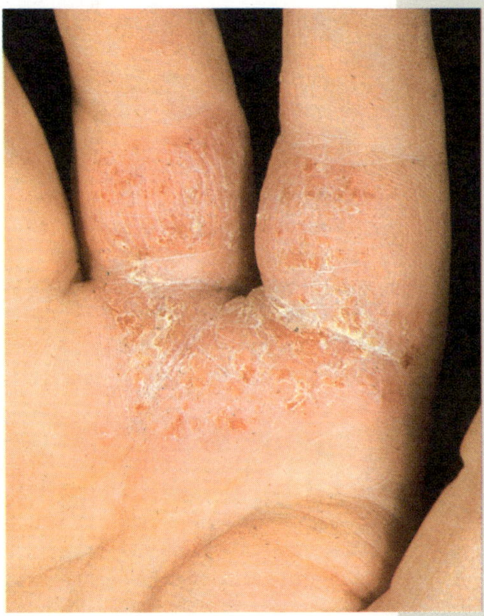

Eczema of the hands is often caused by an allergic reaction to detergents and washing-up liquids. It usually improves if you wear rubber gloves over cotton gloves, while in contact with the offending substance.

ASK THE DOCTOR

DYSPAREUNIA

Q Is intercourse ever painful for men?

A Yes. If a woman is suffering from a dry, tight vagina, then penetration and movement can be painful for her male partner. Other possible causes of discomfort could be an infection or inflammation of the penis and a few men have too tight a foreskin: this can easily be put right by a simple operation. If there is no obvious physical cause, the problem is likely to be emotional and your doctor should be able to help by discussion or by reference to a skilled psychotherapist.

1 As they enter the system, the allergens attach themselves to white blood cells.

2 The converted white cells start releasing their antibodies.

3 Antibodies connect up with mast cells located in the tissues where allergens first arrive.

4 When there's a fresh attack, the antibodies 'capture' the allergens, causing the mast cells to explode and release histamine. The histamine causes the symptoms to appear.

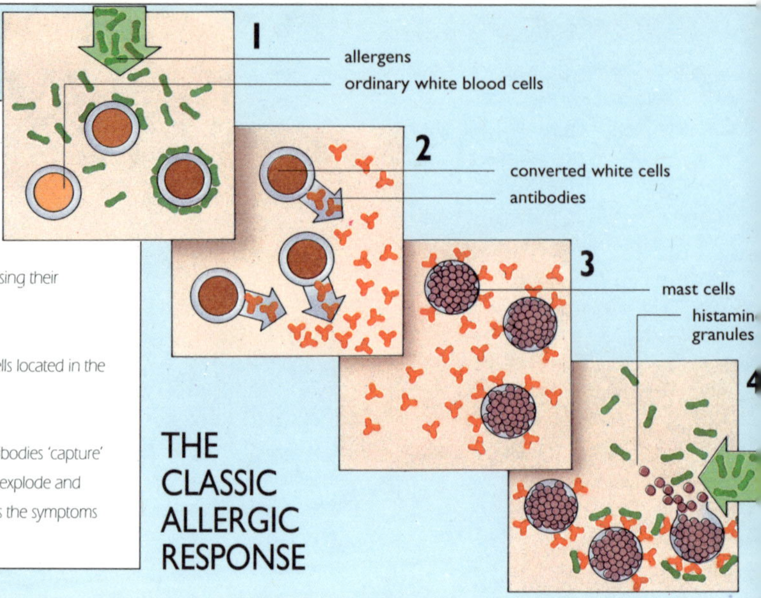

THE CLASSIC ALLERGIC RESPONSE

Self **Help**

ECZEMA

Wear rubber gloves when washing-up. If you're allergic to rubber, wear cotton gloves next to your skin. Dry your hands thoroughly after washing and use a hand cream. If your child has eczema, ensure that his/her clothes are made of cotton. Use a very mild soap for washing, keep bathtimes as short as possible and use emollient in the bath. Oily calamine or lanolin may prove helpful – but you may be allergic to these so proceed with care. Homeopathic remedies may be worth a try.

Contact eczema. You may get contact eczema after contact with a substance to which you are allergic – for example, jewellery, certain plants or cosmetics. The skin becomes red and itchy and tiny blisters start to appear – all within 48 hours of contact.

Irritant eczema (also known as housewives' eczema) is something anyone can get if they expose their hands for long enough – household detergents, washing-up liquids and shampoos are the biggest culprits. The skin may crack, flake and itch.

TREATMENT: Your doctor will probably prescribe steroid cream or lotion. Occasionally, s/he may suggest antihistamine tablets to relieve the itching. Be careful with these as they can cause drowsiness. Any bad case of eczema accompanied by bacterial infection will also need antibiotics.

ELECTRIC SHOCK

Electric shocks can be fatal and need urgent first aid and medical attention.

CAUSES: Contact with live electric current.

SYMPTOMS AND SIGNS: If an electric current passes through a body, it can knock someone to the ground, stop the heartbeat and breathing, and leave the victim unconscious. The current can cause widespread internal damage. Burns are visible at points of entry and exit of current.

TREATMENT: Turn the electric current off at the mains. If this is not possible and the person is still in contact with the source of electric current, isolate him/her from it using a non-conducting object such as a wooden chair – if you touch the person, s/he may still be 'live' and you could also receive an electric shock.

Next, check that the victim is still breathing. If not, begin mouth to mouth respiration at once. Check the heartbeat if the victim's breathing does not begin again after five breaths. Cardiac massage may be needed to get the heart going again. If the victim is breathing, turn him/her over into the recovery position. Call a doctor or ambulance.

EMPHYSEMA

Emphysema is a disease of the lungs. Healthy lungs have a spongy texture with millions of alveoli (air sacs) where oxygen and carbon dioxide are exchanged in the bloodstream. In emphysema, the air sacs are damaged and work less efficiently.

Causes: The alveoli can be damaged through constant high pressure caused by long-standing lung diseases such as chronic bronchitis and asthma. Certain occupations also bring a risk of emphysema: mining, glass blowing and trumpet playing, for example. Ten times more men than women suffer from it and those who smoke or live in highly polluted atmospheres are also more susceptible, but it is relatively rare in people who do not already suffer from bronchitis or smoke.

Symptoms and signs: Shortness of breath which gets worse over the years is the main symptom. This, in turn, can lead to non-functioning of the lungs, pneumothorax (lung collapse) and heart failure because the blood supply to the heart is impaired. The chest may become barrel-shaped and the sufferer wheezes and coughs. There is a constant risk of recurrent lung infections.

Treatment: There is no cure for emphysema but the symptoms can be relieved and slowed down. Doctors may prescribe courses of antibiotics for each chest infection. You may have to inhale a bronchodilator, which helps to widen the airways and makes breathing easier and more efficient. Occasionally, severe sufferers are given a heart-and-lung transplant

ENCEPHALITIS

Encephalitis is an inflammation of the brain. In its milder forms, encephalitis is quite common.

Causes: It is usually caused by a virus. In rare cases encephalitis can be a complication of a more common disease such as measles, mumps or glandular fever.

Symptoms and signs: Headache, fever, loss of appetite, neck or backache are the usual symptoms. The neck may be rigid and there may be a sensitivity to light. In many cases, the symptoms resemble those of any mild viral illness. In severe cases, the patient may have muscular weakness and may even have a seizure.

Treatment: If you develop a bad headache, combined with rigid neck and fever – call the doctor immediately. You may need to be admitted to hospital and prescribed anti-viral drugs. Plenty of rest is essential until the patient has recovered fully. In severe cases, this may take several months.

ENDOMETRIOSIS

Endometriosis affects women – more commonly when they are over 30 and especially when they haven't had children. It may cause infertility.

Causes: Sometimes cells from the endometrium (the tissue that lines the womb) become displaced and grow somewhere else. They may pass out of the Fallopian tubes to surround the ovaries, the intestines or other organs.

Just as the normal lining tissue of the womb bleeds each month, so do the endometrial deposits, and scar tissue can form between the deposit and other nearby organs, often adhering to them and interfering with their function. If one of the Fallopian tubes is affected, fertility can be impaired.

Displaced endometrial glands (white) in the muscle that supports the glandular uterine lining (pink).

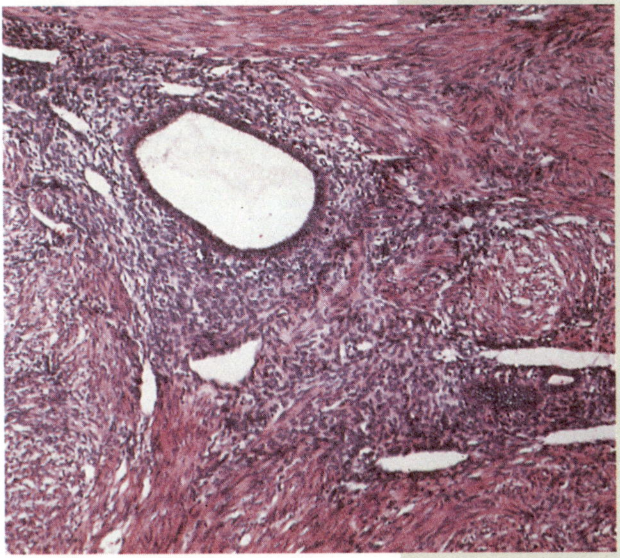

Self **Help**

EMPHYSEMA

Smokers should stop. Take regular exercise and keep away from polluted air.

Useful Addresses

ENDOMETRIOSIS

Endometriosis Society
65 Holmdene Avenue
LONDON
SE24 9LD
071 737 4764
071 737 0380

Symptoms and signs: The usual symptoms are very painful periods caused by the build-up of blood from the endometrial deposits. Sexual intercourse is usually painful as well, and you may suffer backache.

Treatment: If you notice symptoms for two or three menstrual cycles, consult your doctor. S/he will probably carry out an internal pelvic examination and if there is any doubt about diagnosis, may arrange for you to go into hospital for a laparoscopy. This involves examining the womb and other reproductive organs while you are under a general anaesthetic by inserting a lighted telescope-like instrument into your abdomen via a small cut made just below the navel.

The first course of action is usually hormonal treatment. If that is not successful, your doctor may suggest an operation to remove the abnormal tissue.

See also DYSMENORRHOEA, DYSPAREUNIA.

ENLARGED PROSTATE

see PROSTATE ENLARGEMENT

EPILEPSY

Epilepsy takes several forms but each type causes seizures (fits). A seizure is a period of excessive and chaotic electrical activity in a part of the brain. Depending on which part of the brain is affected, this causes disturbance of movement or sensation and/or consciousness. The best-known types of epileptic fits are *grand mal*; and *petit mal*, (now known as 'absence' seizure), to which children are far more prone than adults. Epilepsy has been viewed with considerable fear and superstition for centuries, but it is not, in fact, rare – in Britain about one in 200 people suffer from it, and many epileptics lead normal lives, with no symptoms between seizures.

Causes: Most forms of epilepsy seem to have no obvious reason for the brain cells to pass their electrical impulses in a disorderly manner, but many neurologists believe that epilepsy does not occur unless the brain has been damaged, either at birth or later, even though the damage may be too minute to detect.

Useful Addresses

EPILEPSY

National Society for Epilepsy
Chalfont Centre for Epilepsy
Chalfont St Peter
GERRARDS CROSS
Bucks SL9 ORJ
02407 3991

British Epilepsy Association
40 Hanover Square
LEEDS LS3 1BE
0532 439393

THE THREE PHASES OF A GRAND MAL SEIZURE

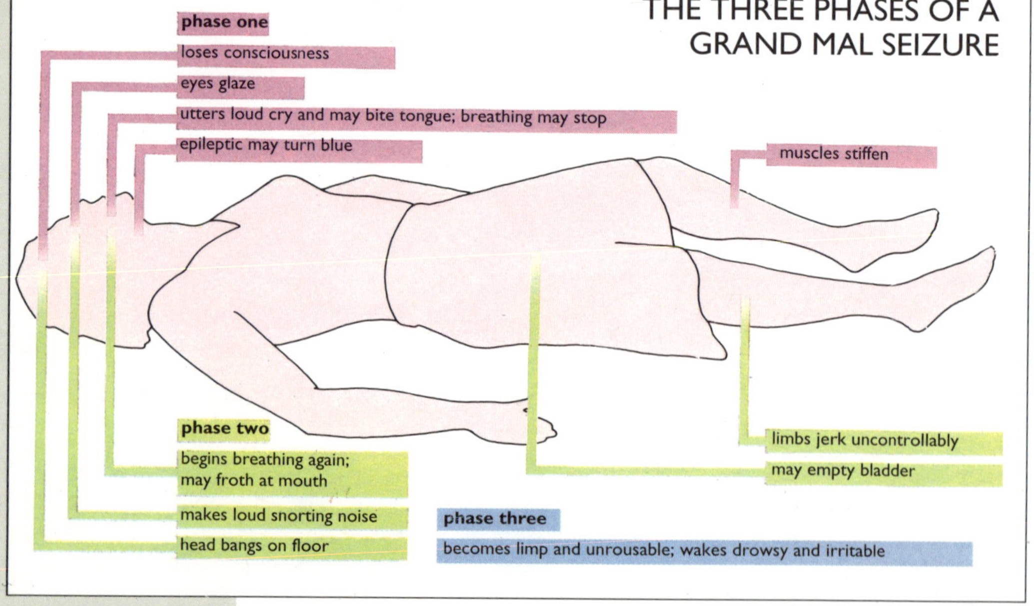

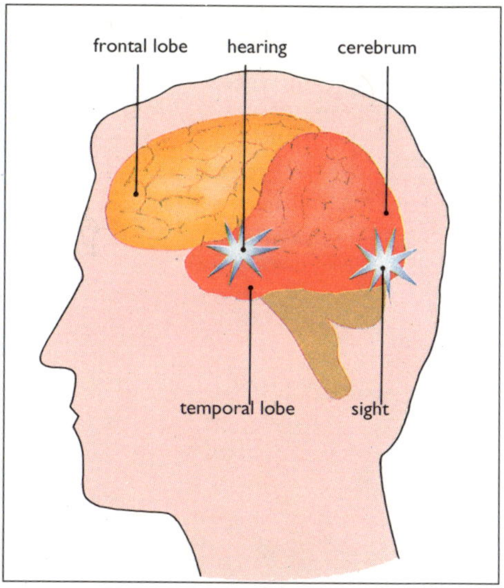

In a petit mal *seizure only certain areas of the cerebrum are affected – in this case hearing and sight.*

An epileptic seizure can sometimes be caused by external factors such as an electric shock, drugs withdrawal, a head injury, high fever and asphyxia. A brain tumour is another possible cause, though this is very rare.

SYMPTOMS AND SIGNS: In a *grand mal* seizure, the person falls to the ground unconscious, and may lose bladder and bowel control. The body becomes stiff and may start to twitch and jerk uncontrollably. A seizure usually lasts from one to four minutes. At the end of it, the muscles relax and the epileptic regains consciousness within a few minutes. The after-effects are a headache and sleepiness. After a few hours of deep sleep, the epileptic usually feels much better, although the after-effects can last for a week.

TREATMENT: Anticonvulsant drugs are the first line of treatment for epilepsy. They are used to control seizures and, if they are taken as prescribed, they are generally very successful. If you are with someone who has a seizure, do not restrain him/her in any way unless s/he is about to injure him/herself. Move hard objects such as furniture. Don't force anything into the mouth – you do not need to stop the person biting the tongue. Once the seizure is over, make sure the air passages are clear and wipe away any froth from the mouth.

Summon medical help if the fit lasts longer than three minutes, or if another one starts as soon as the first one ends, or if the person has not been diagnosed as epileptic. Once the seizure is over, place the person in the recovery position and allow him/her to sleep undisturbed. If s/he has wet or soiled him/herself, you should provide clean clothing.

EYE CYST

A cyst, or chalazion, can sometimes form inside the upper or lower eyelids. If it becomes infected, it will be inflamed and painful, but when the infection has subsided, a cyst usually remains as a painless lump.

CAUSES: A cyst is usually the result of a bacterial infection. It is not contagious.

SYMPTOMS AND SIGNS: A swelling on the eyelid which is inflamed and painful.

TREATMENT: Hot-water compresses to relieve pain and antibiotic drops or ointment to help clear up the infection, but the cyst itself may need to be removed by surgery if it is irritating or obscures vision, as few disappear of their own accord. This operation is simple and will leave no noticeable scar.

f

FACET JOINT STRAIN

Facet joints are the small joints that link the vertebrae in the back together. If one of them is strained or pushed slightly out of position, it can cause back pain, usually in the neck or lower back. Each facet joint is contained in a capsule which, if it is sprained, may

Self **Help**

EPILEPSY

If you are prescribed anticonvulsant drugs you should limit your alcohol intake to an occasional glass of wine. Make sure to eat regular meals and don't become dehydrated. If you have photosensitive epilepsy, avoid strobe light exposure and watch television from at least two metres away, as the flickering screen can precipitate a seizure too.

ASK THE DOCTOR

EPILEPSY

Q If I suffer from epileptic seizures, may I drive?

A No, you must be fit-free for two years or have fits only at night for three years before you can have a driving licence.

swell up and press on a nerve.

Causes: As with many causes of back pain, facet joint injury often results from reaching or twisting or bending awkwardly. In middle age, the facet joints may slip out of alignment because the discs have started to degenerate.

Symptoms and signs: Pain can be severe and, if the injury is in the lower back, may spread to your hip, thighs and buttocks. In the neck, the pain will restrict side-to-side turning movements of the head.

Treatment: Rest, painkillers and an exercise programme will usually solve the problem, especially if your general health and muscle tone are good. If the problem is in the neck, it may be necessary to support it with a special collar. Manipulation may help if the pain continues. It will also help if you can relax and not tense up due to the pain.

FAINTING

Fainting is a sudden and temporary loss of consciousness.

Cause: It occurs when the pressure of blood flow through the arteries of the brain is reduced. It may be as a result of a hot or stuffy atmosphere, prolonged standing in the same position, pregnancy, a heavy period, hunger, heart disease or a sudden emotional upset.

Symptoms and signs: A sudden light-headed feeling and collapse.

Treatment: If you faint and fall to the ground, it is more than likely that you will become conscious again. If you are lying on the ground, your heart no longer needs to defy gravity and blood can be pumped more easily back to the brain. If you feel faint, sit or lie down at once, loosen your clothing and put your head on a lower level than your heart. If you faint regularly, you should check with your doctor that all is well, as repeated fainting can be a sign of anaemia or rarely, of a heart condition.

FEVER

A fever is a raised body temperature, known medically as pyrexia. It is a symptom and not a disease.

Causes: The normal body temperature is around 37°C (98.4°F) but may vary slightly from person to person. It also varies half a degree or so throughout the day, and is usu-

ASK THE DOCTOR

FAINTING

Q Do you recommend the use of smelling salts when someone faints or is this an old wives' tale?

A Smelling salts work because they give off a strong smell of ammonia, which will make you gasp. The sharp intake of air means that more oxygen reaches the blood, which can then be taken to the brain. However, smelling salts are unnecessary as a few sharp intakes of breath will have the same effect.

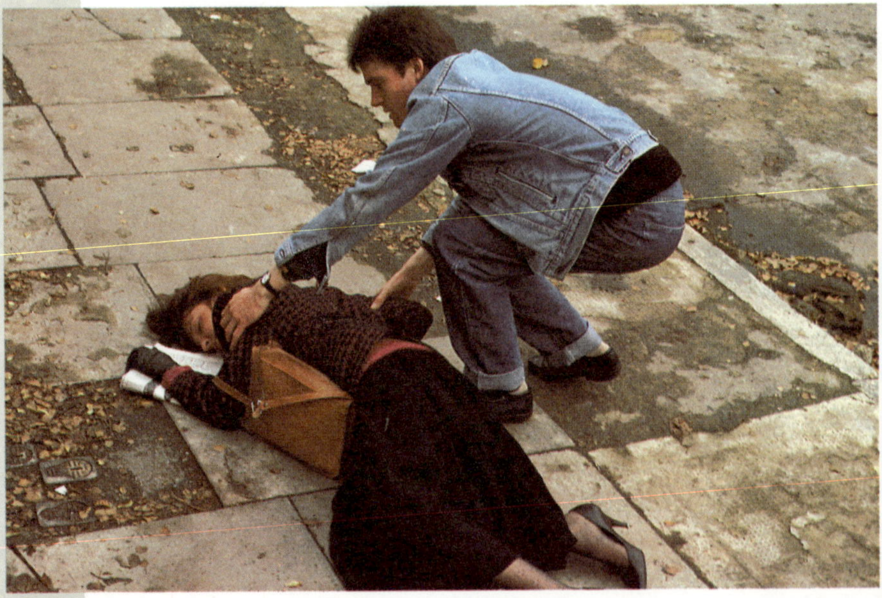

Loosen tight-fitting clothing around the neck, chest, legs and waist of a person who has fainted. Raising the legs above the level of the heart also helps.

The majority of fevers are the result of bacterial or viral infections.

ally at its lowest first thing in the morning. In very hot weather, the body temperature may rise a bit, also after strenuous exercise, but usually a rise in temperature of a degree or more is caused by some form of infection.

SYMPTOMS AND SIGNS: A temperature over 37.4°C (99.4°F) may be considered a fever. The person's face will probably be flushed, the eyes may be glazed, the body hot to the touch. The person may either feel hot or, if the temperature is still rising, extremely cold and shivery as the body tries to lose heat. When a temperature is falling, the body often sweats profusely.

TREATMENT: Treatment will, of course, depend on the disease causing the fever. In the absence of any other symptom, the extent and duration of the fever may indicate when medical intervention is necessary.

For adults, it's wise to contact your doctor for temperatures over 40°C (104°F) or for any fever that lasts for more than three days.

Children are more prone to running temperatures than adults – and they tend to be higher, even for fairly trivial complaints. If a baby under one year old has a fever, contact your doctor immediately. For older children, it's wise to contact your doctor for temperatures over 39.4°C (103°F) or for low-grade fevers that last for more than two or three days.

Many things can be done to keep a fever down. This is especially important for children under the age of five, where temperatures over 39.4/40°C (103/104°F) can be very dangerous; they can cause convulsions and even brain damage. So it is important to keep the temperature below this point.

- Put the patient to bed and keep the coverings fairly light, even if s/he is feeling cold and shivery.
- Dose adults with paracetamol or aspirin to bring the temperature down. Children can be given special infant's, or junior paracetamol, depending on their age, but NEVER give a child aspirin. In all cases, repeat the dose if necessary, but take care not to exceed the stated prescription.
- If the temperature continues to rise, strip the patient and sponge down the body with tepid water. If the temperature shoots up every time you stop the sponging, it may help to cool the patient with an electric fan.

Finally, give the patient plenty of liquids to drink to replace fluids lost through sweating.

TAKING A CHILD'S TEMPERATURE:
It's unwise to put a thermometer in a young child's mouth.
- Use a standard thermometer under the armpit or in the groin. Leave the thermometer in place for five minutes. Temperatures taken here will be about one degree lower than temperatures taken by mouth.
- Alternatively, use a temperature indicator strip. This should be held against the patient's forehead for about 1½ minutes. This method is less reliable, however, as the strip may be influenced by the surrounding temperature.

FIBROIDS

Fibroids are swellings in the wall of the womb, consisting of muscle and fibrous tissue. They develop into lumps which can be smaller than a pea or, very rarely, bigger than a football. They can protrude into the womb or, if they get very large, out into the pelvic region and then into the abdomen. Apart from taking up space, they do no direct harm and it is very unlikely that they will become cancerous. Around 20 per cent of all women have fibroids at some time in their lives, often without even knowing they have them.

The areas shaded in grey show how fibroids can distend the natural Y-shape of the womb.

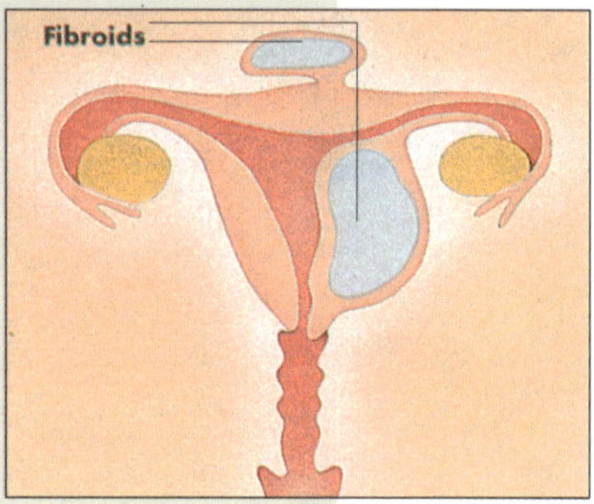

CAUSES: No one knows how or why fibroids grow.

SYMPTOMS AND SIGNS: Usually fibroids give no trouble, but if they push into the womb, they can cause heavier and longer periods, and possibly abdominal swelling.

Fibroids don't usually prevent you becoming pregnant, but if there are several sitting under the womb lining, there could be an increased risk of early miscarriage. If the egg does succeed in becoming properly embedded and you become pregnant, the baby may not be able to get into the ideal head-down position before birth because fibroids are in the way. In this case, a Caesarean delivery is sometimes necessary.

TREATMENT: If the fibroids are small, they are usually best left alone, but if they have made the womb large enough to be felt above the brim of the pelvis – about equivalent in size to a three months' pregnancy – they are generally dealt with by surgery.

Where just a single fibroid has developed (one, say, the size of a tennis ball, hanging on the outside of the womb), it can be removed on its own by an operation called a myomectomy.

If, however, you have several fibroids, and particularly if you are past child-bearing age, doctors often recommend a hysterectomy – an operation to remove the whole of the womb. This not only gets rid of fibroids that have already developed, but ensures that any tiny ones too small to detect won't have a chance to grow.

ASK THE DOCTOR

FIBROIDS

Q I have several fibroids but am still young enough to have children. Will my doctor insist on a hysterectomy?

A If you want to start or add to your family, it is extremely unlikely that your doctor will recommend a hysterectomy unless the fibroids show signs of cancerous growth.

FIBROSITIS

Fibrositis is now called trigger point phenomenon. It is a painful knotting of muscles, most common in the neck and shoulders.

CAUSES: This is often a secondary complication to facet joint strain, and spinal injury. The pain of the first injury causes you to tense the muscles, which become extremely tight and hard at certain recognised trigger points. Poor posture can also tense the muscles and cause the phenomenon.

SYMPTOMS AND SIGNS: Pain in the shoulders and neck, hard, knotted muscles which, when pressed, may twitch and spread pain down the arm, neck or shoulder.

TREATMENT: If the pain is caused by a facet joint injury, this must be sorted out first. If it

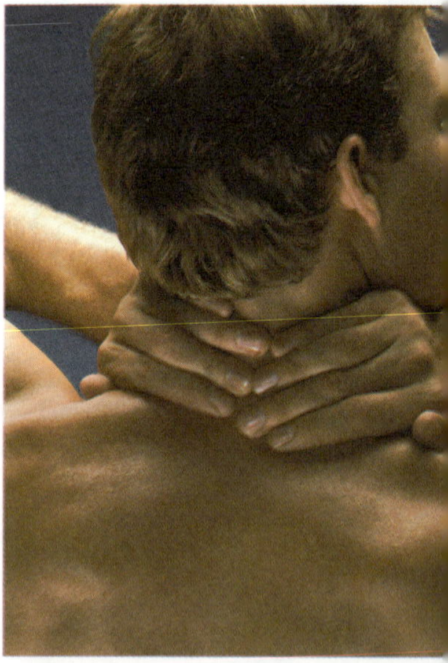

Fibrositis can be caused by tension. In the first place, try self massage or stretching exercises.

is due to tenseness, the muscles need to be relaxed through physiotherapy, massage, or passive stretching exercises. If the pain continues, you may need a painkilling injection to relax the muscles.

See also FACET JOINT STRAIN, SPINAL INJURY.

FLAT FEET

In flat feet, the arches are underdeveloped; the arch sinks down so that the inner edge of the foot comes to rest on the ground. This condition may go unnoticed in youth but can cause much discomfort later on.

Causes: Babies are born with flat feet and the arches develop gradually over the next six years. Factors that may influence poor development are: an inborn weakness in the area; starting to walk before the child's feet are ready; being overweight; and the wrong sort of shoes. Dietary deficiency can be another cause, but this is rare in western countries.

During adolescence, arches may drop when sudden and rapid growth puts new strains on the feet, especially after prolonged standing or walking. In middle age, a tendency to put on weight and to take less exercise can encourage flat feet. Prolonged standing, pregnancy, fashion shoes with high heels or chronic arthritis can also play a part.

Symptoms and signs: It's easy enough to tell whether a child is suffering from flat feet. S/he may be very slow – even reluctant – to walk, or pain in the legs and feet may make the child limp. Flat feet often go together with knock-knees, and the feet may roll in. Sometimes the child walks with a 'rolling gait'.

The clues in adolescence are: a change in gait; aches or pains around the ankle or up the calf, or the walk may become a shuffle or look heavy and flat-footed. Flat-footed adults complain of uncomfortable, burning feet which tire easily; after long periods of standing or walking, the legs become very painful.

Treatment: Flat feet need medical attention. In the case of a young child, the doctor may recommend that s/he goes barefoot whenever possible, and may prescribe exercises to strengthen the feet. Shoes should be well-fitting and supportive, preferably with laces. Sometimes it's necessary to raise the inner side of the heel, especially if the child has knock-knees.

In adolescence, arch supports may be recommended to relieve the acute foot strain. The problem is often corrected with special exercises. In rare cases, an operation may be necessary. Great care should be taken when choosing footwear.

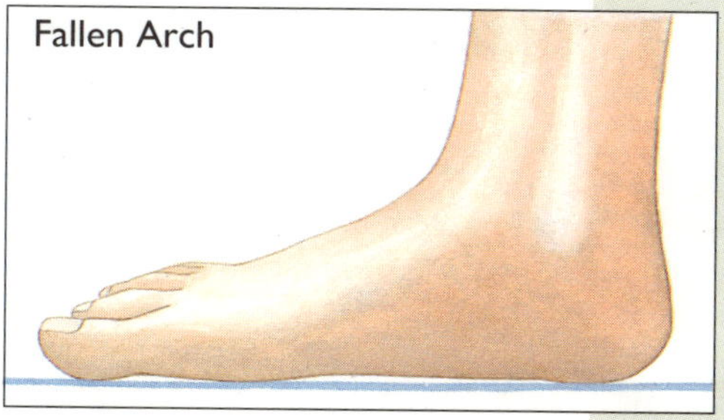

When the arch of the foot touches – or almost touches – the ground, exercise is the best remedy.

Treating adults can be more of a problem. A sensible choice of shoes, together with some form of corrective padding, may give relief.

FLATULENCE

A harmless, but embarrassing problem, which involves uncontrollable expulsion of air through the rectum.

Causes: On very rare occasions, flatulence may be caused by a peptic ulcer or irritable bowel syndrome, a hiatus hernia or Crohn's disease, but far more likely it is as a result of eating foods that are high in fibre, such as eggs, onions or beans, or too much protein or fat.

Symptoms and signs: Passing wind frequently.

Treatment: Avoid foods that upset you. Avoid drinking lots of fizzy drinks and try not

Self Help

FIBROSITIS

The condition can be caused by poor ergonomics, such as incorrect height of work surfaces or bad seating, so tackle these problems if you feel uncomfortable when sitting down.

ASK THE DOCTOR

FLAT FEET

Q I am told that there are exercises to help children with flat feet. Can you suggest one?

A Try putting a few marbles on the floor, and invite the child to pick them up using the toes. This can easily be made into a game or competition, while helping the child to develop stonger arches in the feet.

Self Help
FLEAS

- Fleas are difficult to catch because they can jump several feet, and difficult to kill with the fingers because of their hard shells. One way of catching them is to use a moistened bar of soap.
- If an animal is frequently troubled by fleas, it can be protected by wearing a special plastic flea collar, impregnated with insecticide.
- Don't forget to treat the cat's or dog's bedding.
- Vacuum all the floors regularly.
- Try not to scratch bites, to avoid them becoming infected.

Self Help
FLUID RETENTION

If you have swollen ankles made worse by standing for long periods – do calf exercises i.e. going up and down on your toes. People with leg oedema or varicose veins usually benefit from wearing elastic support hose.

to rush meals. Fibre is an important part of diet, but don't increase the amount you eat too quickly – give your bowel time to adapt.

FLEAS

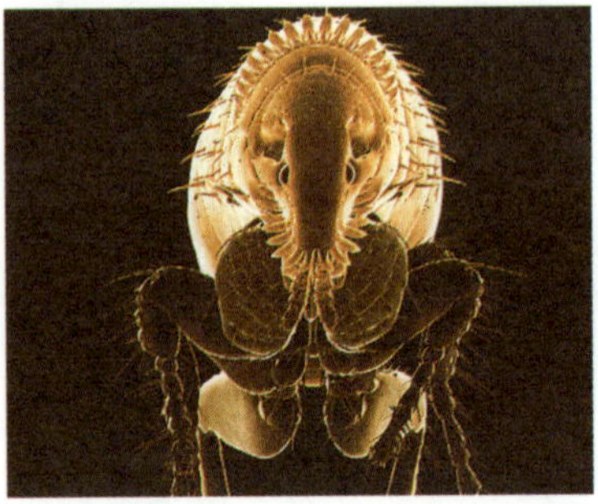

Although they usually ignore people, cat fleas will bite humans if the host animal is removed.

Fleas are small, brownish, blood-sucking insects with thin bodies and six legs. Different kinds of animal, such as dogs, cats and rats, have different kinds of flea, but most fleas will bite people if their favourite animal is not available. There is a human flea, but it is now very rare in developed countries, as are most of the diseases spread by fleas. Small tapeworms from dogs or mice can be carried to humans by fleas, and children handling their pets sometimes swallow an infected flea, though this does not often result in ill-health.

SYMPTOMS AND SIGNS: The most common symptom of flea infestation (apart from dogs or cats which scratch a lot) is intensely itchy bites around the ankles and lower legs. Children are often affected by flea bites more than adults.

TREATMENT: The irritation caused by flea bites can be relieved temporarily with applications of calamine lotion. But, more importantly, the bites will not stop until the fleas themselves are destroyed. If the problem is severe, you should have your house de-infested by the local environmental health office, by means of an insecticidal spray which will ensure that any fleas in the carpets or upholstery are dealt with.

FLUID RETENTION

Fluid retention can occur in a number of conditions that interfere with the normal circulation of fluid, as it travels around between the tissue cells in the body and the bloodstream.

CAUSES: The swelling that accompanies fluid retention is known as oedema. It particularly affects the legs and ankles where excess fluid can collect very easily. However, some con-

In some cases fluid retention can cause a woman temporarily to go up a dress size.

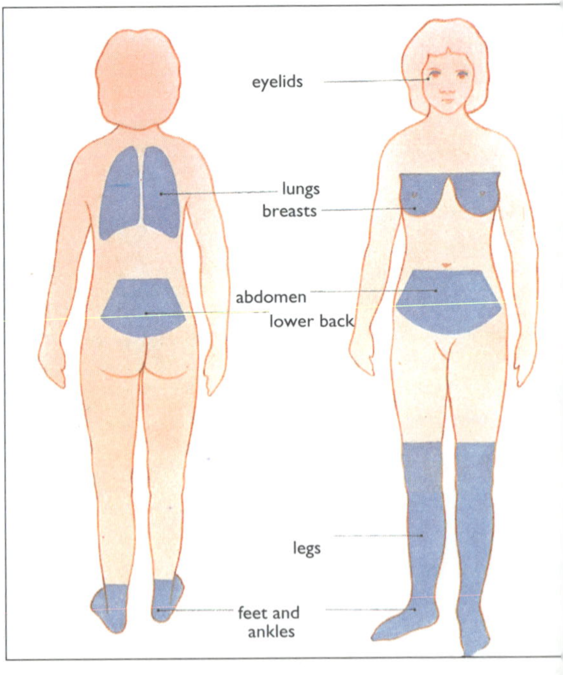

ditions cause generalised fluid retention. Without exercise, blood tends to collect in the leg veins, and eventually causes excessive fluid to leak out of the distended veins and capillaries into the surrounding tissues from which it drains downwards, producing oedema in the ankles and feet. Because of this, people who are immobilized or disabled often get swollen limbs. Fluid retention is also associated with varicose veins, kidney disease, liver and heart disease. Premenstrual fluid retention is due to a relative rise in the oestrogen level and many women notice that they put on a pound or two in weight.

Symptoms and signs: Places where fluid collects include the breasts, abdomen, legs, feet and ankles, lower back and the eyelids. Limbs may appear fatter and skin will feel stretched and taut.

Treatment: Try to restore the natural distribution of fluids around your body. If the fluid has collected in the lower limbs, take your shoes off and put your feet up above the level of your heart. If you are travelling on a plane or coach, take your shoes off and wriggle your toes from time to time. However, don't leave your shoes off for long periods of time and avoid taking alcohol. Premenstrual fluid retention may be helped by reducing the salt content in your diet. If this doesn't work, the doctor may prescribe a diuretic to be taken a week before your period is due.

FRACTURES

A fracture is a break in a bone – known as either simple, impacted, compound, stress, comminuted or greenstick fracture – depending on the nature of the break.

Causes: Fractures most commonly occur in sports injuries and road accidents, as well as in falls.

Symptoms and signs: It is not always easy to tell if you have a fracture or a sprain. The pain caused by a sprain usually covers a general area, whereas a fracture will cause a localised pain. If the break is serious, the bone may stick out at such an angle that it creates a visible lump. Sometimes the fractured ends of the bone audibly rub against one another. However, an X-ray may be necessary to exclude a fracture.

Treatment: Keep the joint or bone completely still. This will stop the jagged broken ends of bones from rubbing against surrounding tissue and creating more damage. In an emergency a fractured arm can be

THE BONES MOST LIKELY TO FRACTURE

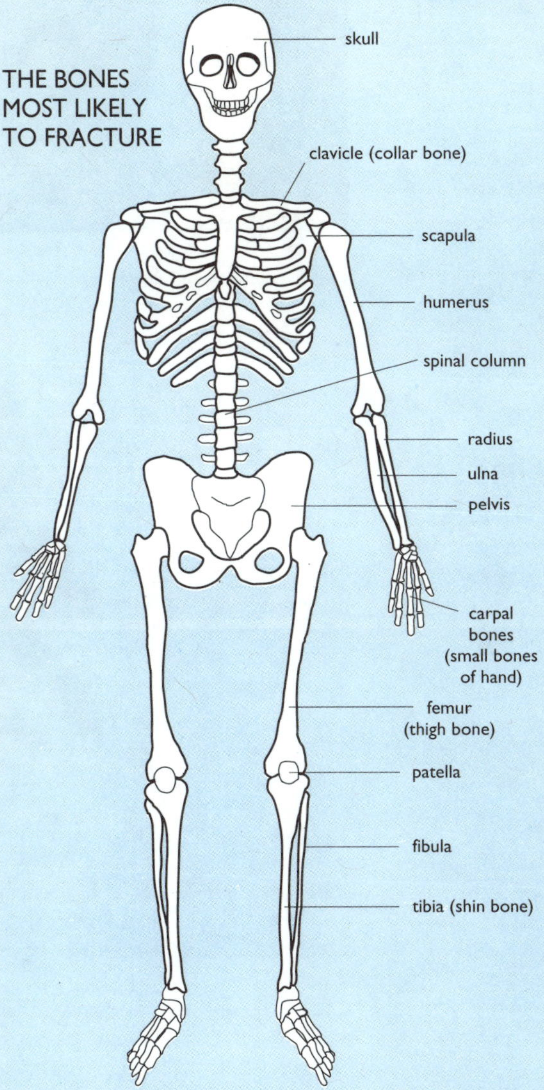

ASK THE DOCTOR

FRACTURES

Q I recently broke my leg and although it wasn't a bad fracture I am afraid of developing arthritis. Is this likely to happen?

A If the fracture was dealt with fairly promptly and there weren't any complications, it is likely that you won't have any problems in later life. If there was a delay in the treatment and a joint was involved, it is more likely that it will wear out more quickly and may lead to arthritis in years to come.

Self Help

FRIGIDITY

Get to know your own body better, especially the genital area, through self-examination and masturbation. Discover what pleases you, then be brave enough to tell your partner.

Useful Addresses

FRIGIDITY

Relate Marriage Guidance
Herbert Gray College
Little Church Street
RUGBY
Warks CV21 3AP
0788 573241

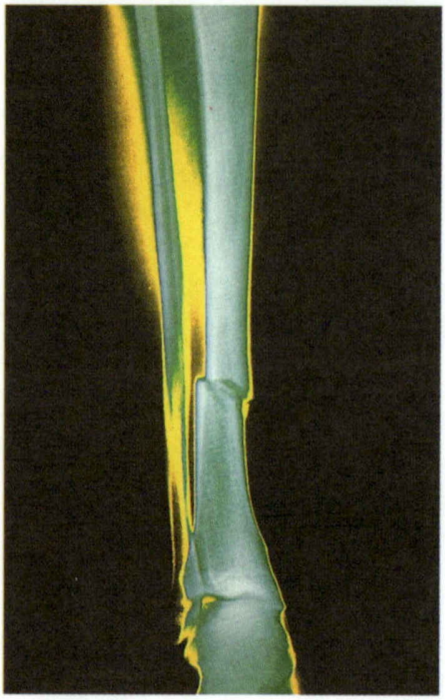

An X-ray of the lower leg, showing a fracture of the tibia, or shinbone (right), the larger of the two bones.

strapped to the body or a leg can be strapped to the other one. Bleeding is likely to occur and treatment for shock may be necessary. In hospital, the bone may need to be manoeuvred so that it can heal and function properly. Traction is used when the muscles in the broken limb are pulling the fracture apart again. Physiotherapy is vital during and after recovery, in order to prevent the wasting of muscles and stiffness in the joints.

FRIGIDITY

Frigidity is the general term used to describe a long-term lack of sexual response. It can affect both sexes but is more usually applied to women.

CAUSES: Anxiety about performance is a major turn-off when it comes to sex. Nearly everyone has occasional worries, but these can become exaggerated when you place too much emphasis on the physical, as opposed to the emotional, side of lovemaking.

Conflict within the relationship is another factor: if a couple is always arguing or one partner is resentful of the other, it can lead to problems in bed. Equally, if you are very tired or worried about other things in your life, you are unlikely to feel sexy.

Other causes of frigidity include having been sexually abused as a child, over-dependence on parents, depression, fear of pregnancy and, conversely, a reluctance to make love unless it is in order to get pregnant. Illness, too, can play a part: certain disorders of the nervous system, such as multiple sclerosis, can affect sexual response, as can diabetes and anorexia.

SYMPTOMS AND SIGNS: Sex drive varies from person to person and fluctuates for all kinds of reasons. A serious lack of response is indicated when you continuously avoid lovemaking or cannot enjoy it even though you find your partner sexually attractive.

Don't bottle up fears or anxieties. The first step in curing frigidity is to talk it through between you.

TREATMENT: Blindly trying to 'do better' in bed is less useful than improving your basic relationship. So talk with your partner. Discuss your hopes and fears, and see if together you can iron out any problems. If you find it hard to communicate, consider consulting your doctor or a trained counsellor.

See also DYSPAREUNIA.

FROSTBITE

Frostbite can affect any part of the body that is exposed to severe cold, but the parts most at risk are the fingers, toes, ears, nose, chin and cheeks. The outer layers of the skin literally freeze, and crystals of ice not only damage the cellular structure but also deprive them of their blood supply. If the tissues remain frostbitten for any length of time, they die and then, when they thaw out, they start to decompose. This condition is known as gangrene.

CAUSES: Prolonged exposure to below-freezing temperatures.

SYMPTOMS AND SIGNS: The skin s normal reaction to severe cold is pain, but if the discomfort suddenly disappears, this may be the first sign of frostbite – a warning sign that may pass unnoticed. It may therefore not be until someone else notices a change in the appearance of the skin that frostbite is suspected. The affected part appears pale, hard, and cold to the touch. The skin looks shiny and may blister. It may also be numb and feel stiff.

TREATMENT: The most important thing is to get into the warm, or at least under shelter, as quickly as possible. Remove any constricting clothing, such as gloves and boots. If warm, but not too hot, water is available, immerse the affected part in it until numbness disappears. If not, use the warmth of your hands to warm it up. If the fingers are affected, hold them under your armpit. Do not rub the affected area with anything – particularly not with snow. Do not give the sufferer alcohol, especially if s/he is suffering from exposure as well. Do not use heated pads or an electric blanket, as these might burn the skin. And do not try to warm the frostbitten part close to fire. As the affected part thaws out, exercise it as much as possible in order to restore the flow of blood.

See also GANGRENE.

Frostbitten toes after treatment. Precautions should be taken against bacterial infection.

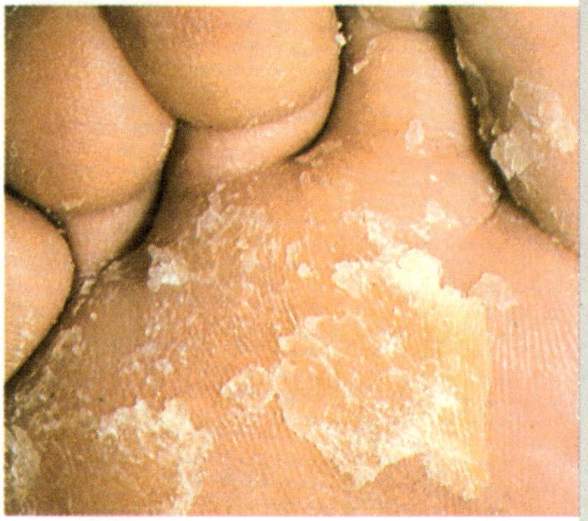

FROZEN SHOULDER

Shoulder pain and severe stiffness that is particularly common among the middle-aged and the elderly.

CAUSES: An inflammation of the capsule that surrounds the shoulder joint. The exact cause is often unknown but may be set off by injury or arthritis.

SYMPTOMS AND SIGNS: You will find it extremely difficult to move your shoulder and it will ache, the pain may be worse at night and your arm will also ache. The pain and stiffness can last from two months to two years.

TREATMENT: Try not to force your arm to move, rest it in a sling but not all the time as lack of exercise will make the condition worse, and take painkillers, as directed on the packet. If the pain doesn't die down, consult your doctor. S/he may arrange for an X-ray or blood test, prescribe painkillers or an injection of a steroid drug to help to relieve inflammation, or arrange physiotherapy or manipulation of the joint under general anaesthetic.

ASK THE DOCTOR

FROSTBITE

Q Are some people more likely to get frostibite than others?

A Yes. People with poor blood circulation and those taking beta-blocker drugs are particuarly at risk. Fatigue, taking alcohol, lack of oxygen etc. will lower awareness levels, which may lead to frostbite going unnoticed.

Self **Help**

FROZEN SHOULDER

Try to relieve the pain yourself by applying an ice-pack or using a heat lamp. Ask your doctor or physiotherapist for an exercise programme you can do yourself at home.

g

GALLSTONES

Gallstones are little pebbles up to about 1.3cm in diameter, which form in the gall-bladder.

CAUSES: The function of the gallbladder is to store bile, which is essential to the digestion of fatty foods. Cholesterol and pigments present in bile may solidify to form stones. The stone starts as a tiny solid particle, which gradually gets larger as more matter solidifies around it. The exact reasons for this condition are not known, but people with gallstones often have a fondness for rich foods and an unusually high level of cholesterol in their blood, and the chance of getting stones increases greatly with age. Chronic inflammation of the gallbladder may be another factor.

SYMPTOMS AND SIGNS: Gallstones usually give no trouble at all. If there are symptoms, they often occur after a rich or fatty meal. Symptoms range from mild discomfort in the upper abdomen, perhaps with wind and a bloated feeling, to severe abdominal pain with nausea and vomiting.

TREATMENT: If the symptoms are mild, a rest and a painkiller to ease discomfort may be the only treatment necessary. To stave off future attacks, care should be taken not to overeat, and fatty foods should be avoided. It is often also advisable to lose some weight. If the attack is severe, consult your doctor. Methods of dealing with gallstones include drugs to dissolve the stones, ultrasound to reduce them to a powder, and surgery.

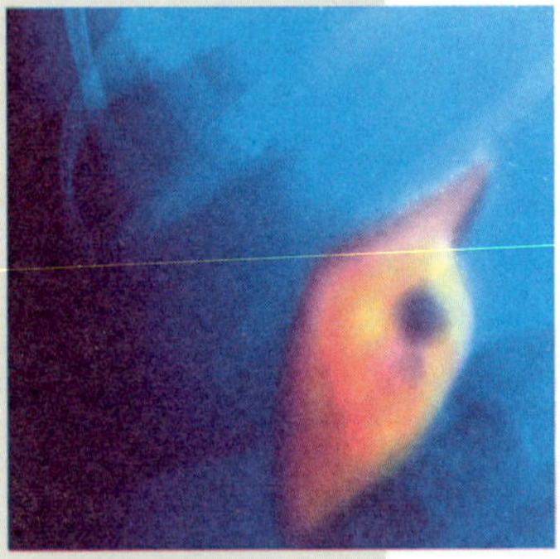

The dark areas show the position of two gallstones within the gallbladder (orange).

ASK THE DOCTOR

GASTROENTERITIS

Q How long does an attack of gastroenteritis last and when should I call a doctor?

A Most attacks last between 24 and 48 hours. If the symptoms have subsided, there is usually no need to call a doctor. Consult your doctor if the symptoms include severe abdominal pain, or continue unabated for longer than 48 hours. Babies and young children dehydrate very easily, so in these cases, consult a doctor if the symptoms persist for six hours, or sooner if you are at all worried.

GANGRENE

Gangrene is the death of tissue. It can affect just a small area of skin, or an entire limb. There are two types – dry and wet.

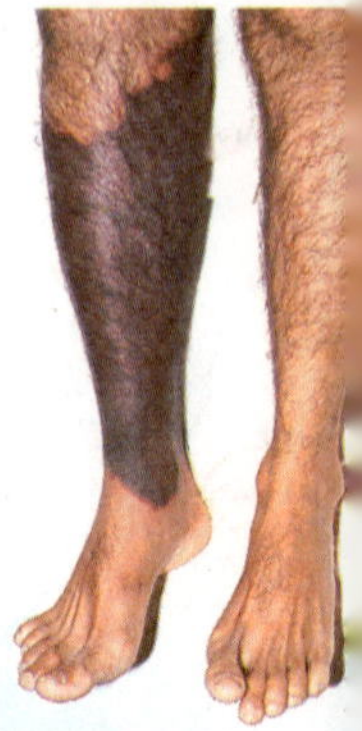

Gangrene turns the affected area black. It also has a tell-tale smell.

CAUSES: Dry gangrene is caused by loss of the normal blood supply to a tissue, which can result from arteriosclerosis, diabetes, thrombosis, embolism or frostbite. Wet gangrene develops when dry gangrene becomes infected.

SYMPTOMS AND SIGNS: Pain is felt, at first, in the dying tissues but once they are dead, there will be loss of feeling. The affected area will turn black, and the surrounding area may become red, with swelling and pus. Gangrene gives off an unpleasant, tell-tale smell.

TREATMENT: In dry gangrene, it is urgent to improve circulation in the affected area before infection sets in, either by drug treatment or surgery. If the area has become infected, antibiotics will be prescribed to prevent the onset of wet gangrene. Once wet gangrene has set in, amputation is unavoidable.

GASTROENTERITIS

Gastroenteritis is an inflammation of the stomach and intestine, which brings about an 'upset stomach'.

CAUSES: Viruses are the most common cause of gastroenteritis. These can easily be passed from one person to another and frequently occur in small epidemics.

Gastroenteritis can also be caused by food or drink which is contaminated by microbes, usually bacteria, causing 'food poisoning'. This is usually caused by poor hygiene in food preparation.

A healthy digestive tract contains bacteria that are either harmless or essential. Gastroenteritis sometimes occurs if the balance of these bacteria is changed through taking antibiotic drugs, altering your diet drastically or by a debilitating illness.

Symptoms and signs: A mild attack of gastroenteritis may make you feel nauseous and give you diarrhoea. Some attacks, however, are more severe. You may vomit and have pains and cramp in the abdomen followed by several bouts of watery diarrhoea. This may be accompanied by a fever and you will probably feel weak.

Treatment: Stay at home, rest, and drink plenty of water to stave off the dehydration caused by diarrhoea and vomiting. If you are vomiting a lot, take only a few sips of water every 15 minutes or so. Drink diluted, unsweetened fruit juice and avoid milk until the symptoms settle, as the sugar (lactose) in milk can prolong diarrhoea. You can add a level teaspoon of salt to every one litre (two pints) of juice to combat dehydration. Alternatively, you can buy a salt and sugar replacement preparation from the chemist. Don't take aspirin or other painkillers, as they would probably make things worse. Kaolin from the chemist will help the faeces to become more solid. Once the symptoms settle down, start eating bland food.

Gastroenteritis is easily passed on to other people, so hygiene is very important. Wash your hands with soap and hot water after every visit to the lavatory. Wash your hands before preparing food.

See also DIARRHOEA.

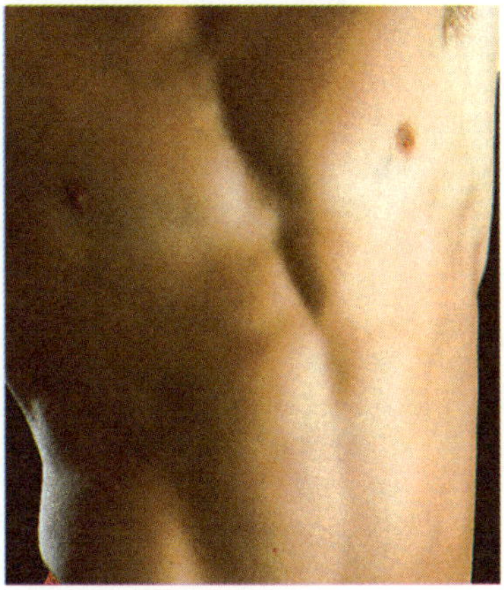

Gastroenteritis is usually caused by a virus but can be the result of food poisoning.

GENITAL HERPES

Genital herpes is an unpleasant, recurring infection, which can affect both men and women. Once the virus is in your body, it stays there all your life. Though some people only get the one attack, others may suffer recurrent attacks. It is usual for attacks to become gradually less and less severe.

Causes: The infection is caused by a virus, usually transmitted by vaginal or anal intercourse, or through oral sex.

Symptoms and signs: A week or so after contact, you may experience an itching and burning sensation on the vulva or penis, and sometimes around the anus. A group of tiny blisters will appear which then burst, leaving small painful ulcers, which should heal in about 10 to 21 days. You may feel generally unwell, possibly feverish, and also run a temperature. Glands in the groin may become enlarged and tender, and women in particular may find passing urine very painful if it comes into contact with the ulcers.

Treatment: It is important to consult your doctor or go to a GU (genito-urinary) clinic as soon as any blisters appear.

There is no cure for genital herpes but antiviral creams and tablets such as acyclovir can alleviate the pain and reduce the length and frequency of attacks. You may also find relief by taking painkillers or bathing the affected area in lukewarm salty water.

GENITAL WARTS

Genital warts are painless, irregular lumps, which can appear on the vulva or penis or around the anus.

Causes: They are caused by a sexually transmitted virus and can take up to 18 months to develop.

Symptoms and signs: Several warts usually form in one particular area. They are small to begin with but may grow quite large if left untreated. Sometimes they grow during pregnancy, but decrease in size again after the baby is born.

Treatment: Genital warts aren't serious in

ASK THE DOCTOR

GENITAL HERPES

Q I have not had an attack of herpes for some time. Should I tell my new girlfriend about the infection before we sleep together, or is it enough for me to avoid sex if and when I have another attack?

A It is possible to infect another person with the virus even when it is not active. You should definitely tell your girlfriend that you have herpes, and reassure her that you will always wear a condom during sex to minimise the spread of infection. However awkward you feel about tackling the subject, it is better to be honest at the beginning of the relationship rather than risk her anger and resentment later. Do, however, give her some literature on the subject so she can learn that herpes is a very common disease, which many people learn to live with and find merely a mild inconvenience.

Useful Addresses

GENITAL HERPES

Herpes Association
41 North Road
LONDON N7 9DP
071 607 9661

Helpline 071 609 9061

themselves, but since they have been linked with cervical cancer, it is a wise precaution for a woman who has had them (or whose partner has had them) to have a cervical smear test each year.

The usual treatment is for a doctor or nurse to paint each wart individually with a preparation of 'podophyllin', which destroys the wart cells. Alternatively, the warts can be removed by freezing them with liquid nitrogen, or by surgery.

GERMAN MEASLES

see RUBELLA

GINGIVITIS

see GUM DISEASE

GLANDULAR FEVER

Glandular fever is a common viral condition in which many of the lymph glands become inflamed. The liver is also often infected.

It is most common in the 15-20 age group. Most people come into contact with it at some time in their lives but only about one-third of them will have the illness severely enough to take the symptoms seriously.

Causes: Glandular fever is caused by a virus, which may be transmitted by sexual intercourse or from a blood transfusion. But since the virus lingers in a person's saliva for several months after recovery, the usual way of passing it on is by mouth-to-mouth kissing.

Symptoms and signs: The first symptoms are rather like those of flu. For the first five days, you'll feel generally tired and unwell. You'll probably have a headache, feel sick and won't want to eat, then you may develop a sore throat and a temperature. Many of the lymph glands may also become enlarged, notably the ones in the neck on either side of the Adam's apple and underneath the jaw. The tonsils often become covered with little yellow spots, and the spleen may swell and protrude below the rib cage on the left-hand side of the stomach. A few people develop a faint, non-itchy body rash.

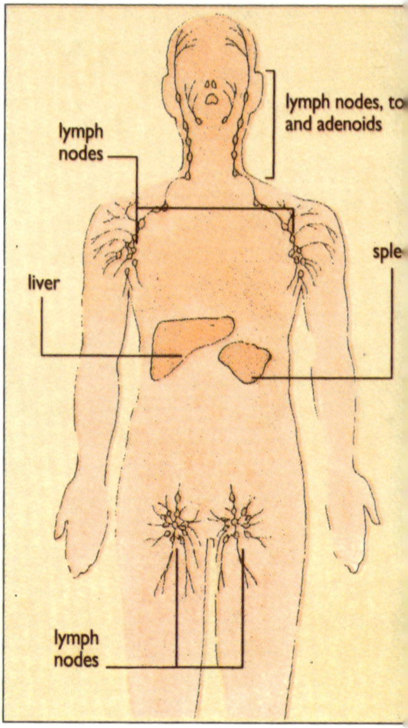

Glandular fever causes the lymph glands and spleen to swell. A rash may also appear.

Treatment: At present there is no specific treatment and, as with most other viruses, you just have to wait for the body's own defences to deal with the infection. In severe cases, it's best to stay in bed for the first week or two, and afterwards take things as easy as possible.

Your doctor may decide to take a swab from your throat to make sure that there aren't any other germs causing the inflammation. S/he may also carry out a special blood test to confirm whether or not you have glandular fever.

The disease usually lasts three to four weeks, but can go on much longer. After a month, most people feel well enough to go back to work or school and have no after-effects, but a few may feel vaguely ill, lethargic and unable to concentrate properly for three months or more.

ASK THE DOCTOR

GLANDULAR FEVER

Q My son has just been diagnosed as having glandular fever. Should he be kept in isolation?

A It is pointless for someone who has had glandular fever to be kept in quarantine as s/he has probably already passed on the virus by the time the condition is diagnosed.

GLAUCOMA

In glaucoma, there is a build-up of pressure inside the eye. If left untreated, this pressure eventually destroys the optic nerve, causing blindness.

CAUSES: Inside the eye there is a delicate balance between the liquids that the eye produces and the draining away of these fluids. This balance is upset when faulty drainage fails to keep pace with production of fluids, thereby causing pressure to build up inside the eye.

Ageing and heredity seem to be the prime factors in this condition, though sometimes glaucoma results from an eye infection which affects the drainage canals.

SYMPTOMS AND SIGNS: Chronic glaucoma often produces no symptoms. There is a slow build-up of pressure and a gradual loss of peripheral vision, which often goes unnoticed. If untreated, the field of vision diminishes with time, until total blindness results. The condition often first comes to light during a routine eye check.

In acute glaucoma, there is a rapid build-up of pressure with pain and aching in and above the eye. Vision may be blurred and the eyeball red and swollen. An acute attack is often accompanied by nausea, vomiting, stomach pains and headaches.

TREATMENT: Chronic glaucoma can usually be controlled with drugs in the form of eye-drops or tablets. But early diagnosis is important as any damage to the optic nerve is permanent. Everyone over the age of 40 should visit an eye specialist for a check-up every two years or so. If there is a history of glaucoma in the family, you should have yearly check-ups.

Acute glaucoma needs urgent medical attention. Drugs are often prescribed, and surgery may be needed to improve drainage.

GOITRE

see HYPERTHYROIDISM, HYPOTHYROIDISM

GONORRHOEA

Gonorrhoea is one of the most common sexually transmitted diseases. It can affect both men and women, following intimate contact with someone infected with these bacteria.

CAUSES: Gonorrhoea is caused by a bacterium which only thrives inside the body, so it cannot be caught from toilet seats or towels. The disease is nearly always passed during sexual contact, including oral and anal sex. Pregnant women can pass on the infection to their babies during birth.

SYMPTOMS AND SIGNS: Since many people, particularly women, have either no symptoms or only very mild ones which quickly subside, they may have no idea that they are infected until they pass on the disease or develop complications themselves.

If symptoms do appear, they are usually noticeable within two to ten days after sexu-

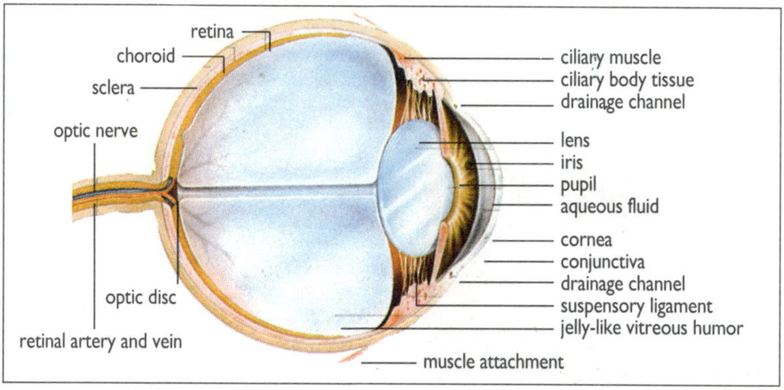

Section through the eye, showing its internal structure.

ASK THE DOCTOR

GLAUCOMA

Q Does glaucoma often lead to blindness?

A Yes, it is responsible for around 15 per cent of cases of blindness in the UK. But if it is diagnosed early enough, blindness can usually be prevented.

Q I am 50. How likely am I to suffer from glaucoma in the future?

A Glaucoma is one of the most common serious eye disorders in people over the age of 60. It is estimated that about two per cent of the over-40s in the UK suffer from it.

Useful Addresses

GLAUCOMA

The International Glaucoma Association
King's College Hospital
Denmark Hill
LONDON SE5 9RS
071 737 3265

ASK THE DOCTOR

GONORRHOEA

Q Can I get gonorrhoea again, once I have been successfully treated?

A Yes, you can. Treatment does not protect you against reinfection.

Self **Help**

GOUT

If you have recurrent attacks, always carry your medication with you. Increased levels of purine are known to raise the levels of uric acid in the blood. If you are susceptible to attacks of gout, it is therefore a good idea to avoid certain foods, such as fish roe, tinned fish, red meat and offal, which are rich in purine.

al contact with an infected person. Men may feel an intense burning in the penis and pain on passing urine; there may also be a thick yellow discharge from the end of the penis.

Women may also feel pain passing urine and may have a vaginal discharge.

Occasionally, anal sex with an infected person can cause infection of the rectum and anus: there may be irritation and some discharge. Infection acquired through oral sex can lead to a mild throat infection.

Babies infected at birth may suffer eye damage.

TREATMENT: The disease can usually be treated with antibiotics. Go to your doctor or nearest GU (genito-urinary) clinic as soon as you suspect you might be infected because, although symptoms tend to disappear in time, you can still be infectious if you have the disease. Also, as with all sexually transmitted infections, you should tell any partner of the risk.

Untreated, gonorrhoea can lead to complications like gonococcal arthritis, which causes pain and swelling in the joints, and septicaemia, which makes you feel feverish and generally unwell.

Men can develop prostatis (inflammation of the prostate) or epididymo-orchitis (inflammation of the epididymides and testes), which may affect fertility. Women can contract PID (pelvic inflammatory disease), which affects the fallopian tubes and can cause infertility.

GOUT

Gout is a type of arthritis which often affects one joint at a time. It can cause deposits of white crystals to form under the skin.

CAUSES: Gout is caused by an abnormality in the way the body deals with a chemical called uric acid. This is a perfectly normal constituent of blood. Gout occurs when there is an unusually high level of uric acid in the bloodstream. This acid then becomes deposited as sharp spiky crystals in various tissues of the body, particularly in the joints but also in the tendons, skin and kidneys. These crystals not only damage the cells but can actually make them disintegrate, as a result of which the cells release various toxic substances, causing more damage and inflammation. Inherited gout is the result of a biochemical abnormality, which causes the patient to produce excessive amounts of uric acid. Certain types of kidney disease can also cause gout.

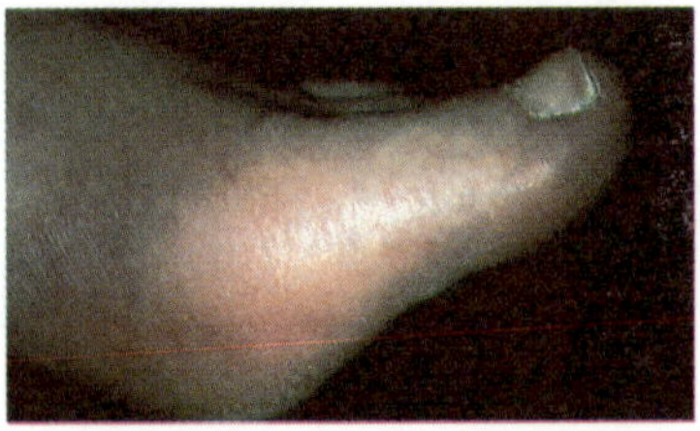

In two-thirds of cases, gout affects the joint at the base of the big toe.

SYMPTOMS AND SIGNS: The first attack of gout usually occurs in early middle age and is often confined to one or two joints. Pain and swelling in the joint usually start suddenly. The joint becomes swollen, hot and inflamed and the skin stretched over it turns bright red. When the pain is at its worst, it is almost impossible to move the joint.

TREATMENT: When an acute attack occurs, the affected joint must be rested, and the patient will probably be given an anti-inflammatory drug, which is normally taken for up to three weeks. However, patients who have frequent attacks will usually be given regular treatment to prevent further attacks.

GUM DISEASE

Inflammation of the gums can cause gingivitis, loose teeth and abscesses.

CAUSES: Plaque and bad oral hygiene are usually responsible for gum disease. Plaque is a mixture of saliva, bacteria and food which coats the teeth. Initially, it is soft and can be brushed off the teeth fairly easily. But some areas of the mouth – the necks of teeth, especially the back teeth and between the teeth – may be missed. In time, the plaque that is left behind hardens into calculus (tartar), which sits round the neck of the teeth. This is a breeding ground of harmful bacteria, which cause the gums to become inflamed – a condition known as gingivitis. Pockets can

1 Plaque forms on the tooth and, if left, calcifies and hardens into calculus. New plaque forms on top of the calculus.
2 The gum becomes enlarged and begins to separate from the tooth. Eventually, calculus forms on the root of the tooth.
3 As gum disease advances, the bone is eaten away and the tooth loosens.

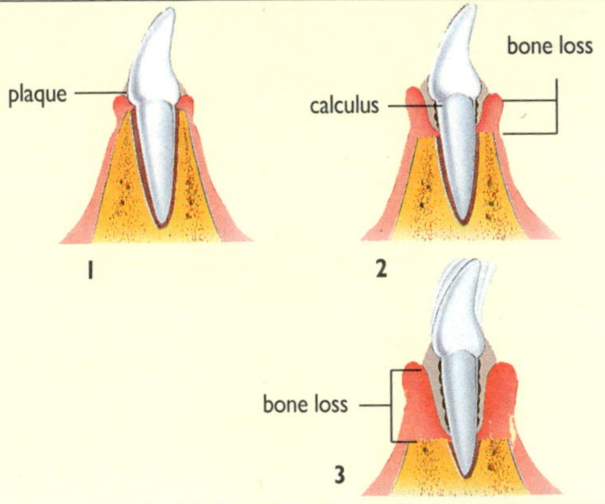

form round the teeth, which allow plaque to attack the connective tissues that hold the teeth firm. Bone loss also occurs. With time, the gums shrink and the teeth become loose.

SYMPTOMS AND SIGNS: Early signs of gum disease are inflamed, spongy, swollen areas around the base of the teeth. Brushing may be painful and the teeth may bleed. Later signs are receding gums and loose teeth. The breath may smell unpleasant and tooth abscesses may form.

TREATMENT: If the dentist diagnoses gum disease, s/he will probably teach you how to keep the teeth plaque-free. The calculus will be removed with a special instrument and the teeth polished. A bacticidal mouthwash may be recommended until the inflammation settles down. Deep pockets may need surgery under local anaesthetic. Good oral hygiene and regular scaling will probably keep further gum problems at bay.

h

HAEMOPHILIA

Haemophilia is a blood-clotting disorder. The blood of a haemophiliac does not contain enough anti-haemophilic globulin, also known as Factor VIII, a chemical that is vital for clotting the blood. As a result, wounds do not stop bleeding, minor injuries tend to bleed profusely and there may be spontaneous bleeding. It is a rare disease – about one male in 50,000 has haemophilia in the UK.

CAUSES: Haemophilia is inherited. It is carried by women and passed on to their sons. There is usually a family history of haemophilia, but, in about 25 per cent of cases, a haemophiliac can be the first in his family because of a sudden mutation in the genes.

SYMPTOMS AND SIGNS: Haemophilia is usually first seen when a male child begins to be active. A baby boy may bruise easily when he begins to crawl. An ordinary tumble can cause internal bruising and bleeding, and joints and limbs can become painfully swollen and usually hamper movement. Cuts tend to

Haemorrhage on the neck of a haemophiliac. The disorder is passed on by women to their sons.

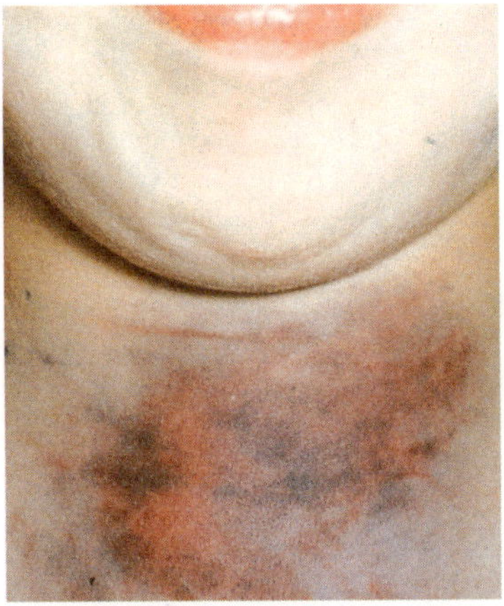

HOW TO REMOVE PLAQUE

Learning to clean your teeth isn't only a matter of brush technique – you need to be sure you remove all the plaque. Plaque-disclosing tablets or solutions that stain the plaque and make it visible are very helpful.

- Use a nylon toothbrush with a small head; you'll find this easier to manoeuvre, especially around the back teeth.
- Clean your teeth first, then use the plaque discloser as recommended.
- Look at your teeth in the mirror. Any plaque that has been missed will be stained by the dye. Check especially the inside surfaces of the back teeth.
- Brush the teeth thoroughly until all traces of dye are removed – this means all the plaque will have gone too. You may find that your gums are now bleeding. Don't let that put you off. You have already taken the first step to healing your gums and preventing disease.

Self Help

HAEMOPHILIA

If you have haemophilia, you should avoid playing high-risk sports, such as rugby, and concentrate instead on activities like swimming or running. Don't take any drugs – not even aspirin – without seeking medical advice.

ASK THE DOCTOR

HAEMOPHILIA

Q If I have haemophilia will I contract HIV through transfusions?

A No, all potential blood donors have been screened for HIV since 1985 and all Factor VIII is now heat-treated to eliminate any possibility of the risk of contracting HIV.

Useful Addresses

HAEMOPHILIA

Haemophilia Society
123 Westminster Bridge Road
LONDON SE1 7HR
071 928 2020

bleed for a long time, although individual haemophiliacs bleed at varying rates.

Treatment: If you are male and bruise or bleed in an unusual way, you should consult your doctor. If you are diagnosed as a haemophiliac, you will be given preventative treatment of regular transfusions of Factor VIII and you may be taught to inject yourself with Factor VIII. Serious injury is still risky to haemophiliacs, but many minor injuries can be treated with extra injections or transfusions of Factor VIII.

HAEMORRHOIDS

Haemorrhoids, or 'piles', are small, bluish swellings, containing enlarged blood vessels located either just inside or just outside the anus. A hundred years ago, the condition was very rare and it is still relatively uncommon in the Third World. However, in countries such as Britain and the USA, up to one-third of all adults now suffer from haemorrhoids.

Causes: The most common cause of haemorrhoids is persistent constipation as a result of poor diet. The straining needed to pass small hard bowel motions causes congestion in the network of blood vessels inside the anal cushions. Eventually, these vessels enlarge and form haemorrhoids. If constipation continues, the persistent straining makes them enlarge until second- or third-degree haemorrhoids develop.

Symptoms and signs: Internal, or first-degree, haemorrhoids, which many people have without even being aware of them, are located just inside the anus. These may occasionally cause some discomfort when a bowel motion is passed, and they may also bleed occasionally. A smear of bright red blood on the toilet paper or drips in the toilet pan is likely to be the only evidence of this.

Second-degree piles usually appear as pea-sized swellings outside the anus after a bowel motion has been passed. They usually return inside the anus of their own accord. They may bleed and cause discomfort when a motion is passed. They may also itch.

With third-degree haemorrhoids, the swollen blood vessels are so enlarged that they remain outside the anus permanently. Known as external piles, these are more troublesome. They may cause soreness and persistent irritation.

Treatment: A high-fibre diet is essential for most haemorrhoid sufferers. The amount of fibre in the diet should be increased gradually until the bowel motion is quite soft and easily passed without any straining.

If the haemorrhoids are painful or causing itching, the doctor may prescribe some cream or suppositories to be inserted inside the anus. However, if the haemorrhoids continue to bleed or cause pain, the doctor may inject them with a chemical that shrivels them. Haemorrhoids may also be treated by freezing. This has a similar effect to the chemical injection but is free of any discomfort, whereas the injection may be painful.

Third-degree haemorrhoids can sometimes be treated successfully by freezing, but an operation is often needed to remove them. The haemorrhoids are removed under anaesthetic and the raw areas sewn back together by the surgeon. This operation is usually successful in curing the problem but, because there is often quite considerable pain for some days after, it is only carried out when other methods of treatment have failed.

HALITOSIS

A harmless condition, commonly known as bad breath.

Causes: Halitosis is usually due to poor teeth and gum care. Eating strongly flavoured

Brushing your teeth regularly and using a mouth wash can help prevent halitosis.

food, such as onions or garlic, can also cause it. It may be linked with constipation, a respiratory infection or very bad sinusitis.

Symptoms and signs: Strong and unpleasantly odorous breath.

Treatment: Make sure you clean your teeth regularly and use a mouth wash. If the condition persists, consult a dental hygienist or your doctor.

HAMMER TOE

When one of the toes, usually the second, is permanently bent downwards at the middle joint, it is called a hammer toe.

Causes: The toe is held in an incorrect position due to crowding by the other toes. This is often caused by shoes that are too tight, either because they are too narrow or because they are too short. A hammer toe can also be caused when a bunion on the big toe bends the second toe into an abnormal position.

Symptoms and signs: The affected toe is permanently bent and a painful corn may develop on the bent joint because of pressure from the shoe.

Treatment: Abandon shoes that may be causing the problem. Schools of thought differ on treatment: if a child has a hammer toe, some people think it best to allow the toe to correct itself. Others think it helpful to manipulate the toe into the correct position and hold it there with a splint.

A protective felt pad may ease the pressure on the joint. In extreme cases, where a toe is badly deformed and prone to ulceration and infection, surgery can help.

See also BUNIONS, CORN.

HAYFEVER

see RHINITIS

HEADACHE

Headaches, along with backpain, are probably the most common of all complaints – but one of the most difficult to define. The great majority of headaches are harmless and of very little significance.

Causes: The causes are so varied that it is often difficult to pin down exactly what physical or emotional problem is the root of the trouble. The most common factors that bring on headaches are various types of tension, fatigue, anxiety or emotional upset. Less commonly, a headache may reflect some disorder or infection elsewhere in the body, or accompany a problem affecting the eyes, sinuses, teeth or neck.

The pain may originate outside the skull, as a result of contraction and tension of the muscles in the neck and scalp – this is thought to be the case with common tension and fatigue headaches. Or it may originate within the skull due to some inflammation, distortion, or some other disturbance of the blood vessels and pain-sensitive membranes surrounding the brain. Tension headaches, usually a result of everyday tensions and fatigue, are normally brief but they tend to recur unless the underlying cause is dealt with. Occasionally, frequent mild headaches may indicate chronic ill-health, such as anaemia, high blood pressure or kidney disease. Headaches may also be due to an infection elsewhere in the body, a blow to the head, eye strains, or severe sinusitis. Very rarely, a headache may be due to a brain tumour.

Symptoms and signs: The ache experienced can vary in intensity from no more than mild discomfort to very severe, stabbing pain.

Treatment: It usually helps to take a painkiller, such as aspirin or paracetamol, but you should not take more than two tablets at any one time. If necessary, these can be repeated about four hours later. If you find you are taking painkillers regularly or in large doses to deal with headaches, you should consult a doctor.

See also MIGRAINE.

ASK THE DOCTOR

HAEMORRHOIDS

Q Is it true that you can get piles from sitting on a hot radiator?

A No - nor is it true that you can get them from sitting on cold concrete.

Self **Help**

HAEMORRHOIDS

Eat wholemeal bread rather than white bread, wholemeal or bran breakfast cereals, and plenty of fresh fruit and vegetables.

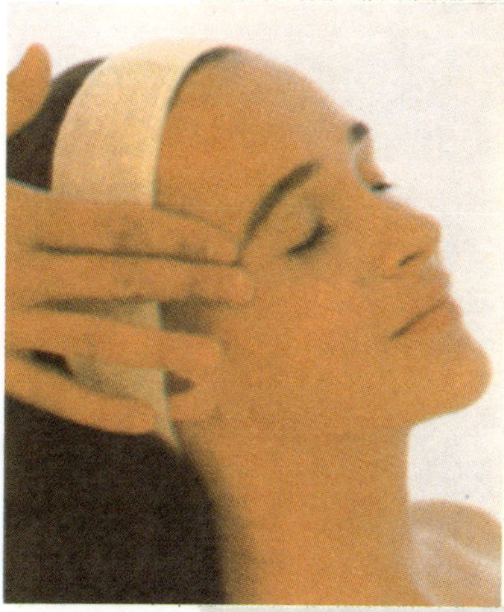

If tension headaches are a problem, use common-sense preventative measures. Try to relax more and avoid stressful situations If simple remedies fail and headaches keep coming back, see your doctor.

HEART ATTACK

A heart attack, more correctly known as myocardial infarction, is when an area of heart muscle tissue dies. As many as 160,000 people in the UK die each year as a result of a heart attack. A further 90,000 people have a heart attack, but survive. It is the most common cause of death in western society today.

CAUSES: The heart is a muscular pump and relies on a regular supply of blood to keep the muscle pumping. If the blood supply to an area of heart muscle is cut off, the tissue dies and the heart ceases to function properly.

There are several reasons why the heart muscle can be deprived of blood. Atherosclerosis or 'furring' of the coronary arteries is the most common cause. The restriction of blood flow causes clots to form and the clotting may stop the blood flow to an area of the heart muscle.

The likelihood of heart attack increases with age. If you smoke, are overweight, do not take enough exercise, have an unhealthy diet high in saturated fats, or you have high blood pressure or diabetes mellitus, you are more vulnerable to heart attack.

SYMPTOMS AND SIGNS: The first sign of a heart attack may be a sudden severe pain across the middle of the chest. The pain may radiate down the left arm or up into the jaw and may last for 30 minutes or more without relief. You may also feel nauseous or vomit, be short of breath, restless and anxious, sweat and have cold, clammy skin. You may collapse and either remain conscious or become unconscious.

If the heart muscle is severely damaged, the heart may reduce its pumping action, causing heart failure. The heart rhythm may become abnormal (arrhythmia). Death may be due to a disturbed heart rhythm, called ventricular fibrillation.

TREATMENT: If you suspect that someone is having a heart attack, call an ambulance at once. If the victim is taken swiftly to hospital, the arrhythmia can be controlled by electrical defibrillation or drugs. In addition to strong painkillers, treatment may also include diuretic drugs to clear the lungs of fluid, and betablocker drugs to lessen the risk of further heart muscle damage. Thrombolytic drugs are relatively new. They can lessen the amount of heart muscle damage by dissolving the clot during an attack. Most people who survive a heart attack are not encouraged to stay in bed for more than four or five days, although they may be in hospital for much longer.

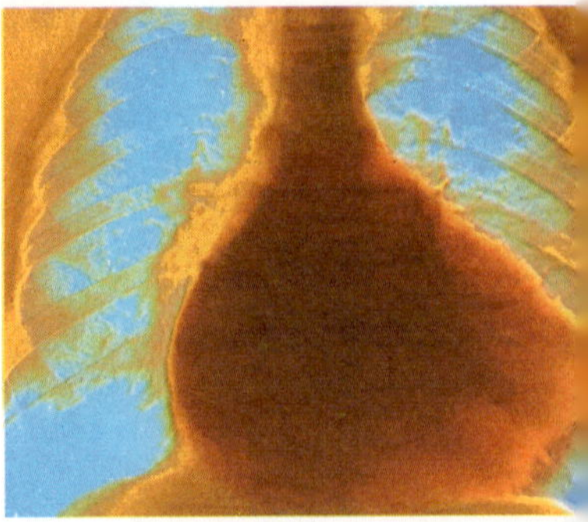

An x-ray of the chest showing the enlargement of the lower left-hand chamber of the heart.

ASK THE DOCTOR

HEART ATTACK

Q If I have had a heart attack, will I have another one?

A There is an increased risk of suffering another heart attack in the years immediately following the first one.

Self **Help**

HEART ATTACK

To reduce the risk of an attack:

- Don't smoke
- Keep to a healthy, low-fat diet
- Ask your doctor to recommend a suitable exercise programme
- Keep your weight down

HEARTBURN

see INDIGESTION

The heart is not a continuous pump – it beats and then relaxes. Five beats are shown here.

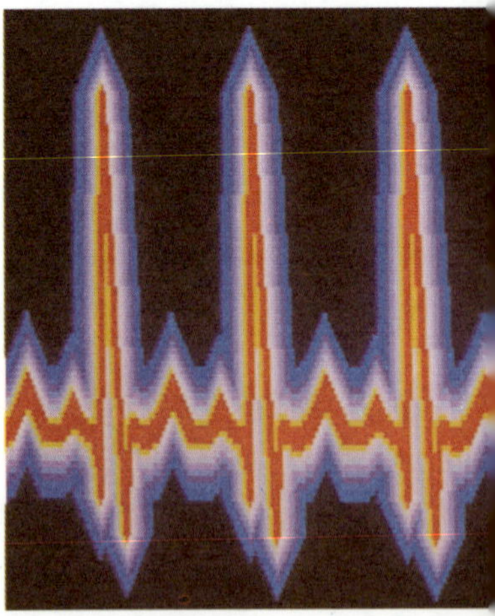

HEART DISEASE

Heart disorders are the most common cause of death in the modern western world. Of these, coronary heart disease, which affects the arteries that supply blood to the heart muscle, is the most common. Other heart diseases include those of the heart muscle, such as myocarditis, and arrhythmia, which is a disturbance in the rhythm of the heartbeat. See also ANEURYSM, ANGINA PECTORIS, ARTERIOSCLEROSIS, HEART ATTACK, HEART FAILURE, HEART VALVE DISEASE.

HEART FAILURE

A condition where the heart cannot work efficiently and fails to pump blood properly to the lungs and the rest of the body. In most cases it is treatable. There are two kinds of heart failure: left-sided and right-sided.

CAUSES: left-sided heart failure: The left side of the heart does not empty or fill properly with each pumping action, which eventually leads to excess fluid in the lungs. Congenital heart defects, anaemia, high blood pressure, heart valve defects, arrhythmia (irregularities of heart beat), heart attack and diseases of the heart muscle can all cause left-sided heart failure.

CAUSES: right-sided heart failure: The back pressure in the circulatory system caused by this type of heart failure leads to fluid retention in the tissues, swollen neck veins and enlargement of the liver. It may be caused by heart valve defects and a congenital heart defect, but the most common cause is a raised blood pressure due to obstruction of blood flow through the lung veins (pulmonary hypertension), usually as the result of lung diseases such as chronic bronchitits and emphysema.

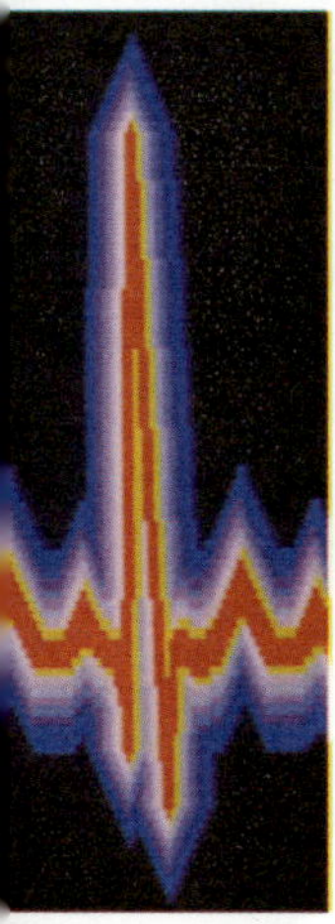

SYMPTOMS AND SIGNS: The earliest symptom of heart failure is general fatigue. In left-sided heart failure, breathlessness is a common symptom. At first, the breathlessness comes after exercise, but eventually is present even at rest. In right-sided heart failure, the breathlessness is less apparent but the ankles and legs swell and you may feel internal discomfort and have indigestion. Left- and right-sided failure often occur together.

TREATMENT: At first you may be given bed rest, sitting up in bed to ease the lung congestion. You may also be given diuretic drugs to reduce the excess fluid in the body. Drugs that ease the burden of work on the heart or make the heart's contractions stronger are sometimes prescribed too. If drug treatment fails, a heart transplant may be the only cure.

HEART VALVE DISEASE

A significant proportion of deaths due to diseases of the heart and circulation are caused by diseased heart valves. These diseases can be prevented, or at least improved, by treatment, if caught early enough.

A system of valves in the heart is required to ensure that the blood is squeezed forward when the heart contracts, and not backwards in the direction from which it came. The right side of the heart, which pumps blood to the lungs, has two valves – the pulmonary valve and the tricuspid valve. The left side of the heart, which pumps blood to the rest of the body, also has two valves – the mitral valve and the aortic valve.

CAUSES: Some kinds of heart valve disorder, such as narrow or abnormal valves, are due to congenital defects. Others are caused by rheumatic fever. A heart attack may cause problems too. Damage to the aortic valve can also result as a complication of syphilis, often many years after infection.

SYMPTOMS AND SIGNS: Breathlessness is probably the most common symptom of

Useful Addresses

HEART DISEASE

The Coronary Prevention Group
102 Gloucester Place
LONDON W1H 3DA
071 935 2889

The Coronary Artery Disease Research Association (CORDA)
Tavistock House North
Tavistock Square
LONDON WC1M 7DG
071 387 9779

The British Heart Foundation
14 Fitzhardinge Street
LONDON W1H 4DH
071 935 0185

ASK THE DOCTOR

HEART FAILURE

Q If I have heart failure, will I be able to lead a normal life again?

A In most cases, after proper treatment, there is no reason why someone with heart failure should not return to an active life as long as the underlying cause is treatable. Although rest is often helpful in the early stages, doctors usually recommend a progressive exercise programme to improve the function of the heart, lungs and circulation.

heart valve disease. This is due to the back pressure of blood, which builds up in the lungs and prevents them working efficiently.

Less blood than usual may be pumped out, because a valve has either narrowed or become incompetent. With disease of the aortic valve, you may suffer from a chest pain similar to that caused by coronary artery disease. The pain is usually in the centre of the chest but may affect the neck and arms.

Dizzy spells or blackouts, which usually develop after exertion, are severe symptoms of aortic stenosis, and occur when there is insufficient blood passing through the narrowed aortic valve to supply enough oxygen to the brain – resulting in faintness.

Abnormal heart rhythms may occur in heart-valve diseases – probably because of back pressure on the area of muscle, which is normally responsible for the maintenance of a regular heart rhythm. These abnormal rhythms may lead to palpitations.

TREATMENT: If you already have heart valve damage, you run a much higher risk of valve infection. Any form of treatment that might release bacteria into the bloodstream should therefore be preceded by a short course of antibiotics to protect the valves from an acute infection.

Breathlessness, ankle swelling, abdominal pain and general malaise can be treated with diuretics, which help to reduce the amount of fluid in the patient's body. Drugs that increase the heart's pumping ability or control abnormal heart rhythms may also be given, as may anticoagulants which reduce the likelihood of blood clots. If a valve becomes infected, the patient will be treated with antibiotics.

If the patient doesn't respond to treatment with drugs, open-heart surgery may be considered necessary.

HOW BLOOD FLOWS THROUGH THE HEART AND ITS VALVES

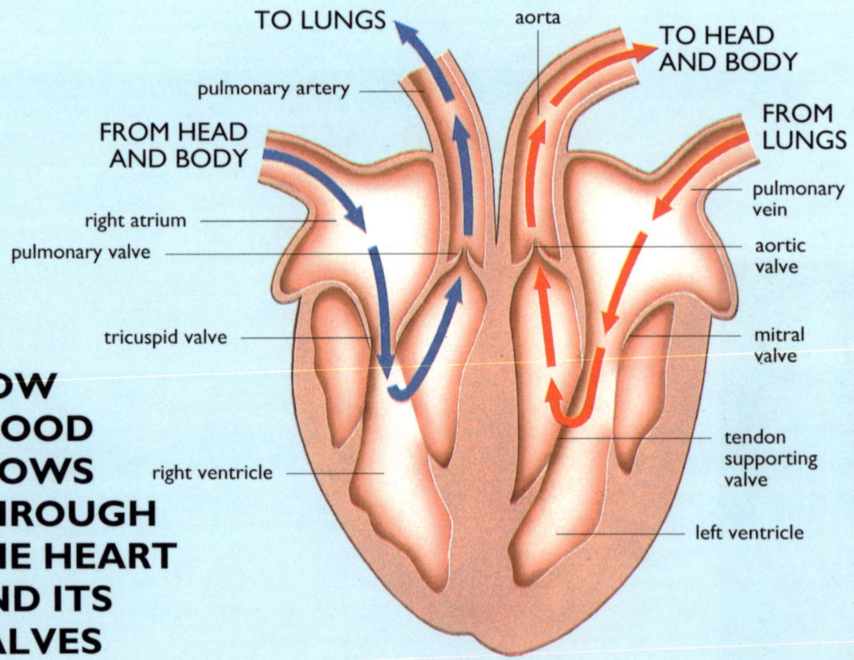

HEPATITIS

Hepatitis means inflammation of the liver. There are two main types of hepatitis. They are commonly known as hepatitis A and hepatitis B. Each disease is caused by a different virus.

CAUSES: Hepatitis A is usually transmitted via contaminated food or water.

HEPATITIS A This is the milder of the two, is more infectious and hence more common.

SYMPTOMS AND SIGNS: The first signs are a fever and headache, followed by nausea, vomiting and discomfort over the region of the liver, which lies under the ribs in the upper, right-hand side of the abdomen. Occasionally, vomiting is so severe that food poisoning is suspected. However, within three or four days of the first symptoms, jaundice will appear and worsen over the next week. The sufferer's urine may become a dark brown colour. Strangely enough, as the jaundice gets worse, sufferers may find that they begin to feel better, and recover over the next week or two.

TREATMENT: Drink plenty of water and rest. It will take a few weeks to recover and you may remain tired and depressed for some time. Maintaining a high level of hygiene is important to prevent the infection spreading.

HEPATITIS B This is caused by a different virus and is contracted from contact with infected blood or through sexual intercourse.

SYMPTOMS AND SIGNS: Symptoms are similar to those of hepatitis A, but those that emerge before the jaundice will be more severe than in hepatitis A. You may experience severe joint pains and aching of the muscles. Convalescence may be prolonged.

CAUSES: Unlike hepatitis A, the B virus requires the transfer of blood or seminal fluid from one person to another. It is either sexually transmitted, passed on via dirty syringes and needles, or contracted through blood transfusion in countries that don't screen or heat-treat donated blood.

TREATMENT: Essentially, treatment is the same as for hepatitis A. As soon as the patient is recovered enough to be eating again, it is important to give as much nourishing food as possible. Usually victims of hepatitis B require a hospital stay. Those who are particularly at risk can easily be immunised against hepatitis B.

Rarely, someone infected with hepatitis B cannot get rid of the virus. Although the patient appears to recover, the virus remains alive and active over time, causing a low-grade continual inflammation of the liver. This gradually causes more and more damage to the liver. These rare cases may be infectious for many years and, if precautions aren't taken, can easily be passed to sexual partners.

HERNIA

A hernia occurs when part of an organ breaks through a weak point in its enclosing wall. The most common type of hernia occurs when part of the bowel protrudes through a weak area of the abdominal wall. Other organs, including the stomach, kidney, ovary, womb or bladder, can also herniate, though this is rare. Hernias are more common in men.

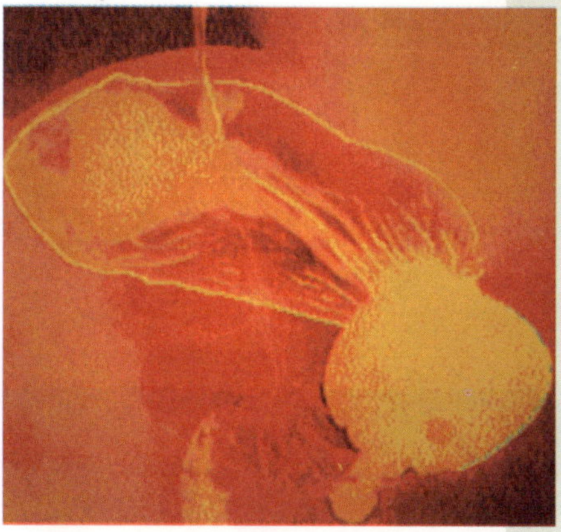

In a hiatus hernia, the upper part of the stomach moves up into the chest. Unlike most hernias, hiatus hernias are more common in women, probably because of the increase in pressure during pregnancy.

CAUSES: An abdominal hernia is usually caused by a congenital weakness in the abdominal wall. Damage may be caused by violent exertion, lifting heavy objects, persistent coughing, or 'straining' when going to the toilet. Being overweight is another possible cause because, when you're fat, you're

ASK THE DOCTOR

HERNIA

Q My husband has had an operation for a hernia. He works for a removals firm. When will he be able to go back to work?

A After an operation for a hernia, it takes time for the muscle wall to become strong again – this can be as long as three months. Your husband's job obviously entails a lot of heavy lifting. If he can be given lighter duties, he can go back after six weeks, but if he cannot avoid heavy lifting, he should probably wait three months.

Useful Addresses

HIVES

Action Against Allergy
43 The Downs
LONDON SW20 8HG
081 947 5082

National Society for Research into Allergy
PO Box 45
HINCKLEY
Leicestershire
LE10 1JY
0455 635212

putting extra strain on the stomach muscles. Pregnancy is another possible source of strain. A hernia can also develop after surgery at the site where the incision was repaired.

SYMPTOMS AND SIGNS: The first symptom is usually a soft bulge in the abdominal wall. Sometimes, the protrusion can easily be pushed back into place. Never try to push it back forcibly.

TREATMENT: If the hernia can be pushed back into place, a supportive truss may be all that is required. If complications develop, such as strangulation or obstruction of the protruding part of the intestine, surgery may be necessary.

HIGH BLOOD PRESSURE

see HYPERTENSION

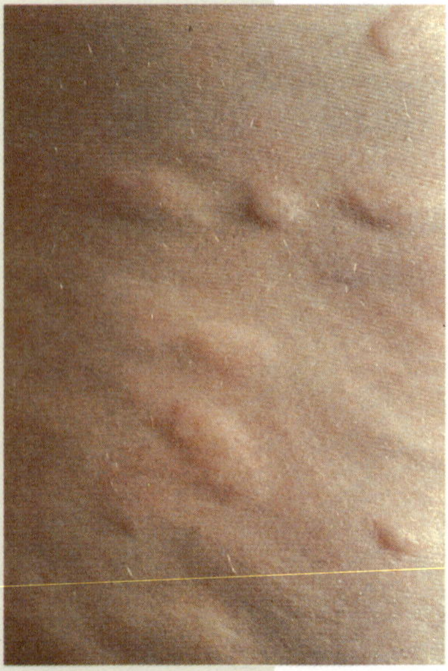

The most important thing to do if you get hives is to identify the cause – and then try to avoid it.

HIVES

Hives, also known as urticaria or nettle rash, is an allergic reaction which produces pale raised areas of skin surrounded by blotchy red patches.

CAUSES: Hives is an allergic reaction, which can have a variety of causes. Foods such as chocolate, nuts, fish, eggs, strawberries and dairy products are common culprits. It also may be a reaction to certain drugs. Other causes include sunlight, insect bites and excessive sweating. Often the victim has no idea what causes the attack.

SYMPTOMS AND SIGNS: A rash resembling nettle rash, with pale weals surrounded by inflamed red patches. It is often itchy and tends to come on suddenly. It can appear anywhere on the body and usually only lasts a few hours; however, as the old rash fades, new patches may appear, and the condition can go on for several days. Sometimes the lips, eyes and tongue swell and in rare cases there may be difficulty in breathing.

TREATMENT: Severe cases, especially when there are breathing difficulties, need urgent medical attention.

Mild cases usually only need medical attention if they recur frequently, or if they last for a considerable time. Antihistamine may be prescribed to relieve the itching. Local applications of calamine, or bathing with a solution of bicarbonate of soda may be helpful.

It helps to identify the allergen so that it can be avoided.

HODGKIN'S DISEASE

Hodgkin's disease is cancer of the lymphatic system. It is fairly rare – about 3,000 new cases are reported in the UK each year – and most patients are cured if treated early enough.

CAUSES: The causes are not definitely known, though recent research suggests that a virus might be responsible.

SYMPTOMS AND SIGNS: The first noticeable signs are commonly enlarged lymph nodes, usually in the neck or armpits. There may also be enlarged nodes in the groin. The patient will probably feel tired and generally unwell, with fever and night sweats. The lymphatic system produces antibodies to fight off infections – so, as Hodgkin's disease pro-

The cause of Hodgkin's disease, also known as Hodgkins lymphoma, is not known.

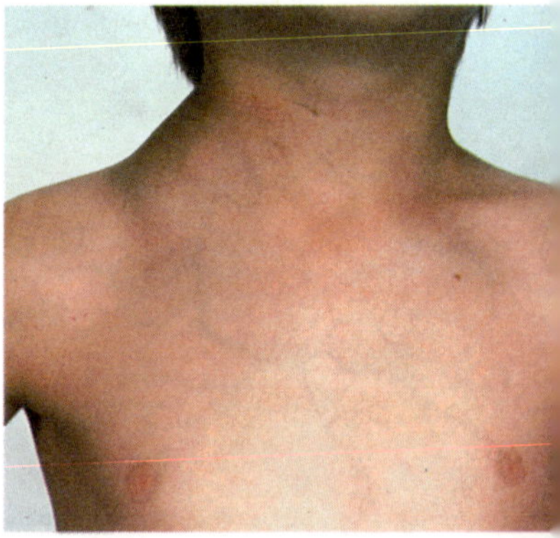

gresses, resistance to diseases decreases and what would normally be trivial diseases may have life-threatening complications.

TREATMENT: Treatment will depend on how far the disease has developed. It may involve radiotherapy or a prolonged course of anti-cancer drugs, or a combination of these, depending on the stage of the disease. In the early months of treatment, patients are advised to keep well away from anyone with any sort of infection. If resistance to disease is low, antibiotics may be prescribed to keep everyday infections at bay until the patient is well enough to cope with these infections.

HOUSEMAID'S KNEE

see BURSITIS

HUNTINGTON'S CHOREA

Huntington's chorea is an inherited disease of the brain which affects about six people in 100,000.

CAUSES: This condition is caused by a dominant gene passed on by a parent with the disease: each of his/her children stands a 50/50 chance of inheriting the gene. As the disease tends to show itself in later years, the parent is usually unaware that s/he carries this abnormality when starting a family.

SYMPTOMS AND SIGNS: Symptoms sometimes appear in childhood, but more often they develop as middle age approaches. Symptoms include uncontrollable jerking of the limbs, clumsiness, facial twitching, loss of memory and personality change.

TREATMENT: There is no cure. Drugs to suppress uncontrolled body movements may be prescribed. It is now possible to identify the gene in many carriers before the disease develops. Anyone at risk is advised to consult a genetic counsellor before having children.

HYPERMETROPIA

Hypermetropia is the medical name for longsightedness – the inability to focus on objects close to the eye.

CAUSES: This condition results when the distance between the front and the back of the eye is too short to enable images to be focused clearly on the retina.

The condition is usually inherited and present from birth. Mild cases may not be noticed until later life, when the ability to focus by altering the eye lens shape is reduced.

SYMPTOMS AND SIGNS: Longsightedness usually comes to light while reading, when small print appears blurred. Small objects are also difficult to see clearly. Later on, there is difficulty in reading larger print and gradually distant vision becomes affected as well. Severe cases are usually noticed at a young age but many people are only aware of the condition as they approach middle age.

TREATMENT: Eyes should be tested by an ophthalmic optician, who will prescribe glasses if necessary.

Hypermetropia, or longsightedness, tends to run in families. It is present from birth but does not usually become apparent until later in life – most commonly after the age of 40.

HYPERTENSION

Hypertension is abnormally high blood pressure. It's a very common condition, which affects up to 20 per cent of adults in the UK.

CAUSES: Blood pressures are given in two figures, for example 120/80 mm Hg. The first, higher figure is called the systolic pressure and the second the diastolic pressure. Pressure is the force needed to pump blood round the body.

The heart is not a continuous pump; it beats and then relaxes. Each beat produces a wave of pressure when blood surges into the aorta from the heart; this is the systolic pressure. The pressure then drops between beats, when the heart chambers relax and fill with blood; this is the diastolic pressure.

There is no set 'normal' pressure. Normal blood pressures vary, and tend to increase with age. 100 to 140 is normal for systolic pressure and 60 to 90 for diastolic. The

Useful Addresses

HUNTINGTON'S CHOREA

Association to Combat
Huntington's Chorea
34a Station Road
HINCKLEY
Leicestershire
LE10 1AP
0455 615558

Chest X-ray in a case of hypertension, showing an enlarged heart at bottom right.

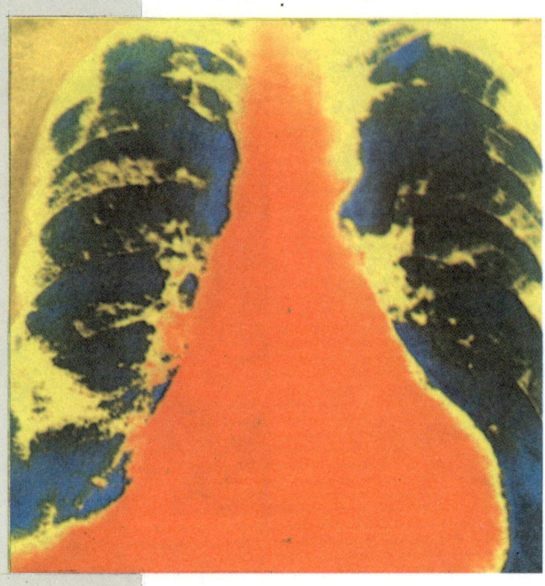

Self **Help**

HYPERTENSION

There are a number of ways in which you can help keep your blood pressure normal.

- Stop smoking
- Keep your alcohol consumption moderate
- Keep your weight down
- Reduce your intake of animal fats
- Take regular exercise
- Learn to relax

ASK THE DOCTOR

HYPERTENSION

Q My father has high blood pressure. Does this mean I'm likely to get it?

A It's a definite risk factor, though everyone should have their blood pressure checked regularly.

blood pressure also increases with strenuous exercise, and for this reason blood pressure should be taken after the patient has rested for a while.

Several factors are associated with a permanently high blood pressure. Being male seems to increase the chances, as well as stress, smoking tobacco, heredity, lack of exercise, over-weight, high alcohol consumption and excessive salt in the diet.

High blood pressure may be caused by a specific condition, such as kidney disease, pregnancy, and certain disorders of the adrenal glands. The contraceptive Pill may also be to blame.

SYMPTOMS AND SIGNS: Mild hypertension often has no symptoms, and may only be noticed during a routine medical examination. When severe, symptoms include headaches, giddiness, shortness of breath.

TREATMENT: Hypertension is a health risk; it puts great strain on the heart and blood vessels. It increases the chances of having a stroke or developing heart failure or coronary artery disease. There can be damage to the kidneys and to the retina of the eyes.

Mild cases are often cured with a change of life style. Dietary changes include cutting down on salt, sugar, caffeine, alcohol, fats. Smoking should be stopped and overweight people are usually advised to lose weight. Some people have found the technique of biofeedback a help.

For severe cases, hypertensive drugs may be prescribed; these include diuretics, betablockers and vasodilators. Drug treatment may need to continue for several years and the doctor may want to check the pressure at regular intervals. Very severe hypertension may require hospitalisation.

HYPERTHYROIDISM

Hyperthyroidism, also known as thyrotoxicosis, is the overproduction of thyroid hormones by the thyroid gland. Graves' disease is the most common form of hyperthyroidism.

CAUSES: In Graves' disease, antibodies produced by the body's immune system stimulate the thyroid gland to produce an excess of thyroxine – one of the thyroid hormones. Hyperthyroidism sometimes results from a tumour in the thyroid gland.

SYMPTOMS AND SIGNS: Excess thyroid hormones cause a rapid pulse and a fine tremor of the hands. There is usually weight loss, despite an increase in appetite. Women may find their periods become either heavy or scanty. Patients also often complain that they are constantly hot and anxious; they may become overactive and develop prominent, staring eyes. The gland may also enlarge, causing a swelling in the neck – a condition known as goitre.

TREATMENT: Consult your doctor if these symptoms appear. If left untreated, hyperthyroidism can cause many serious complications, such as mental illness and heart failure. Treatment will depend on the cause of the condition. It may include drugs that inhibit the production of thyroid hormones, given for several months, and betablocker drugs to bring the symptoms under control. Sometimes, a single dose of radioactive iodine is

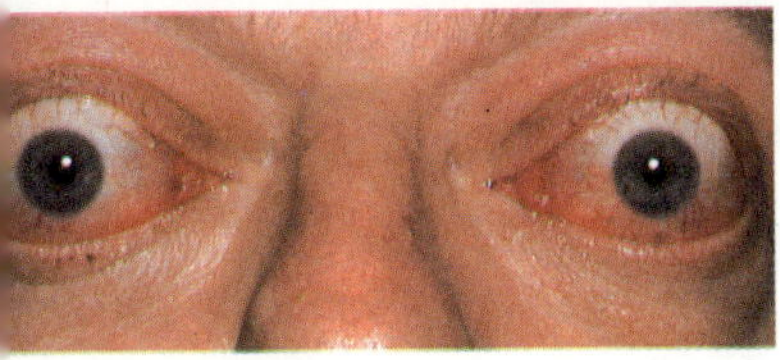

A person suffering from hyperthyroidism may develop staring, bulging eyes.

prescribed; the iodine is taken up by the gland and stored, and acts gradually over four to six weeks to make the gland less active. Sometimes surgery is the answer. If the eyes have become very prominent, surgery may also be needed to preserve eyesight by relieving pressure on the optic nerve at the back of the eye.

HYPOGLYCAEMIA

Hypoglycaemia is an abnormally low level of glucose in the blood.

CAUSES: The main cause is too much insulin – one of the hormones that control glucose levels in the blood. Diabetics are the usual victims, when they have taken too high a dose of their drugs – insulin injections or hypoglycaemia tablets, used to correct a high blood glucose – for the amount of food they have eaten.

Very rarely, hypoglycaemia results from drinking too much alcohol or eating highly refined sugary foods, which cause a surge of insulin release from the pancreas; or from diseases of the pituitary gland and Addison's disease. Occasionally, children suffer from this condition for no apparent reason.

SYMPTOMS AND SIGNS: These include sweating, dizziness, general weakness, trembling, bad temper and aggression. If the sugar level is dangerously low, the victim may go into a coma.

TREATMENT: Eating sugary food or drinking a sweetened beverage reverses the condition. Diabetics who are being treated with drugs should eat regular meals to ensure that these attacks don't happen and should always carry some sugar on them just in case they do. Most diabetics learn to recognise the beginnings of an attack so that they can take immediate action.

If the person is unconscious, call a doctor at once – an injection of glucose or glucagon may be needed. Also consult your doctor if you are diabetic and hypoglycaemic attacks happen frequently – this may be an indication that the drug dosage needs to be adjusted.

See also DIABETES.

HYPOTENSION

Hypotension is the medical name for low blood pressure.

CAUSES: Persistently low blood pressure is not a common complaint, though it may occur as a symptom of some rare disorders such as Addison's disease. An acute drop in blood pressure can be caused by shock, serious burns and injuries, heart attacks or adrenal failure.

Postural hypotension is the name given to the dizziness some people experience if they stand up or sit down very abruptly. This is a fairly common complaint, which can be caused by certain drugs – in particular, antidepressants and antihypertensive drugs – and is experienced by some diabetics.

SYMPTOMS AND SIGNS: Tiredness, dizziness and fainting.

TREATMENT: Treatment of hypotension will depend on what is causing the condition.

ASK THE DOCTOR

HYPERTHYROIDISM

Q I've been told I have an over-active thyroid gland. What and where is the thyroid gland?

A It's in the neck, just below the level of the larynx, and is visible as the Adam's apple. Its function is to manufacture thyroxine, which is taken into the bloodstream and thence into the cells of the body. The exact function of thyroxine is not clear, but it is known to be essential to the general working of the body.

Regular blood pressure checks may be given to check that all is as it should be.

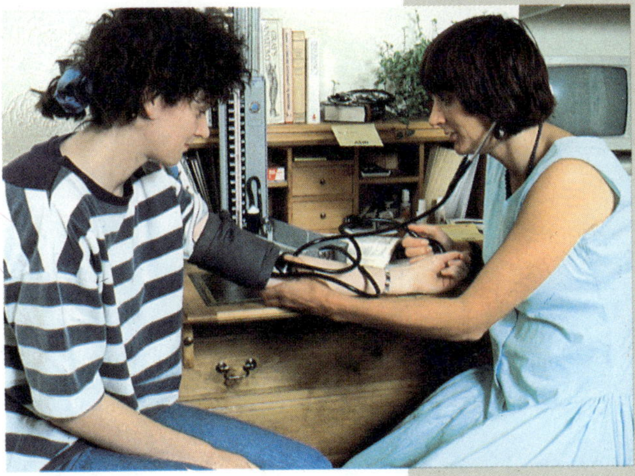

ASK THE DOCTOR

HYPOTHYROIDISM

Q I was treated for hypothyroidism last year and feel fine. Do I still have to take my medication?

A Probably. In most cases the patient has to take thyroxine for life, even after a full recovery.

Q My grandmother feels the cold very badly in the winter, although her house is quite warm. Could this be due to hypothyroidism?

A It is possible. Some of the old people who develop hypothermia in winter have this complaint and need to start treatment immediately to make them less vulnerable to the cold.

HYPOTHYROIDISM

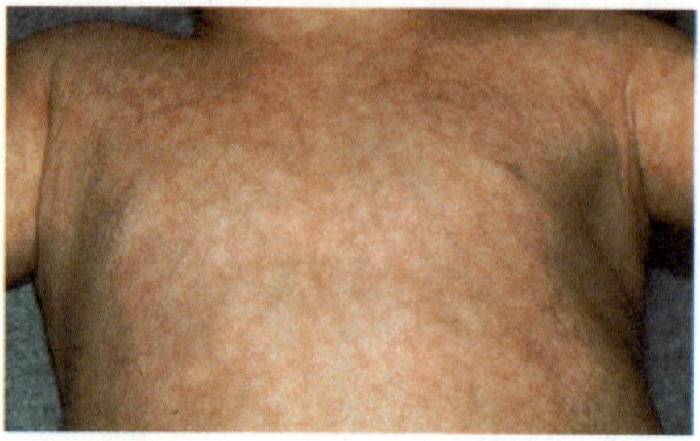

Hypothyroidism can cause a coarse skin rash known as myxoedema.

Hypothyroidism means the underproduction of thyroid hormones by the thyroid glands. This under-activity can result in the condition of myxoedema and a goitre may form in the neck.

CAUSES: Sometimes the body produces antibodies against its own thyroid gland, so making the gland underproductive. This takes place in the condition known as Hashimoto's thyroiditis. Very occasionally, hypothyroidism occurs after treatment for an over-active thyroid gland.

SYMPTOMS AND SIGNS: A mild deficiency of the thyroid hormones often produces no obvious symptoms. More severe deficiencies may cause fatigue, lethargy and drowsiness, together with a dislike of cold weather. The skin becomes dry, hair is lost from the head and eyebrows, the voice becomes deep and gruff, and there is usually weight gain. Myxoedema – a condition where the skin and other body tissues thicken – can occur. The thyroid gland may become enlarged, forming a goitre in the neck.

TREATMENT: Hypothyroidism can be successfully treated with doses of thyroxine – one of the thyroid hormones. Sometimes the goitre needs to be operated on.

If left untreated, hypothyroidism can cause the patient to go into a coma, suffer severe heart failure, anaemia or hypothermia.

See also HYPERTHYROIDISM.

HYSTERIA

Hysteria is a general term describing unusual, inexplicable behaviour. More specifically, it can refer to a severe mental or physical reaction out of proportion to the cause.

CAUSES: There is no physical cause, but sufferers are often trying to attract attention – although, confusingly, their reaction to symptoms can be supreme indifference as well as intense concern. They may also be avoiding an unpleasant situation or trying to forget one by, say, developing amnesia (loss of memory) after a dreadful accident. If someone merely over-reacts in moments of stress or over-dramatises his or her feelings, this is not classed as hysteria.

SYMPTOMS AND SIGNS: A whole range, from vague pains to paralysis or blindness.

TREATMENT: Treat sufferers firmly and without fuss and, when possible, distance them from the cause of hysteria. If the symptoms continue, sufferers should see their doctor, who will want to eliminate the possibility of any physical cause before trying sympathetic counselling. In very rare cases, when hysteria is caused by a single emotional shock, drugs are used to put people into a hypnotic state in the hope that they can re-live the experience, work through it, and overcome the problem.

Mental stress gives rise to a range of symptoms described by the term hysteria.

i

IMPETIGO

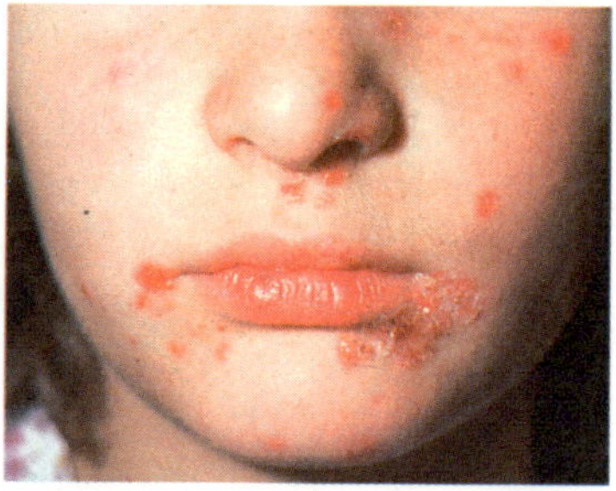

Spots infected with impetigo should be kept scrupulously clean.

Impetigo is a highly contagious skin infection, which appears as yellow scabby sores, usually around the mouth and nose. Children are more likely to be infected than adults.

CAUSES: The staphylococcus bacterium is usually responsible. In most instances, the infection develops through contact with an infected person – usually a child – or through picking a spot or scab with contaminated fingers.

SYMPTOMS AND SIGNS: The first sign is a red spot, usually around the mouth and nose. This turns into a blister which bursts and weeps. Yellow crusts form round the edges. The infected area may spread or other spots develop, usually on the face, hands or knees.

TREATMENT: To avoid spreading the infection, it's important to consult a doctor as soon as possible. Antibiotic ointments or tablets will usually cure the condition in a few days. Wash off loose crusts gently with soap and water or bathe them with a mild antiseptic, to keep the area clean. To stop the infection spreading, children are advised to stay away from school and playmates until the condition has cleared. Try not to touch the infected areas, as this is a sure way of spreading the infection.

IMPOTENCE

Impotence is the failure of a man to achieve or maintain an erection, and is more common in older men. Occasionally the term is also used when a man can have an erection but cannot ejaculate any semen.

CAUSES: The usual reason a man fails to get an erection is psychological: he might be overtired, overstressed, worried about something, or just desperately lacking in confidence: maybe his partner is making excessive demands on him or criticising his 'performance'. Any kind of hostility, anger or resentment towards his partner may also be a factor, or he might fear making a woman pregnant or hurting her.

Guilt (perhaps about an affair) is another cause, as is any negative feeling about sex, possibly due to a restrictive upbringing or having been sexually abused as a child.

Sometimes impotence is linked to an illness, such as diabetes or severe depression or adverse reaction to some types of drug; quite a few men also become impotent after a prostate operation because they are worried about the effect it's going to have on their potency. Occasional impotence can happen simply because a man has had too much to drink.

SYMPTOMS AND SIGNS: There are many different degrees of impotence. If failing to get an erection is an isolated, short-lived occurrence, then it's probably nothing to worry about. When it becomes a longer-term problem, though, it has usually developed

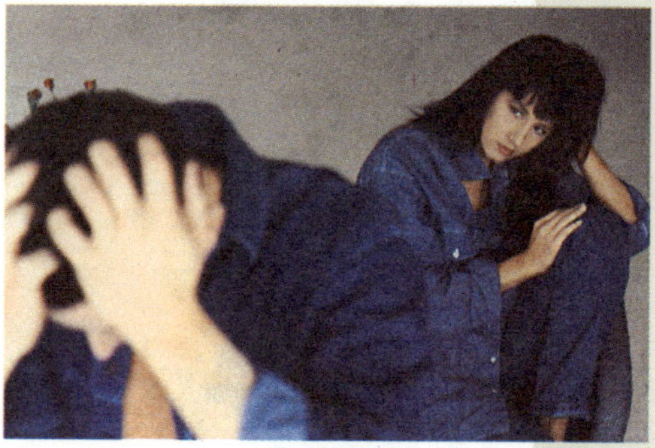

Fear of failure and feelings of rejection can increase the problems of impotence.

Self **Help**

IMPETIGO

To avoid re-infection, be sure to boil your pillowcases, towels and facecloths after use.

ASK THE DOCTOR

IMPOTENCE

Q Can a man be impotent with one woman but sexually all right with another when he's attracted to both?

A On rare occasions, a man may be impotent, say, with one partner but quite normal with another. This could be because he has become bored with the first partner and no longer finds her attractive, or because he 'splits' women into two categories – love objects and sex objects.

Self **Help**

INDIGESTION

Some people have trouble digesting particular foods, such as green peppers, cabbage, baked beans, garlic and cucumber. Try to avoid these if you suspect they are to blame for your indigestion.

after a period of normal sexual function. There are a small number of men who, right from adolescence, have had difficulty achieving an erection firm enough for intercourse.

TREATMENT: A sympathetic partner can contribute a great deal in helping a man overcome this problem; equally, the man should reassure his partner that he still very much wants to show and receive affection.

If the cause is psychological and the couple cannot work it out together, it's worth asking a doctor's advice and maybe having specialist counselling sessions or sex therapy.

If a physical cause is found, appropriate medical treatment will be given. In some cases, a man can be offered a penile implant or a drug can be injected into the penis to help produce and maintain erection.

INDIGESTION

Indigestion, also known as dyspepsia, is a vague term used to describe any discomfort in the upper abdomen brought on by eating. Most people suffer from it from time to time and it is often no more than a sign of overindulgence. Sometimes, though, it may indicate the presence of a more serious complaint.

CAUSES: Indigestion, as the name suggests, indicates that food is being digested with difficulty. The reasons for this are many. Common causes include overeating, eating too quickly, and too many rich fatty or spicy foods which can irritate the stomach lining.

In the case of heartburn, the cause is acid which finds its way up from the stomach into the gullet. Other common causes of indigestion include pregnancy and stress (nervous indigestion). Occasionally, indigestion is a symptom of some other problem: peptic ulcers, gallstones or hiatus hernia, for example.

SYMPTOMS AND SIGNS: The symptoms come on shortly after eating and may last for a couple of hours. Depending on the severity of the attack, you may feel vague discomfort or tenderness or get quite severe stomach pains. You may feel bloated and nauseous; burping is another sign. The discomfort is made worse by wearing tight clothes.

The symptoms of heartburn are a scalding, burning or boring sensation in the chest or gullet, sometimes brought on by leaning forward.

TREATMENT: Treatment will depend on the cause. The occasional attack of mild indigestion doesn't usually require treatment and will pass in a couple of hours. More severe discomfort, especially if accompanied by heartburn, may be relieved by taking antacid medication.

Heartburn during pregnancy can safely be relieved with antacids, provided you don't take too many.

If abdominal pains continue for more than three hours, or if there are other symptoms such as vomiting, consult a doctor immediately.

Also consult your doctor if indigestion is persistent, it may be a symptom of a more serious problem.

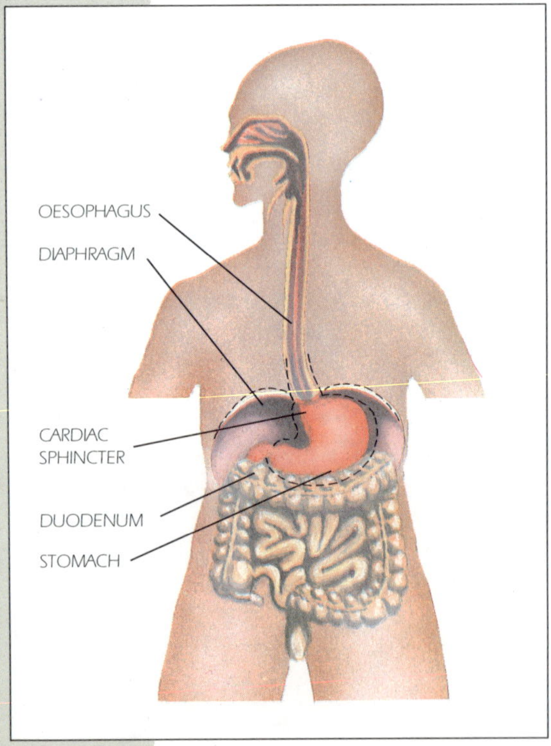

After a heavy meal, the stomach can become distended, allowing food to rise and causing heartburn.

Roughly one-third of all couples attending fertility clinics eventually succeed in having a baby.

INFERTILITY

Infertility is the inability in a woman to conceive, or in a man to induce conception. This is more likely to be a problem for older couples.

CAUSES: Infertility can be due to factors affecting one or both partners. The man's sperm have to be healthy, there have to be enough of them, and they need to be deposited high enough in the woman's vagina to make their way to an egg. If there is trouble with conception, it could be because the man's sperm count is low, or because there is a blockage in his spermatic tubes; similarly, the woman may not be producing eggs or her Fallopian tubes may be blocked. Sometimes her womb can be retroverted (tipped backwards) or filled with fibroids, or her cervical mucus can be hostile to the sperm.

There are many other reasons why conception doesn't take place, including the fact that the couple are not making love properly or not around the time of ovulation.

SYMPTOMS AND SIGNS: If a couple have had normal, regular intercourse without using contraception for a year and the woman has not become pregnant, the chances are that there is a fertility problem and they should consult their doctor, who may refer them to a fertility clinic.

TREATMENT: After a thorough physical examination, both partners will probably be offered fertility tests to see what the problem might be: this could involve them making love either the night before or during the morning of the day they go for the tests.

Sperm and egg production can sometimes be increased with pills or injections; tube obstructions can be dealt with by surgery.

If infertility continues, there is the option of other remedies such as artificial insemination and *in vitro* fertilisation.

INFLUENZA

Influenza is a viral infection which affects the respiratory tract. While many people are quick to label bouts of the common cold as flu, true influenza is far more rare and far more serious; the flu epidemic in 1918 killed more people worldwide than the First World War.

CAUSES: Flu is caused by a virus, which spreads by droplets in the air, as the germs are coughed or sneezed out by those who are infected.

There are three main groups of flu virus, known as A, B and C, but usually only one type of virus is going around at any one time. Unfortunately, some of the flu viruses have the ability to change in the course of time so that they bypass the body's existing antibodies. For example, the virus A causing the Spanish flu epidemic of 1918 turned up as

The spiky surface of the flu virus attaches itself to the walls of the respiratory tract, causing infection.

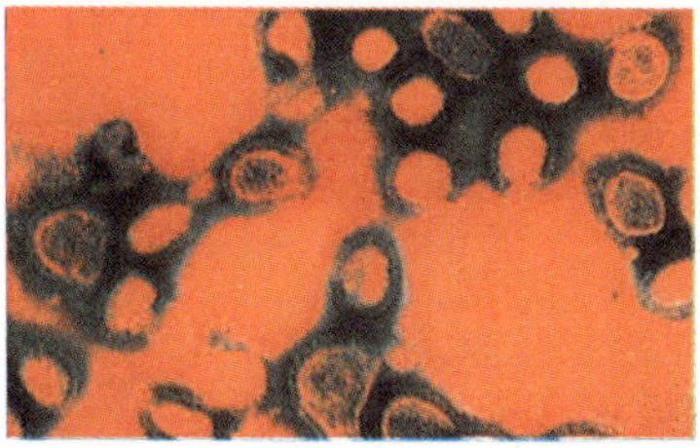

INF

Useful Addresses

INFERTILITY

National Association for the Childless
318 Summer Lane
Birmingham
B19 3RL
021 3594887

Society for the Study of Fertility
141 Newmarket Road
Cambridge
CB5 8HA
0223 351870

ASK THE DOCTOR

INFERTILITY

Q You often hear of couples who believed they were infertile and so adopted a child. The woman then went on to conceive almost immediately. Why should this happen?

A **It is possible for a couple to get themselves into such a state about problems they're having conceiving a child that their anxiety compounds the problem. The removal of the worry, simply by adopting a child, may be all they need to restore their fertility.**

ASK THE DOCTOR

INFLUENZA

Q I suffer from flu every winter. Is there a vaccination I can have?

A Yes, there is an anti-influenza vaccine, which can help give some immunity against the viruses currently circulating. These are recommended for elderly people and for anyone suffering from respiratory disease, a heart condition, or any other chronic illness.

Self **Help**

INFLUENZA

- Go to bed
- Keep warm
- Drink plenty of fluids
- Take one aspirin or paracetamol every four hours
- When the temperature returns to normal, get up but take things easy for a while

Regular exercise and an established night-time routine can help you relax and overcome insomnia.

the Asian flu of 1957, only to reappear as Hong Kong flu in 1968.

Symptoms and signs: Initial symptoms include high fever, often with shivering, aching all over the body, muscular weakness, headache, loss of appetite and general fatigue. A sore throat, cough and runny nose may follow.

Treatment: Bed rest is important. In a true case of flu, you usually feel so weak that there is no other option anyway. Paracetamol will relieve aches and pains and help control fever. Inhaling steam helps with lung congestion. Generally the symptoms clear in 5-10 days.

If there is a very high fever or if the patient's condition deteriorates, call the doctor immediately. Also call the doctor if the patient is elderly or has a history of heart or lung disease. The antiviral drug amantadine is sometimes helpful and antibiotics may be prescribed for secondary infections, such as bronchitis or pneumonia.

INSOMNIA

Insomnia means difficulty either with getting to sleep or staying asleep, or waking in the early hours of the morning and being unable to get back off to sleep.

Causes: Worry is the usual cause, but you may also be over-excited, ill, or prey to a mental illness such as depression. You could also be adjusting to drug withdrawal of some kind, be using sleeping pills in the wrong way, have had stimulants, such as caffeine, late in the evening, or simply be sensitive to light or noise in your bedroom.

Symptoms and signs: Constantly not getting enough sleep. Not everyone, however, needs the same amount: the average may be eight hours, but some people need more and others far less.

Treatment: Make sure you take some exercise during the day and, at bedtime, try a malted-milk drink, a warm bath, relaxation techniques or anything else that quietens your mind. If the problem continues, keep a note of your sleeping times, then consult your doctor in case there's a physical or psychological cause that can be treated. S/he may recommend sleeping pills, but it's best to look on these as short-term help to break a pattern rather than a long-term solution.

INTESTINAL CANCER

see BOWEL CANCER

IRITIS

Iritis more commonly affects younger adults than older people and usually occurs in only one eye.

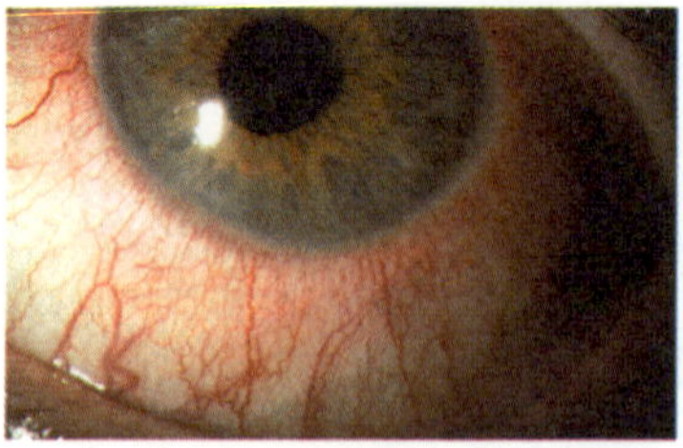

Iritis is an inflammation of the iris, which is the coloured part of the eye that lies behind the transparent cornea. It is a serious, though rare eye disorder, which blurs the vision in the affected eye and, if not treated promptly, may permanently impair sight.

Causes: In most cases, iritis is caused by an autoimmune disorder in which the body's immune system fails to recognise its own tissues as friendly and attacks them, but occasionally it is associated with a disease such as syphilis or tuberculosis.

Symptoms and signs: The eye becomes red around the edge of the iris, and there is often a good deal of pain either in the eye itself or in the forehead above the eye.

Treatment: If you suspect you may have iritis, you should consult your doctor without delay. S/he may examine the eye with a special microscope, and will probably prescribe a course of corticosteroid drugs to suppress the inflammation.

IRRITABLE BOWEL SYNDROME

Sufferers of irritable bowel syndrome, also known as spastic colon, experience bouts of abdominal pain with irregular bowel movements. This is the most common disorder of the intestine and it affects twice as many women as men.

Causes: No actual disease or abnormality of the bowel can be diagnosed. The syndrome involves a disorder of the involuntary muscles in the colon and causes are uncertain. Sufferers are often tense individuals, and a bout may follow emotional stress. The condition may be irritated by unsuitable foods and excessive smoking.

Symptoms and signs: Symptoms usually appear around the age of 30 and recur from time to time throughout life. A bout may last anything from a few days to a few months.

Symptoms range from mild discomfort to fairly severe pain in the lower intestine (usually to the left), together with a feeling of fullness in the area. Discomfort usually increases after a meal.

There may be constipation or diarrhoea, or alternating bouts of both. Excessive flatulence and mucus in the stools are other symptoms. Depression and anxiety are also commonly present.

Treatment: Similar symptoms appear in some other more serious bowel conditions, so it is essential to go to a doctor to get these excluded. Drugs may be prescribed to relieve diarrhoea, abdominal spasm, depression and anxiety. Constipation can be relieved by drinking more fluid and eating a high-fibre diet.

ISCHAEMIA

Ischaemia is an insufficient supply of blood to specific organs or tissues in the body. It most commonly affects the heart, kidneys and legs.

Causes: Ischaemia is usually caused by atherosclerosis, which is a narrowing of the arteries, brought about by deposits of fatty materials. Insufficient blood supply may also be caused by an injury to a vessel, a narrowing of a vessel due to muscle spasm or an inadequate pumping action from the heart.

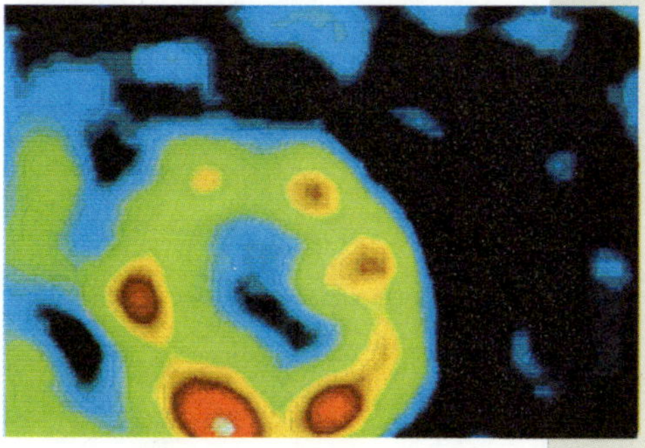

A false-colour image of a human heart, showing the result of ischaemia. The red areas are healthy muscle, while the green areas show tissue that has died because of lack of blood.

Symptoms and signs: The symptoms vary according to which part of the body is affected. If ischaemia affects the heart, you will feel a severe chest pain; if the disease affects your legs, you will feel a cramping sensation when you exercise. Renal failure will result if your kidneys are affected, or you may suffer a stroke if ischaemia affects the brain.

Treatment: Your doctor may prescribe drugs that widen the blood vessels. If the condition has affected the heart, a heart specialist may perform an operation using a 'balloon', which is passed into the narrowed vessel in order to unblock it.

See also ANGINA PECTORIS, STROKE.

Self **Help**

IRRITABLE BOWEL SYNDROME

Take regular exercise (as sedentary workers are the most frequent victims). This suggests that a lack of exercise plays a part in causing irritable bowel syndrome.

ASK THE DOCTOR
JAUNDICE

Q When I feel particularly tired, my skin looks slightly yellow. Might I be suffering from a mild form of jaundice?

A Some people have higher levels of bilirubin than others. This could mean that you are suffering from a syndrome known as Gilbert's, syndrome, an inherited disease that affects two per cent of the population. It manifests itself as long-term jaundice, and becomes worse when you are suffering from infection or do not eat enough. If you take good care of your health, it shouldn't cause you any problems.

j

JAUNDICE

Jaundice is common in newborn babies. It is also the chief symptom of many disorders of the liver and gallbladder. It may develop suddenly, over a few days, or take longer.

CAUSES: Jaundice may occur when the flow of bile from the liver, through the biliary system to the intestine, is blocked. The bile stagnates in the liver, which in turn means that the yellow pigment, bilirubin, flows back into the circulation.

Obstructive jaundice is caused by gallstones or cancer of the pancreas. It usually happens when the bile ducts become blocked and the bile cannot pass into the intestines. Haemolytic jaundice occurs when too much bilirubin is produced, by the breakdown of red blood cells. Liver damage, as a result of hepatitis or malaria, may also cause jaundice. Alcoholism and poisons are rarer causes. Jaundice is also very common in perfectly healthy newborn babies, because of an immature liver.

SYMPTOMS AND SIGNS: The first signs of jaundice are yellowing of the skin and the whites of the eyes, darkened urine and sometimes cream-coloured stools. The skin may become itchy before turning yellow.

TREATMENT: Whatever type of jaundice you have, your doctor will probably treat the underlying cause. Babies with jaundice will be given extra fluid and phototherapy. In extreme cases, they may need a blood transfusion.

k

KIDNEY STONE

Kidney stones vary in size from a fleck of gravel to a huge 'stag-horn' stone, so-called because it resembles the horns of a stag.

CAUSES: In the majority of patients, there is no obvious reason why a kidney stone has developed, but there are a few cases in which the cause is fairly clear. For example, some people with severe and chronic gout have such a high level of uric acid in the blood that the acid crystallises in the kidneys to form stones. Similarly, patients with an overactive parathyroid gland may develop kidney stones because the calcium content of their blood and urine is much higher than normal. A kidney infection may cause cells to be shed from the kidney lining, which form a focus around which a stone may develop. People who are bedridden or who live in a hot climate and do not drink enough fluid may also end up with kidney stones, because their urine becomes highly concentrated.

SYMPTOMS AND SIGNS: Some kidney stones produce no symptoms at all but are discovered during a routine check-up – these are known as 'silent' stones. If, however, a kidney stone gets into the urinary tract, blocks off

If a stone moves out of the kidney into one of the ureters, it will cause renal colic, causing sudden pain.

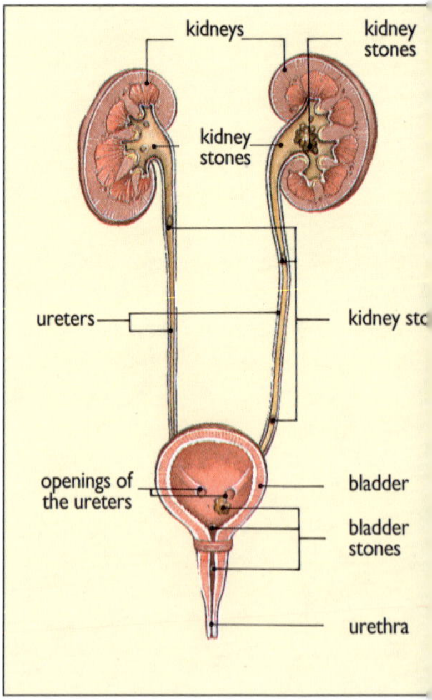

the flow of urine or starts some infection, it can cause intense pain, which demands immediate treatment

TREATMENT: Silent stones, which remain painlessly in the kidneys, need little or no treatment, especially in the old or infirm. Surgeons usually advise younger, fitter people to have the larger stones removed, as these are most likely to cause future trouble and they're best dealt with while a person is still well. Kidney stones that are causing a blockage or infection are usually removed by surgery. If a stone is obstructing the flow of urine, it is either removed at once by an emergency operation to prevent or minimise kidney damage, or the kidney is drained and the stone removed later when the patient is in better health.

If a stone has set up a chronic kidney infection, antibiotics will be prescribed. They may have to be taken for several weeks before the infection clears.

Patients with high levels of uric acid or calcium in the blood will need special treatment to prevent new stones forming once the original stones have been removed.

l

LARYNGITIS

Laryngitis is an inflammation of the larynx (voice box).

CAUSES: Acute laryngitis is a short-term viral or bacterial throat infection, often caused by a cold. It may also be caused by some other irritation, such as smoking. Some people may suffer from chronic laryngitis, such as those who have smoked excessively, who work in a dusty environment, or who use their voices continuously.

SYMPTOMS AND SIGNS: The characteristic sign is a hoarse voice, which may lead to total voice loss. A sore throat and difficulty in swallowing are also common. Chronic laryngitis develops over a period of time and sufferers may cough and clear their throats

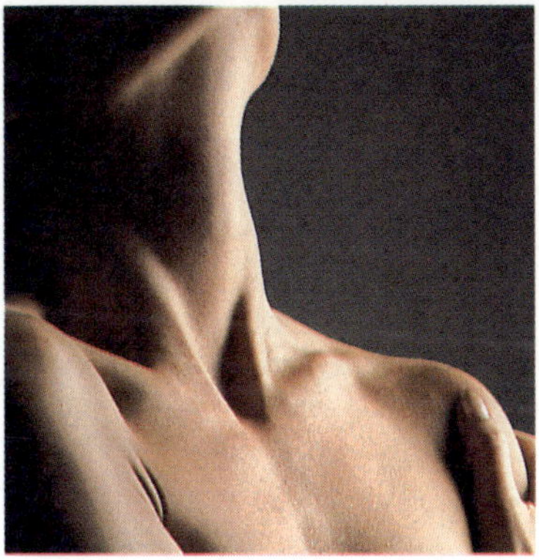

constantly, and always have a hoarse voice.

TREATMENT: Acute laryngitis is uncomfortable, but is not a serious condition. The hoarseness and irritation may last for up to a week and can be eased by resting the voice and stopping smoking. They can also be relieved by inhaling eucalyptus or other soothing preparations and by drinking plenty of liquids.

People with chronic laryngitis should consult their doctor.

LEGIONNAIRES' DISEASE

Legionnaires' is a bacterial infection, which is often hard to recognise. Unfortunately, a delay in diagnosis and proper treatment may be fatal.

CAUSES: The organism responsible for this disease is called *Legionella pneumophila.* It grows in a moist atmosphere and is commonly caught by breathing in droplets of contaminated water. The bacterium is particularly fond of water and of air-conditioning systems that are not properly sterilised.

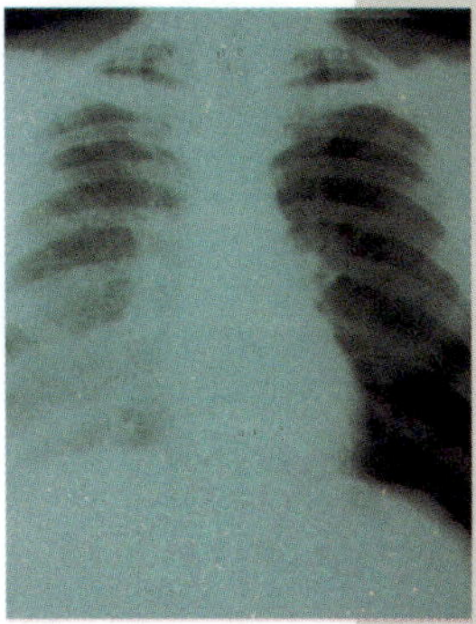

SYMPTOMS AND SIGNS: The incubation period is three weeks for Legionnaires'. The symptoms are much the same as those of pneumonia. You will

The characteristic signs of chronic laryngitis are a sore throat, difficult swallowing, and a hoarse voice.

ASK THE DOCTOR

LARYNGITIS

Q Are growths on the voice box necessarily cancerous?

A No, this is rare. Small, fibrous growths – known as nodules or polyps – which sometimes grow on the larynx, are usually non-cancerous and will not spread. The growths can easily be surgically removed but speech training may be required afterwards.

ASK THE DOCTOR

LEGIONNAIRES' DISEASE

Q Where did the name Legionnaires' come from?

A This disease was named after a spate of deaths in the 1970s, when 29 people died of this pneumonia after attending a conference of Legionnaires in Philadelphia, USA.

Legionnaires' disease is an infection of the lungs, affecting mainly men over the age of 50.

ASK THE DOCTOR

LEUKAEMIA

Q My six-year-old niece has just developed leukaemia. What are the chances of her being cured?

A Her chances will depend on the type of leukaemia that is diagnosed. However, most cases of childhood leukaemia are the acute lymphocytic type. With this form of leukaemia, there is a 50 per cent chance of a complete cure.

Useful Addresses

LEUKAEMIA

Leukaemia Care Society
PO Box 82
EXETER, EX2 5DP
0392 64848

develop a nasty cough, a high fever and feel short of breath.

TREATMENT: Legionnaires' is treated with high doses of antibiotics.

LEUKAEMIA

Cancer of the blood is known as leukaemia. It is relatively rare and accounts for only three per cent of all cancer deaths.

CAUSES: Leukaemia usually involves the white blood cells which are responsible for fighting disease. Leukaemic cells lose their ability to function properly but continue to divide in the bone marrow inside the cavities of the bones where normal blood cells are made. These then find their way into the blood.

There are four main types of leukaemia: acute lymphocytic, chronic lymphocytic, acute myeloid and chronic myeloid. The terms lymphocytic and myeloid refer to the different types of white cell involved. In acute leukaemia, the abnormal cells multiply rapidly; in chronic leukaemia, the disease progresses more slowly.

In most cases, the reasons for this happening are not known. Factors that may influence the condition include exposure to certain chemicals (in particular benzene), irradiation from X-rays, and certain viral infections. There may also be a hereditary factor at work.

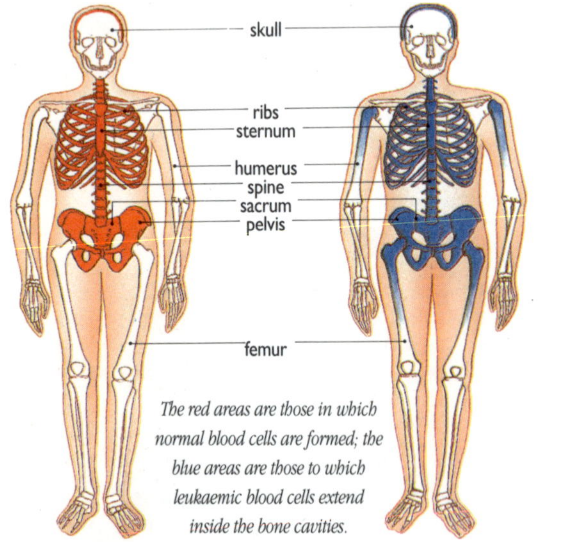

The red areas are those in which normal blood cells are formed; the blue areas are those to which leukaemic blood cells extend inside the bone cavities.

Exposure to atomic radiation can be another cause. There was a marked increase in the number of cases of leukaemia in Japan after the atomic explosions in 1945. Some children with chromosome abnormalities, such as Down's syndrome, appear to be susceptible. X-rays in early pregnancy may also increase the chances of children developing the disease.

SYMPTOMS AND SIGNS: With rapidly dividing white cells, not enough red cells may be produced. This leads to anaemia, causing tiredness and headaches and, in severe cases, dizziness and breathlessness.

Because of white cell malfunction, sufferers are more susceptible to sore throats and flu-type infections. Other symptoms may include enlarged lymph nodes in the neck, armpits and groin; excessive bruising; bleeding gums; blood in the urine; heavy periods; enlarged spleen; tenderness or pain in certain bones; fever; and night sweats.

TREATMENT: Leukaemia is diagnosed by blood and bone marrow tests. Acute leukaemia needs immediate treatment and hospitalisation; untreated, it can be fatal within a few weeks or months.

Blood transfusions are usually necessary and antibiotics may be needed to fight off infections. Anti-cancer drugs and radiotherapy can be used to kill the cancerous cells. Treatment with drugs will continue until no further leukaemic cells are detected – this may be several weeks. If there is a relapse, treatment may need to be restarted. In this case, a bone marrow transplant may be considered.

Chronic lymphocytic leukaemia is incurable but not necessarily fatal. The disease progresses very slowly and may need no treatment at all in the early stages. More severe cases may need treatment with anti-cancer drugs or radiotherapy. Blood transfusions and antibiotics may also be given.

Chronic myeloid leukaemia is usually treated with anti-cancer drugs. This disease can develop into the acute form and will then be treated as acute leukaemia. Sometimes chronic cases are given bone marrow transplants to prevent further development.

LICE

If you've got young children at school, the head louse (*Pediculosis humanus capitus*) is a fact of life. Unfortunately, cleanliness is no guarantee against infestation as head lice thrive in clean hair.

CAUSES: Head lice are small, brown, wingless insects about the size of a pinhead, which live on the human scalp. They are caught by being in close contact with someone who has them.

SYMPTOMS AND SIGNS: The usual sign is an itchy scalp. There may also be an itchy red area at the back of the neck.

Most young children become infected by lice at some time in their early years.

Nits, the empty eggs of the head louse, show up as white flecks firmly attached to the hair shaft – these are particularly noticeable on dark hair. You may see lice on the scalp; favourite spots are behind the ears and at the nape of the neck. Dead lice can often be spotted in the rinse water after washing the hair.

TREATMENT: Head lice should be treated immediately with a lotion or shampoo containing carbaryl or malathion insecticide; ask your local chemist which of these insecticides is currently recommended. It is important to follow the instructions very carefully when applying these preparations.

To be sure of getting rid of the lice, treat the whole family, not just the person known to be infested. Inform your child's school and any close contacts.

LISTERIA

Listeria monocytogenes is the name of the bacterium that causes listeriosis. It is found naturally in soil and vegetation. Ingestion of large numbers can cause an infection in both animals and humans. Dairy products are a breeding ground for the bacterium - however, most of the bacterium are killed at pasteurising temperatures. Listeriosis may be fatal in young children and the elderly, and in other vulnerable people who are less able to fight off infection.

CAUSES: The disease is caused when the bacterium continues to multiply once the food has been refrigerated. This is why you should never eat foods that have exceeded their sell-by dates. The bacterium is found in animal and dairy products, and in ready-made salads. You can also catch listeriosis by coming into contact with an infected animal. An unborn child can become infected through its mother and may be stillborn or suffer meningitis, which is why pregnant women should avoid foods likely to be contaminated with large amounts of these bacteria, such as soft or blue-veined cheeses.

SYMPTOMS AND SIGNS: A fever may be accompanied by diarrhoea, vomiting and generalised aches and pains. In severe cases, meningitis, pneumonia and septicaemia may develop.

TREATMENT: Antibiotics are used to treat this type of food poisoning, but may not be successful in those cases where complications have already set in.

See also FOOD POISONING.

LOCKJAW

see TETANUS

LONGSIGHT

see HYPERMETROPIA

LOW BLOOD PRESSURE

see HYPOTENSION

ASK THE DOCTOR

LICE

Q Can people have head lice without knowing it?

A Yes. Most people's scalps itch uncomfortably when they are infested, but there are people, usually adults, who show no such reaction.

Self **Help**

LICE

If you have school children, there is a lot you can do to help keep down the lice population.

- Comb hair thoroughly in the morning and last thing at night.
- Examine your child's scalp weekly – more often when lice are about.

If you see a head louse on your child:

- Treat him/her immediately.
- Also treat the whole family.
- Inform the school immediately, and any person with whom the child has been in close contact.

ASK THE DOCTOR

LUNG CANCER

Q I have been smoking 20 cigarettes a day for 20 years. Will it help if I kick the habit now?

A Yes, it may well do. Once a heavy smoker stops smoking, s/he becomes progressively less likely to develop lung cancer as time goes on. And after 15 years, the risk will have become extremely small.

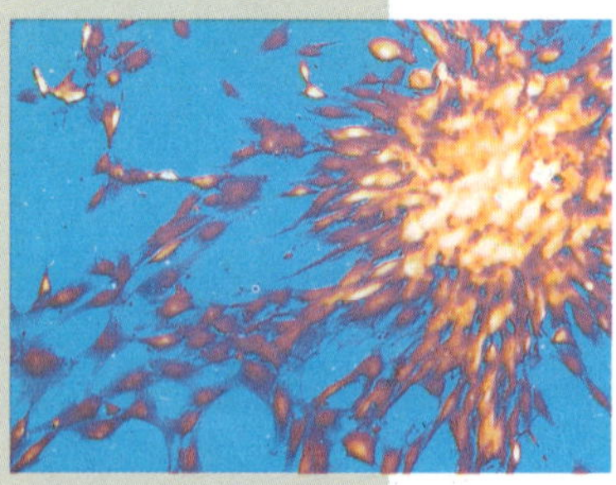

False-colour light micrograph of a malignant tumour, showing cancerous cells breaking away from the site and migrating to surrounding tissue.

Useful Addresses

LUPUS ERYTHEMATOSUS

LUPUS GROUP
Arthritis Care
5 Grosvenor Crescent
LONDON SW1X 7ER
071 235 0902

LUMBAGO

see BACK PAIN

LUNG CANCER

Lung cancer is the most common form of cancer in the UK. The peak age for contracting this disease is between 60 and 75 years. There are few cases under the age of 40.

CAUSES: Cigarette smoking is the major cause of lung cancer. The more cigarettes a person smokes and the younger s/he takes up the habit, the greater the chances of developing this disease. Cigar and pipe smokers are also at risk but not to the same extent. Passive smokers – non-smokers who are regularly exposed to cigarette smoke – also seem to be at greater risk of developing the disease.

SYMPTOMS AND SIGNS: The most common symptom is a persistent cough which usually produces a small amount of sputum, sometimes containing flecks of blood. Increasing shortness of breath is another common sign. There may also be wheezing, tightness in the chest, or a persistent aching behind the breast bone.

TREATMENT: To be cured, lung cancer needs early treatment. If your doctor suspects lung cancer s/he will arrange for an X-ray; anything suspicious will need further investigation.

In the early stages, it may be possible to remove the tumour through surgery. Anti-cancer drugs and radiotherapy are also used to treat the disease. Fewer than 10 per cent of lung cancer patients are alive five years after the disease is diagnosed.

LUPUS ERYTHEMATOSUS

Lupus erythematosus is a disease that inflames the connective tissue in our bodies. There are two types of lupus erythematosus: discoid lupus erythematosus (DLE), which is more common and affects exposed areas of the skin; and systemic lupus erythematosus (SLE), which spreads to affect many parts of the body. The term *lupus erythematosus* is Latin, which literally means 'red wolf'. This describes the characteristic rash that appears on the face of those suffering from it. Nine times as many women as men suffer from this condition.

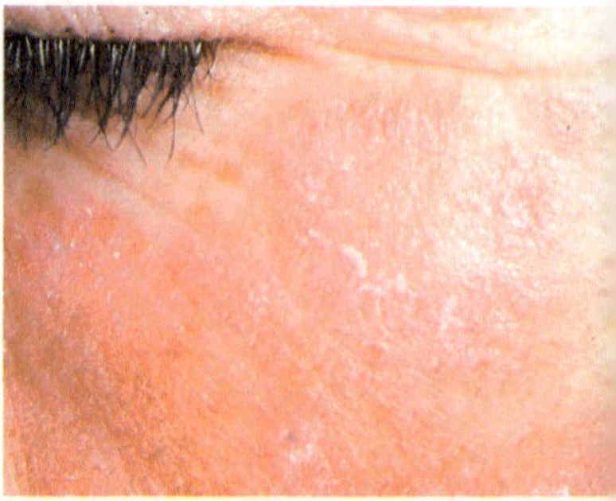

The red scaly rash of systemic lupus erythematosus (SLE) affecting a person's cheek.

CAUSES: Lupus is thought to be an autoimmune disease. For some reason, the body's immune system begins to regard the connective tissue as a foreign body and attacks it. It may be that the disease is hereditary or that hormones play a part in upsetting the immune system. Certain drugs, especially when taken by elderly people, are thought to be another cause of SLE and some people develop it as a result of a viral infection or as a reaction to strong sunlight.

SYMPTOMS AND SIGNS: DLE manifests itself as red marks around the cheeks, ears and on the backs of the hands. SLE, which is the most severe form of the disease, also causes red marks across the nose and cheeks, which form a 'butterfly rash'. You may also feel feverish, sick, lose weight and your joints may ache. The disease can lead to arthritis, hair loss, stroke, miscarriage, damage to the heart and lungs, and kidney failure.

TREATMENT: The doctor may prescribe anti-inflammatory drugs or a drug to suppress the immune system, but there is no cure for SLE. The rash may be treated with drugs that are also used to treat malaria and, if the sun aggravates the condition, s/he may advise that you stay out of the sun.

m

MALARIA

Malaria is a serious illness – the often violent fevers, debilitating anaemia and damaged blood vessels it brings in its wake can weaken its victims to such an extent that they are unable to resist other infections. The disease mainly occurs in central and southern Africa, Asia, south-eastern Asia and South America.

CAUSES: Malaria is caused by a tiny, single-celled parasite. It is transmitted by the bite of an infected mosquito, which can also spread other diseases. The malarial parasite belongs to the family *Plasmodium*. The most dangerous member of this family is *Plasmodium falciparum*, whereas the disease caused by other members of the family is rarely, if ever, fatal.

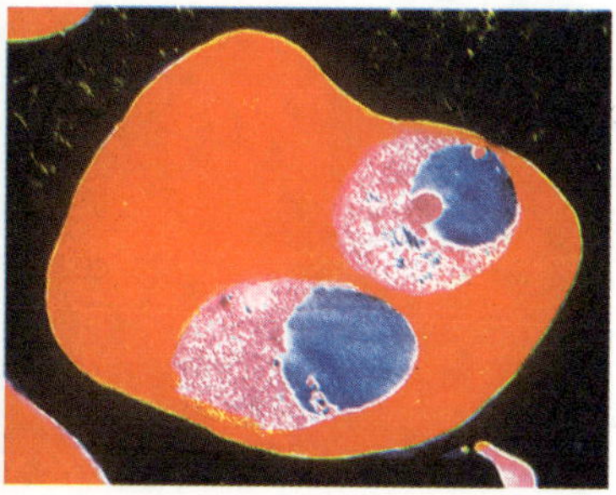

False-colour transmission electron micrograph of two Plasmodium parasites colonising a red blood cell.

SYMPTOMS AND SIGNS: Malaria usually begins with flu-like symptoms, including a severe headache, aches and pains in muscles, shivering and a high temperature. The shivers usually take the form of full-blown rigor. Your temperature will rise dramatically, and you may vomit. This is followed by a phase of heavy sweating and a fall in temperature. These periods of fever may come and go. Stomach pain, diarrhoea, jaundice and nose bleeds are all early symptoms of malaria.

TREATMENT: A short course of anti-malarial drugs may be all you need to rid yourself of malarial parasites. In extreme cases, a blood transfusion may be necessary. The flu-like symptoms are treated in the same way that flu might be, with aspirin or paracetamol to alleviate the pain and to reduce the patient's temperature. Once anti-malarial treatment has started, it will take three or four days to get rid of the parasites in your bloodstream.

MANIC DEPRESSION

Manic depression is a severe mental disturbance associated with pronounced mood changes with intermittent episodes of mania and depression. The condition is relatively rare and affects men and women equally.

CAUSES: The tendency to manic depression can be inherited. It may also be caused by certain drugs and some brain disorders. Just because someone has a personality characterised by 'high' and 'low' moods, though, doesn't necessarily mean that s/he is a manic-depressive or will ever become one. Some people function well at either end of the scale of excitability and yet are perfectly normal.

SYMPTOMS AND SIGNS: Mania is a psychological and emotional state in which the sufferer feels 'high' or unusually elated and energetic, in contrast to a state of depression in which s/he feels 'low' and lethargic. A manic-depressive can experience periods either of mania or depression, or alternate one with the other. Most sufferers, however, have many more periods of depression than mania and some experts believe that occasionally people who have repeated depressive attacks are really manic-depressives who haven't yet had a manic episode.

TREATMENT: It is important that someone with manic-depressive symptoms receives medical treatment as soon as possible. Unfortunately, not all manic depressives end up at a doctor's surgery and it is a tragic fact that many of them may end up committing suicide.

If someone suffering from manic depression displays alarmingly irrational behavior or a tendency towards suicide, he may need to be admitted to hospital.

Self **Help**

MALARIA

The most sensible course of action is to avoid malaria in the first place. If you are intending to travel, ask your doctor if there is any chance of catching malaria in the countries you are visiting. No matter how short your stay, you should take a course of anti-malarial tablets. The type and quantity of these drugs will depend on the area you are visiting, whether you are pregnant, and your age. It is very important to follow the directions on the bottle. While you are away, use a good mosquito repellent, particularly at night, and a mosquito net if possible.

Useful Addresses

MALARIA

London School of Hygiene
and Tropical Medicine
Keppel Street
LONDON WC1E 7HT
071 636 8636

HELPLINE
071 636 7921

Useful Addresses

MANIC DEPRESSION

Mental After Care Association
Bainbridge House
Bainbridge Street
LONDON WC1A 1HP
071 436 6194

Mental Health Association of Ireland
6 Adelaide Street
DUN LAOGHAIRE
Co Dublin
Republic of Ireland
(Dublin) 1284 1166

Self **Help**

MEASLES

It is because of the risk of severe complications that the measles vaccine was introduced into the childhood immunisation programme. Make sure your child has protection.

ASK THE DOCTOR

MEASLES

Q I am pregnant and my son has just gone down with measles. Is it serious if I catch the disease from him?

A Fortunately measles doesn't cause birth defects, but there is a 20 per cent chance of a miscarriage if you develop the disease.

Fortunately, once it has been properly diagnosed, manic depression can be treated very successfully with drugs or ECT (electroconvulsive therapy), and regular lithium therapy may be used to prevent further attacks. Later, individual or group therapy may help someone return to normality.
See also DEPRESSION.

MEASLES

A childhood disease, measles (rubeola) is one of the most contagious of all infections. One attack usually gives immunity for life.
Causes: A virus which is spread through the air by coughing and sneezing. People can spread the infection to others as early as a day after making contact with the disease and remain infectious for about a week after the symptoms first appear. Nowadays, children are routinely vaccinated against measles.
Symptoms: Symptoms appear seven to 14 days after being in contact with the virus. They start with a fever, runny nose, sore eyes and a general feeling of not being well. A cough and sore throat soon follow.

After a couple days, small pink spots with whitish centres appear inside the mouth on the cheek area. These are the first definite indication of measles. A couple of days later, these are followed by the blotchy measles rash, which usually starts on the head and neck and gradually spreads down to cover the whole body. The lymph glands are usually enlarged at this stage. The rash typically fades after three to four days.
Treatment: If measles is suspected, put the patient to bed. Give him/her plenty of fluids to drink and dose with paracetamol to keep down the fever. Contact the doctor to confirm the diagnosis and, in the case of school children, inform the school.

While the measles virus itself doesn't usually cause complications, the original infection may be followed by secondary bacterial infections – some of which are very serious indeed. So keep a close look at the condition of the patient. Common complications include ear and chest problems. There may be diarrhoea, stomach pains and vomiting. One in a thousand cases develop encephalitis.

MELANOMA

see SKIN CANCER

MENINGITIS

Meningitis is a brain disease caused by inflammation of the coverings (the meninges) of the brain and the spinal cord.
Causes: The brain and spinal cord are covered by three layers of tissue known as the meninges. Between the two inner membranes is a fluid called cerebro-spinal fluid (CSF), which protects and lubricates the brain and spinal cord. Meningitis occurs when a germ enters the CSF via the bloodstream. The meninges become swollen and exert pressure on the brain and spinal cord.

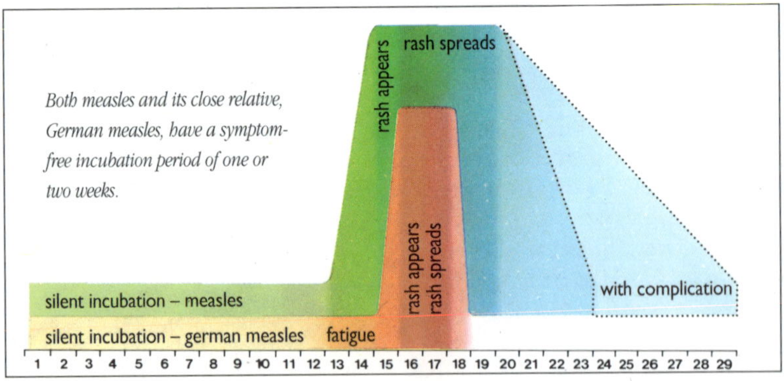

Both measles and its close relative, German measles, have a symptom-free incubation period of one or two weeks.

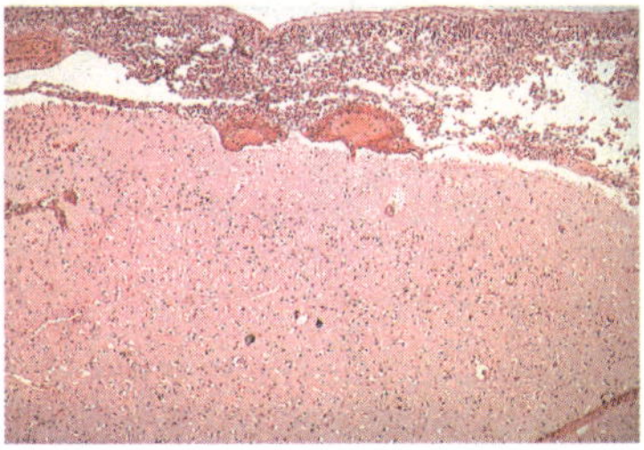

Light micrograph of a section of brain showing the inflammation of the connective tissue, which lines the skull and vertebral canal.

The infection can be caused by a virus which spreads from person to person through the air, or by viruses which cause other general infections such as mumps, measles and glandular fever. This type of meningitis is the most common.

Bacterial meningitis is rarer and much more serious. It occurs when bacteria reach the brain, via the bloodstream from other parts of the body such as lungs. The bacteria can also enter the brain directly through cavities in bone from infected ears or sinuses, or from a fractured skull. However, in most cases, none of these factors is present and the infection happens 'out of the blue'.

SYMPTOMS AND SIGNS: Viral meningitis is the less dangerous form of the disease. Symptoms vary according to the viral strain, but sufferers generally experience flu-like symptoms accompanied by a severe headache, neck stiffness and photophobia (dislike of bright lights). Bacterial meningitis is far more serious. In addition to the above symptoms, some sufferers may also get a rash and their symptoms tend to be worse.

TREATMENT: Viral meningitis cannot be treated with drugs. In most cases, the patient's natural defence system gradually copes with the infection and the sufferer recovers after two or three weeks.

Bacterial meningitis can be fatal and prompt treatment is essential. Most people recover fully, but some are left brain damaged, deaf or blind. All treatment must be undertaken in a hospital, where large doses of antibiotics are given over several weeks.

MENOPAUSE

The term menopause is used to describe the whole range of physical and emotional changes that occur around the time a woman's monthly periods, and therefore her fertility, come to an end. Generally, this 'change of life' happens between the ages of 45 and 55, and can take up to five years.

CAUSES: The ovaries stop producing eggs and there is a marked change in hormone levels – notably a reduced level of oestrogen.

SYMPTOMS AND SIGNS: Symptoms may include hot flushes and night sweats, vaginal dryness, and an increased need to pass water; there can also be an increase in facial hair, and the skin all over the body may become drier.

Later on, bones can become more brittle, (osteoporosis) and the arteries narrower.

TREATMENT: If symptoms are getting you down, go to your doctor. S/he may give you an oestrogen cream to help with vaginal dryness and might recommend hormone replacement therapy (HRT). HRT can be a great help, but your doctor will discuss with you the small increased risk of breast and uterine cancer, so you can weigh up the pros and cons.

See also ATHEROSCLEROSIS, DYSPAREUNIA, OSTEOPOROSIS.

ASK THE DOCTOR

MENINGITIS

Q Are the risks of meningitis greater for babies and young children?

A Yes, but mainly because their inability to communicate may mean that the symptoms are not detected early enough. If the infection is bacterial, and it is not treated, the chances of brain damage are much increased.

Self **Help**

MENOPAUSE

Keep busy, well exercised and well nourished, eating plenty of green vegetables and drinking plenty of milk to keep up your calcium intake. Apply a rich moisturiser and night cream to your skin, and consider electrolysis to remove any facial hair. Use a lubricant when making love,

Some women sail through the menopause, but others may need medical help.

ASK THE DOCTOR

MENORRHAGIA

Q I have very heavy periods every month. Can this make me anaemic?

A Yes, it is possible. In fact, blood loss is one of the main causes of iron deficiency – which is not surprising when you consider that the normal loss of blood during menstruation is about 60ml, but in an abnormally heavy period, it can be as much as 90ml. If you're feeling unusually tired and are worried about this, you should see your doctor.

ASK THE DOCTOR

MIDDLE EAR EFFUSION

Q What are the chances of a child suffering permanent deafness due to glue ear?

A Total deafness is unlikely, but treatment is important because partial deafness may interfere with the language development and performance of the child at school.

MENORRHAGIA

Menorrhagia is the heavy loss of blood during menstruation. Some women have menorrhagia regularly, while others suffer from it only rarely, if at all.

CAUSES: In some women, there is no obvious physical cause for menorrhagia. In others, it can be caused by a hormonal imbalance, a uterine disorder such as fibroids, a pelvic infection, or an intra-uterine device (IUD).

SYMPTOMS AND SIGNS: Excessive blood flow during menstruation.

TREATMENT: This depends on a number of things, including the underlying disorder, the severity of blood loss, the woman's age, and whether or not she wants to bear children. In a minor case and if the woman is still young, the doctor may prescribe hormones. In a serious case and if the woman is older, s/he may advise a hysterectomy.

See also DYSMENORRHOEA.

MENTAL BREAKDOWN

see NERVOUS BREAKDOWN

MIDDLE-EAR EFFUSION

Middle-ear effusion, also called glue ear, is one of the most common causes of temporary deafness in young children.

CAUSES: Glue ear often occurs when an infection of the nose and throat, such as a cold or tonsillitis, passes along the eustachian tube from the back of the nose to the middle ear cavity. The eustachian tube may become blocked and swollen, and the thick, sticky substance that is secreted from the lining of the middle-ear cavity may accumulate in the middle ear.

SYMPTOMS AND SIGNS: Glue ear is often accompanied by enlarged adenoids, colds and other respiratory infections. The main symptom, however, is slight deafness, often in both ears. Sometimes there is a dullness in the ear, but there is usually no discharge or pain, unless the eardrum perforates under the build-up of pressure.

TREATMENT: Your doctor will examine the child's eardrums to see whether fluid has accumulated. If it is only minimal, decongestants may be prescribed to improve drainage down the eustachian tube. In more severe cases and if the deafness persists for several weeks, the fluid will have to be removed in hospital under a general anaesthetic. A tiny plastic tube, called a grommet, is then inserted into the eardrum and left for several months. This allows air to enter and to dry out the middle ear. Removal of the adenoids may also be required, as these can block the eustachian tube.

MIDDLE EAR INFECTION

see OTITIS MEDIA

MIGRAINE

Migraine is an intensely severe headache. It is not a dangerous complaint but is often incapacitating. Women are more prone to it than men. Attacks can last anything from two hours to two days.

CAUSES: No one is sure what causes migraine, but the basis of an attack is thought

Migraine attacks can last up to two days. Relaxation techniques may shorten the period of suffering.

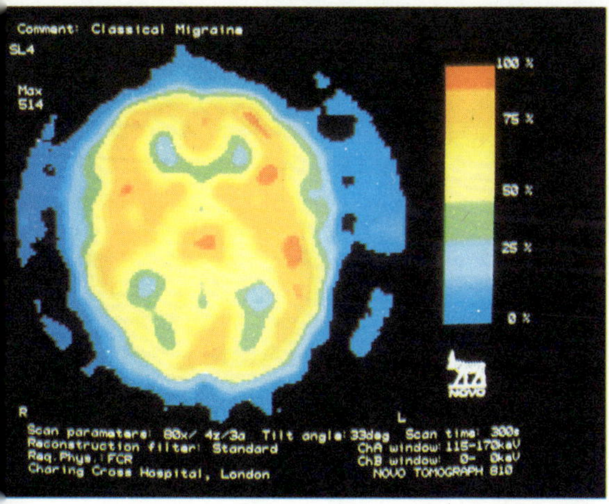

Image of the brain in a patient during an attack of classical migraine.

to be a change in sensitivity of the blood vessels in the head. A tendency to attacks can be inherited, and they can be triggered by certain foods such as citrus fruits, chocolate, cheese and other dairy products, and red wine. The Pill and menstruation are sometimes thought to be causes, too.

Symptoms and signs: The headache is often confined to just one side of the head, but it can be more general and is usually accompanied by disturbances of vision, nausea, and vomiting. There may also be visual disturbances, such as blurred vision or partial blindness.

Other symptoms may include giddiness, fainting and excruciating, stabbing pain around an eye, ear or cheek. The migraine may be accompanied by watering of the eye, nasal congestion and flushing on the affected side.

In the much rarer 'classical' migraine, there are warning symptoms that may include partial or temporary blindness, flashing lights, vomiting, and extreme sensitivity to light and sound. There may be other warning signs before an attack, such as weakness and tingling in the limbs and changes in mood.

Treatment: During any form of attack, it is advisable to lie down in a quiet, darkened room and try to sleep. Painkillers such as aspirin or paracetamol can be extremely effective if they are taken as soon as the attack is recognised; they work more quickly when taken in soluble form. Your doctor may prescribe drugs to be taken regularly to prevent or diminish attacks, or perhaps tranquillisers to be used during an attack. A preparation containing a painkiller and an anti-nauseant or sedative drug may be prescribed to relieve sickness. See also HEADACHE.

MISCARRIAGE

A miscarriage occurs when a pregnancy ends before the 28th week of pregnancy. This is known medically as a spontaneous abortion. If the baby is born dead after the 28th week of pregnancy, it is termed a stillbirth.

Medical research shows that about one-third of all pregnancies abort spontaneously within four weeks of conception. In the majority of these cases, the woman does not even know she is pregnant as the miscarriage occurs four or five weeks after the onset of her last period.

It is not uncommon for a woman to experience a 'threatened' miscarriage early on in pregnancy. In many such cases, the pregnancy will continue and result in a healthy baby. However, if the foetus becomes dislodged from the womb, or if it dies in the womb, then a miscarriage is 'inevitable'. A 'missed' miscarriage occurs when the foetus dies in the womb, but there are no other noticeable symptoms. Often the only way this type of miscarriage is detected is when your doctor discovers that your womb has not increased in size since the last ante-natal examination.

Causes: Miscarriages are nature's way of ending a pregnancy that is in some way

Self **Help**

MIGRAINE

Preventative treatment is well worth pursuing - the frequency and severity of attacks can often be reduced if trigger factors can be identified and avoided. Your doctor may be able to help with suggestions on how you could set about this: you can, for instance, try to find out if something you eat is producing an attack by cutting out all the most common dietary triggers, then starting to re-introduce them one by one into your diet. You may then be able to establish a link between a particular food and the frequency of attacks. Relaxation techniques, such as yoga, may also be useful, in that they help to reduce the tension that can cause or prolong attacks.

Useful Addresses

MIGRAINE

The Migraine Trust
45 Great Ormond Street
LONDON WC1N 3HZ
071 278 2676

British Migraine Association
178A High Road
WEST BYFLEET
Surrey KT14 7ED
0932 352468

Self Help
MISCARRIAGE

- Avoid strenuous sporting activities, although gentle exercise is encouraged.
- Avoid unnecessary fatigue.
- It may also be wise to avoid sexual intercourse at the time when periods would normally occur.

ASK THE DOCTOR
MISCARRIAGE

Q I am two months pregnant and bleed very slightly near the time of my period. Am I having a miscarriage?

A Not necessarily. It is not uncommon for women to notice a very slight loss of blood during the first three months of pregnancy. 'Spotting' may occur at about the time when the period would usually be due. However, consult your doctor to ensure that the foetus is developing normally.

Q I have been told that my womb has a structural problem and cannot support a developing foetus. Can anything be done to correct this?

A Yes. If you have a structural abnormality of the womb, this will show up on an X-ray. The abnormality can usually be corrected surgically.

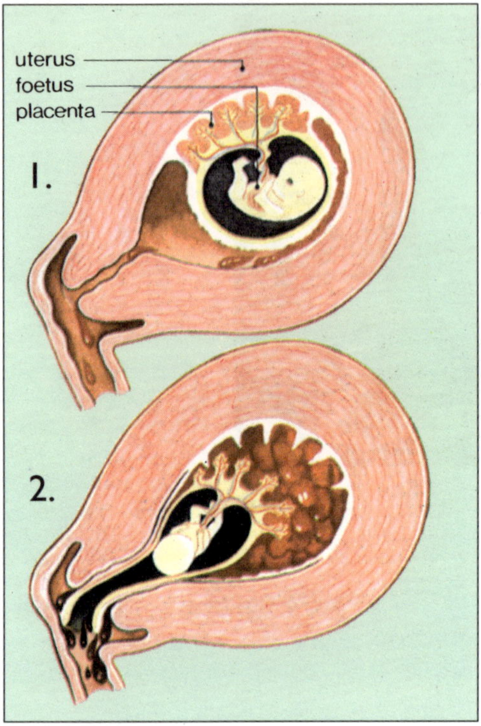

If bleeding is slight and stops quickly, this is a 'threatened' miscarriage **(1)** *and the chances are that the pregnancy will continue. But if bleeding is severe and there are strong, painful contractions, miscarriage becomes inevitable* **(2)**.

unsatisfactory – for example, if the foetus has some abnormality or the mother has a hormone imbalance. Miscarriages resulting from minor accidents or falls are rare, because the foetus is protected inside the womb.

Symptoms and signs: The most common symptom of a miscarriage is bleeding from the vagina. This can be just a few drops or a heavy flow, and may start without warning or be preceded by a brownish discharge. There may also be some pain in the lower abdomen or back, similar to small labour pains.

Treatment: At the first sign of bleeding, the woman should tell her doctor and go to bed, as rest is essential. If the bleeding stops, or is very light, the doctor may take no further action and simply tell her to continue resting. After a 'threatened' miscarriage, the doctor may recommend another pregnancy test or ultrasound to ensure that the foetus is developing normally. S/he may also recommend avoiding sexual intercourse for a few weeks. If the bleeding is heavy and the miscarriage 'inevitable', the doctor will send the woman to hospital. The doctor may recommend an evacuation of the womb to ensure that all of the foetus, placenta and membrane are removed and cannot cause infection. This is carried out under general anaesthetic. When a 'missed' miscarriage is detected, the remains of the foetus must be removed under general anaesthetic.

After a miscarriage, most women feel very low and may be depressed about their loss. Support and understanding from their partners is essential to recovery at this time.

MITES

Mites are tiny insects, which are found as parasites on many different animals. The mite *sarcoptes scabiei*, which causes scabies, is the one most commonly found in humans. Although similar mites affect dogs, horses and other animals, these rarely infect people.

There are also large numbers of tiny mites present in house dust. Some of these mites live in bedding, and feed off the dead scales of skin, which are always rubbing off from people's bodies. Many people with allergic asthma or rhinitis are, in fact, allergic to the faecal pellets excreted by house dust mites, which are breathed in along with dust. Careful control of house dust, especially in bedrooms, by vacuuming, sometimes relieves the symptoms. You can also buy a spray from the chemist to kill off the dust mites.

See also ASTHMA, RHINITIS, SCABIES.

MOLES

see SKIN CANCER

MOTOR NEURONE DISEASE

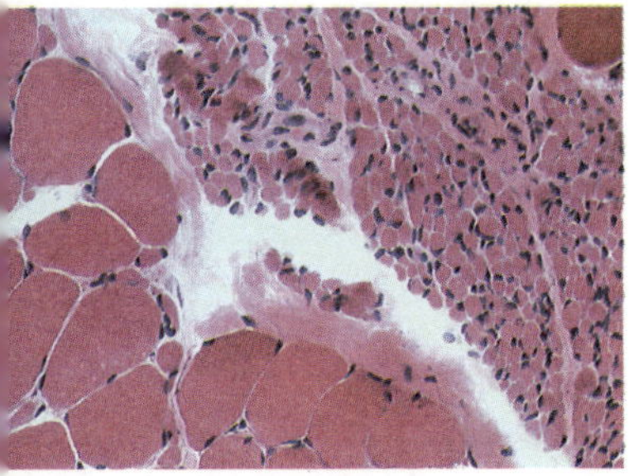

Light micrograph of human muscle showing wasting caused by motor neurone disease.

Motor neurone disease is, in fact, a group of disorders, causing degeneration of the nerves that control the muscles. The most common type of motor neurone disease is ALS, or Lou Gehrig's disease. It is a rare disease, which is diagnosed in only one or two per 100,000 people in the UK each year. It affects more men than women, and usually people over the age of 50.

CAUSES: Not known.

SYMPTOMS: The first symptoms are usually weakness in the hands and arms, sometimes with cramps and stiffness. Diagnosis is confirmed by various types of X-ray, the measurement of electrical activity in the muscles, blood tests, and analysis of a sample of muscle tissue under the microscope.

TREATMENT: There is currently no treatment available for motor neurone disease and nerve degeneration cannot be halted, or even slowed down. Physiotherapy may help maintain certain functions for as long as possible. Eventually, the disease affects the muscles involved in breathing and swallowing. In the later stages of the disease, the sufferer may be unable to move, speak or swallow, and the best form of psychological and physical support may be provided in a home or hospice. Normally, death occurs within two to four years of outset.

MOUTH CANCER

Malignant tumours may develop anywhere in the mouth, with the exception of the teeth. Five per cent of cancerous growths are mouth cancers, with the lips and tongue the most common sites. If caught early, there is a good chance of a complete cure.

CAUSES: Tobacco smoking, especially in the form of pipe and cigars, is one of the main causes. Drinking alcoholic spirits, chewing tobacco, wearing badly fitting dentures, and poor oral hygiene may also increase the risk of cancerous growths in the mouth.

SYMPTOMS AND SIGNS: The first sign of a tumour is usually a small, pale, painless lump. This may turn into an ulcer which bleeds easily. The ulcer can grow and spread to surrounding tissues. The tongue may become stiff.

TREATMENT: Surgery and radiotherapy are the usual methods of treatment. If surgery is performed early enough, there is a 75 per cent chance of a complete cure.

MOUTH ULCER

CAUSES: A mouth ulcer is an open sore caused by a breakage in the lining (mucous

Ulcers on the tongue are likely to be unpleasant rather than dangerous.

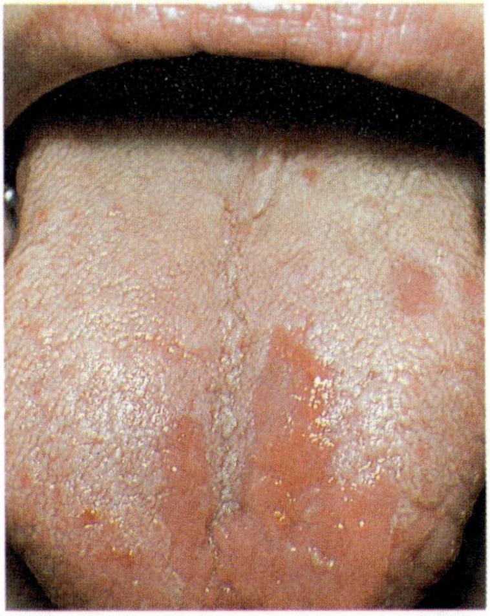

Useful Addresses

MOTOR NEURONE DISEASE

Motor Neurone Disease Association (MNDA)
PO Box 246
NORTHAMPTON
NN1 1UE
0604 22269

ASK THE DOCTOR

MOUTH CANCER

Q A rough edge on my tooth has irritated my tongue and I now have a small sore there. Does it matter?

A Yes, it does matter. Constant irritation in one form or another is a possible cause of mouth cancer, so ask your dentist to smooth down the tooth.

Useful Addresses

MOUTH CANCER

Cancer Aftercare & Rehabilitation Society (CARE)
21 Zetland Rd
Redland
Bristol, BS6 7AH
0272 427419

membrane) of the mouth. Ulcers vary in their cause and severity. The most common types are aphthous ulcers, which tend to form as a result of stress or becoming run down; and traumatic ulcers, which are caused by an injury to the mouth, such as biting the tongue or abrasion from a toothbrush.

SYMPTOMS AND SIGNS: You may feel pain even before the ulcer appears, often when eating or drinking something acidic. Aphthous and traumatic ulcers look very similar. They are very small and are round or oval in shape with a pale grey base. Typically they have white or yellow spots and a red inflamed edge. Sometimes ulcers appear in clusters on the tongue or on the roof or the side of the mouth. They may last for up to 10 days. Traumatic ulcers tend to be larger and last for a week or more.

TREATMENT: Aphthous ulcers can be treated with applications, lozenges and mouthwashes which are readily available from chemists. Traumatic ulcers will only be cured if the cause, such as a jagged tooth, is removed. Although painful, most ulcers will heal by themselves or with self help.

ASK THE DOCTOR

MOUTH ULCER

Q I often suffer from mouth ulcers, should I consult a doctor?

A Yes, if your ulcers haven't cleared up after about a month, if they keep coming back or if they are situated in the grooves alongside your gums. Your doctor or dentist will probably prescribe a special mouth-wash or steroid cream. If, however, there is some underlying reason, a biopsy of the ulcer may be required. In very rare cases a mouth ulcer may be an early stage of mouth cancer.

MULTIPLE SCLEROSIS

Multiple sclerosis (MS), also known as disseminated sclerosis, is a disease of the central nervous system, which affects 80,000 people in the UK. The symptoms are caused by the progressive destruction of myelin – the fatty sheaths that protect the nerve fibres of the central nervous system.

Women are more susceptible to MS than men, there being about three female sufferers to every two males, and most cases begin in early adulthood.

CAUSES: There are several theories about the causes of this condition, but few proven facts. It is thought by some to be an autoimmune disease, where the body's defence system, designed to fight harmful bacteria and viruses, starts to attack the body's own tissues. Some scientists think it is caused by a slow virus, which takes a number of years to develop. There is definitely a heredity factor involved; brothers and sisters of affected people are 15 times more likely to get MS than the rest of the population in that area of the country.

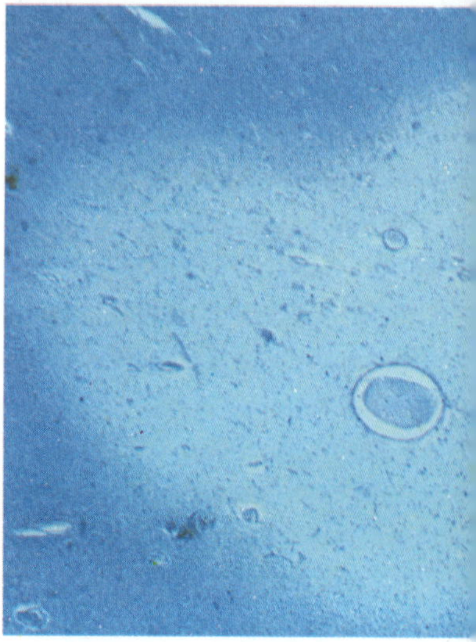

Light micrograph of nervous tissue (white matter) in multiple sclerosis.

Where you live is also important; the further you live from the equator, the more likely you are to contract MS.

SYMPTOMS AND SIGNS: When the myelin sheaths are destroyed, patches of scarring, called plaques, form in the areas where the myelin is damaged. These plaques can occur anywhere in the brain, spinal cord or optic nerves of an MS sufferer, and symptoms vary according to where the plaques form.

There are usually periods where symptoms are bad, followed by periods of remission when they almost clear up completely. Common symptoms include eye pain, blurred vision and double vision. There may also be uncontrolled flickering of the eyeballs (nystagmus).

Other symptoms include weakness or paralysis, dragging a leg after exertion, tingling and numb areas particularly in the feet and legs. There may be incontinence and malfunctions of the bowel. When badly affected, there may be paralysis resembling a stroke.

The pattern of the symptoms varies greatly,

ASK THE DOCTOR

MULTIPLE SCLEROSIS

Q My mother died of MS. Does that mean that I am more likely to get it?

A Oddly enough, no. While the disease tends to run in families, the children of MS sufferers very rarely contract the disease.

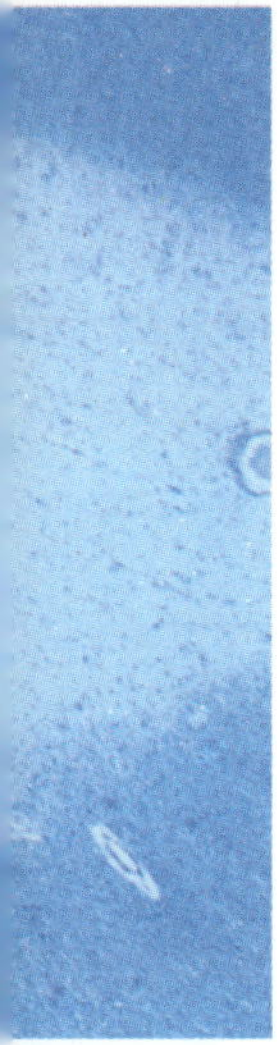

too. The symptoms may come on singly or in combination. They may last anything from a few weeks to a few months or more. Some people suffer no more than the odd mild attack, leading a perfectly normal and long life. Occasionally there is a steady gradual deterioration from the first attack.

Treatment: Several different tests may be needed to establish the condition, these include a lumbar puncture, brain scan, and electrical tests, which measure the speed of response in the brain.

As yet, there is no cure. During severe attacks, drugs may be given to alleviate symptoms; these may include corticosteroids and antidepressants. Physiotherapy can be helpful where there is muscle weakness. Some people find specialised diets help.

Multiple sclerosis destroys patches of nerve fibres in the spinal cord. It is more common in women.

Anyone with MS should try to preserve the good health s/he has by sensible eating, getting plenty of rest, and taking care not to abuse the body with excessive alcohol and nicotine.

MUMPS

Mumps is an infectious illness, which can affect a number of different glands in the body, but most commonly the salivary glands.

Causes: It is caused by a virus, which is easily transmitted from one person to another by 'droplet spread' – via the small droplets of saliva that form in the air when someone speaks or coughs, particularly if the infected person is close to other people for a long time in a poorly ventilated room. Anyone who hasn't already had mumps risks catching it if they're exposed to the infection. Most people contract mumps during childhood, though the incidence is likely to drop markedly since the introduction of routine mumps immunisation in 1988.

Symptoms and signs: There is an incubation period of 12-26 days between infection and the appearance of symptoms. In a mild case, these may include feeling slightly unwell, with discomfort in the glands situated just inside the angle of the jaw. In more serious cases, there may be inflammation and swelling of the glands, with pain and tenderness. There may also be fever, headache and difficulty in swallowing. In most cases, the fever falls after two or three days, and the swelling goes down after seven or eight days. Children rarely develop complications, though there is occasionally a possibility of meningitis, which usually clears up without any long-term effects.

In males after puberty, about one in four develops swelling and tenderness in a testicle. This can be very

Useful Addresses

MULTIPLE SCLEROSIS

Multiple Sclerosis Society of Great Britain & Northern Ireland
25 Effie Rd
LONDON SW6 1EE
071 736 6267

Action for Research into Multiple Sclerosis (ARMS)
4A Chapel Hill
STANSTED
Essex
CM24 8AG
0279 815553

Self **Help**

MUMPS

If a man's testicles are affected, he may find supporting underpants helpful in relieving discomfort caused by the swelling.

ASK THE DOCTOR

MUMPS

Q I had mumps as a child. Can I catch it again?

A No, once you have had mumps your body's immune system recognises the virus, giving you immunity for life.

painful. In rare cases, it can affect both testicles, and, very rarely, leads to infertility.

Pancreatitis, or inflammation of the pancreas, occurs in about one in 10 adults who have mumps. A patient with this complication may vomit, as well as developing pain in the upper part of the abdomen.

TREATMENT: There are no effective drugs against mumps, so the illness has to be left to run its course. An affected child may be given paracetamol and should drink plenty of fluids,

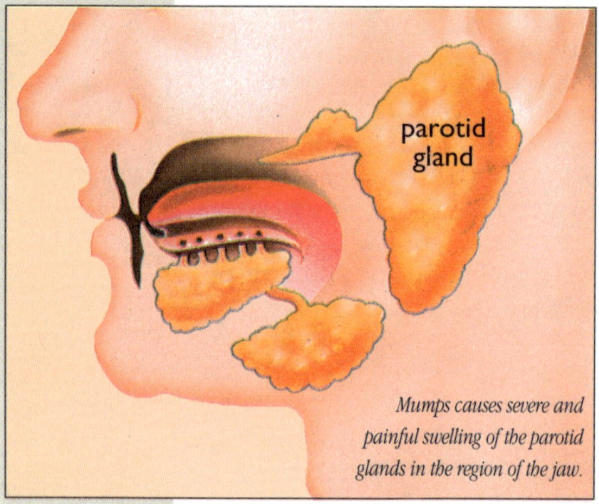

Mumps causes severe and painful swelling of the parotid glands in the region of the jaw.

particularly as s/he may find it difficult to eat.

An adult male whose testicle is swollen will probably need to take painkillers. If the pain is severe, the doctor may prescribe a steroid drug to be taken in tablet form, which can help to relieve the inflammation.

Anyone with mumps who develops pancreatitis and has persistent abdominal pain and vomiting should be seen by a doctor, so that s/he can assess whether the patient is absorbing enough fluids to make up for those lost through vomiting. Pancreatitis as a result of mumps usually clears up after a few days.

MUSCULAR DYSTROPHY

There are many different kinds of muscular dystrophy, but the most common is Duchenne muscular dystrophy, named after the French doctor who first described it in 1868. It is a condition in which the muscles gradually become progressively weaker until the patient dies. Duchenne muscular dystrophy becomes apparent in childhood, affects only boys, and is found in about 30 out of 100,000 baby boys.

CAUSES: In about 70 per cent of cases, Duchenne muscular dystrophy is genetically inherited from the mother, who is usually herself completely well. In the remaining cases, there is no evidence that it has been inherited from the mother and the disease is thought to have arisen because of a new gene mutation.

SYMPTOMS AND SIGNS: Usually the first thing that worries parents about their son is that he seems unusually clumsy when he starts to walk, and trips up more often than the average toddler.

It soon becomes obvious that the child's walking is not getting any better as he gets older. He begins to complain of feeling tired when he walks. He never really learns to run and, by the age of about three or four, he has difficulty climbing stairs. In time, the loss of strength shows itself very clearly and, by the age of about 10 or 12, the boy is likely to have become so weak that he needs a wheelchair.

The disease eventually affects all muscles in the body. Most boys die before they reach the age of 21, usually as a result of contracting a chest infection due to the weakness of the muscles controlling breathing.

TREATMENT: There is no known cure. Parents of an afflicted child should encourage him to take regular exercise so that he remains mobile for as long as possible. They must try to stop him becoming obese, and encourage him to sit correctly and to breathe properly.

Useful Addresses

MUSCULAR DYSTROPHY

Muscular Dystrophy Group
of Great Britain
35 Macaulay Road
LONDON SW4 0QP
071 720 8055

MUSCULAR STRAIN

see STRAIN

MYALGIC ENCEPHALOMYELITIS

Also known as ME, myalgic encephalomyelitis

is a very controversial disease, which affects more women than men.

Causes: The causes are unknown, but it is thought to be brought on by repeated viral infections or damage to the immune system following viral infection. Some people believe that it is caused by neurosis.

Symptoms and signs: Muscle tiredness, fever, headaches and aching limbs are common symptoms. As well as feeling generally unwell physically, you may also feel slightly depressed. The condition usually passes in time, but may last for several years.

Treatment: No known treatment. However, you may be advised to take some rest as soon as the condition starts and then gradually build up to taking plenty of exercise. A change of diet may be recommended.

MYOCARDIAL INFARCTION

see HEART ATTACK

MYOPIA

Myopia is the medical name for shortsightedness – a condition in which near objects can be seen extremely clearly while things in the distance appear blurred.

Causes: This condition results when the distance between the front and back of the eye is too long; when distant objects are viewed they are focused in front of the retina, instead of on it, and appear blurred. Shortsightedness is often inherited.

Symptoms and signs: Shortsightedness usually develops around the age of 12 and is inclined to get gradually worse until the age of 20, when it tends to stabilise. It is often first noticed when school children have trouble reading the blackboard. People with uncorrected short sight tend to screw up their eyes to see things in the distance. The condition may not be noticed at first and only picked up during a routine eye test.

Treatment: Eyes should be tested by an ophthalmic optician, who will prescribe glasses or contact lenses to correct the defect. There should be frequent tests to check for deterioration, especially in the early years, as the wrong type of lens can strain the eyes still further.

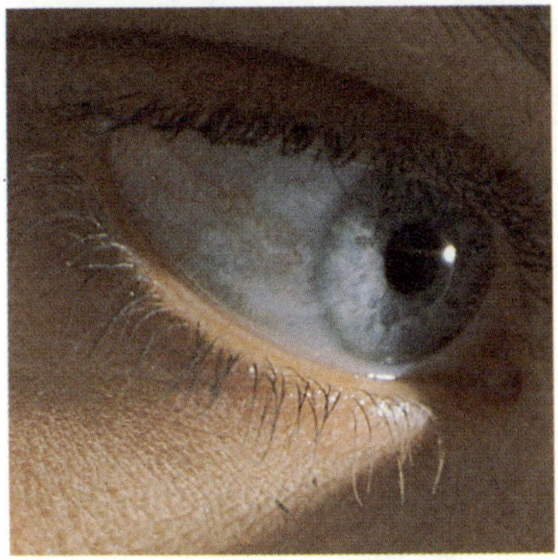

Myopia is a common eye condition, which is usually inherited.

MYXOEDEMA

see HYPOTHYROIDISM

Useful Addresses

MYALGIC ENCEPHALOMYELITIS

Myalgic Encephalomyelitis Association (MEA)
PO Box 8
STANFORD-LE-HOPE
Essex
SS17 8EX
0375 642466

Shortsightedness can easily be corrected with concave glasses or contact lenses.

HOW MYOPIA IS CORRECTED

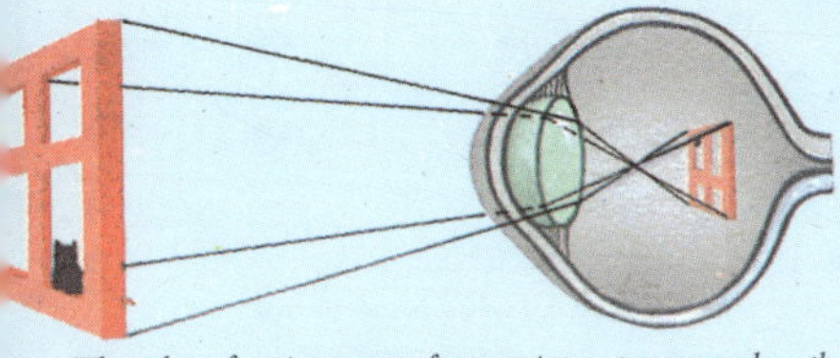

When the refractive power of an eye is too strong or when the eyeball is elongated, the image becomes focused in front of the retina.

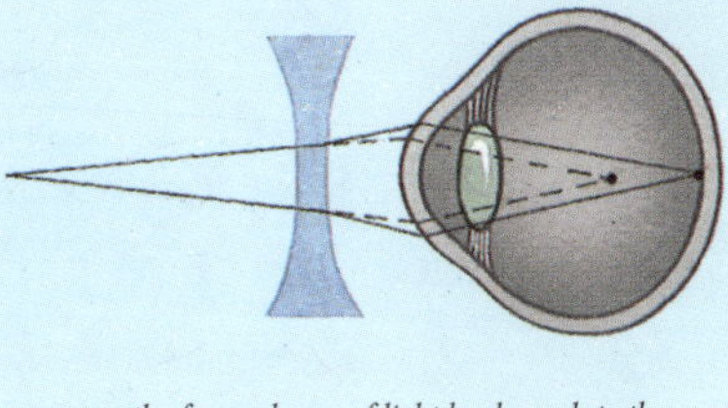

A concave lens moves the focused rays of light backwards to the retina so that the image becomes clearly focused.

ASK THE DOCTOR

NEURALGIA

Q My mother suffers from trigeminal neuralgia. Is there anything she can do to prevent an attack?

A Yes. Neuralgia may be prevented by avoiding activities that irritate a particular nerve. For example, trigeminal neuralgia is often caused by exposure to cold wind. If your mother has to go out in cold weather, she should be sure to protect herself with warm clothing.

Self **Help**

NEURALGIA

Regular dental check-ups should eliminate tooth trouble as a cause of trigeminal neuralgia.

ASK THE DOCTOR

NON-SPECIFIC URETHRITIS

Q Once I've been cleared of NSU, can I get it again?

A Yes, and sometimes quite soon after the first attack. For this reason, you might be advised to go for follow-up visits to your doctor for a couple of months or so.

n

NERVOUS BREAKDOWN

Nervous breakdown is a common term for mental illness that prevents the sufferer coping with work or day-to-day activities. Its main cause is severe anxiety or depression. See also DEPRESSION.

People suffering a nervous breakdown are unable to cope with everyday situations.

NEURALGIA

Neuralgia is a severe pain which results from a nerve being irritated or compressed. It can often be felt along the length of the nerve and usually occurs in brief bouts. Trigeminal neuralgia is a recurrent facial pain, which mainly affects the elderly.

CAUSES: Any infection or inflammation that affects a nerve can lead to a neuralgia attack. One possible cause of the condition is a slipped disc or fractured bone pressing on a nerve. Migraine sufferers may have attacks of intense pain around the eye. Shingles is another common cause, with pain being felt in the same area as the shingles rash. A condition known as post-herpetic neuralgia may sometimes persist after all other symptoms of shingles have disappeared.

Trigeminal neuralgia is caused by an irritation to a nerve in one side of the face. This can occur when a tooth becomes infected and the resultant abscess presses on a nerve.

SYMPTOMS AND SIGNS: The pain of a neuralgia attack may be felt anywhere in the body, depending on which nerve is damaged and what part of the body it affects. It may follow the path of the nerve or it may be a general pain over a larger area. The pain tends to be excruciating and very hard to bear and, although they may only last for a second, attacks can occur in quick succession.

TREATMENT: Treatment depends on the location of the damaged nerve, and on the cause and extent of the damage. If the pain is mild, it can be treated with painkillers such as paracetamol. If, however, it is severe, consult your doctor who will probably prescribe strong painkillers to relieve the symptoms. S/he will examine you to find the cause of the pain and will recommend an X-ray if a fractured or displaced bone is suspected. S/he may send you to a neurologist for further diagnostic tests and treatment or, in some very rare cases of persistent pain, s/he may recommend that the nerve be killed by injection or removed by surgery.

NON-SPECIFIC URETHRITIS

Non-specific urethritis (NSU), sometimes called non-gonococcal urethritis, is a urinary tract infection and is the most common sexually transmitted disease. More often reported by men, it also affects women but often NSU is only recognised if it produces complications like salpingitis, which is inflammation of the fallopian tubes.

CAUSES: Passed via sexual intercourse, NSU is caused by chlamydiae, tiny organisms similar to bacteria.

SYMPTOMS AND SIGNS: Symptoms appear in men about one to five weeks after infection has taken place.

There might be a slight tingling at the tip of the penis when urinating, and a clear or pus-filled discharge. Women sometimes have a

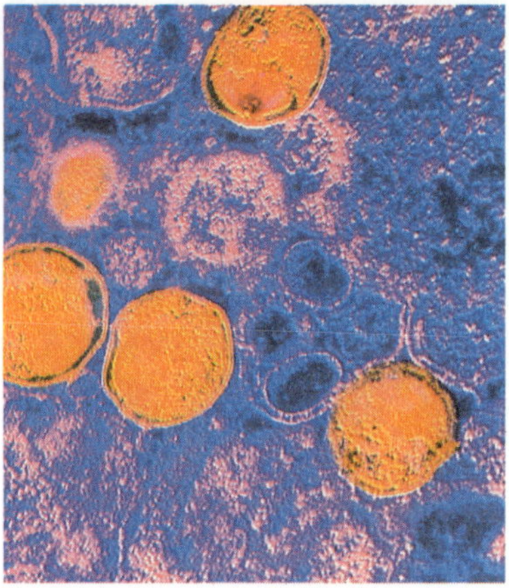
The chlamydia bacteria (orange) are responsible for 50 per cent of cases of non-specific urethritis.

little vaginal discharge.

TREATMENT: If you or your partner have NSU symptoms, go to your doctor or GU (genito-urinary) clinic. Both of you will usually be given a course of antibiotics.

See also CHLAMYDIA INFECTIONS, SALPINGITIS.

NOSE BLEED

Although nose bleeds can happen to everyone, they are most common in children and older people. The blood usually comes from blood vessels in the mucous membrane that lines the nose.

CAUSES: Nose bleeds can start when you blow your nose, especially when you have a heavy cold and the crusts that have formed on the mucous membrane are dislodged; fragile blood vessels can be another cause. Very rarely, nose bleeds can be a symptom of high blood pressure or a more general bleeding disorder called thrombocytopenia, but in this last case, there may also be a great deal of bleeding in other places such as the gums or under the skin. A heavy head injury from a fall or violent blow that has caused a small fracture may also cause a nose bleed.

SYMPTOMS AND SIGNS: Noses usually bleed from one nostril only, and the amount of blood lost is not great – although it can seem so to the sufferer.

TREATMENT: In most cases, there should be no need for concern, though more attention should be paid to older people. If someone who has just had a head injury starts a nose bleed, s/he should be taken to hospital straight away.

NSU

see NON-SPECIFIC URETHRITIS

A nose bleed can start when swollen blood vessels in the mucous membrane burst.

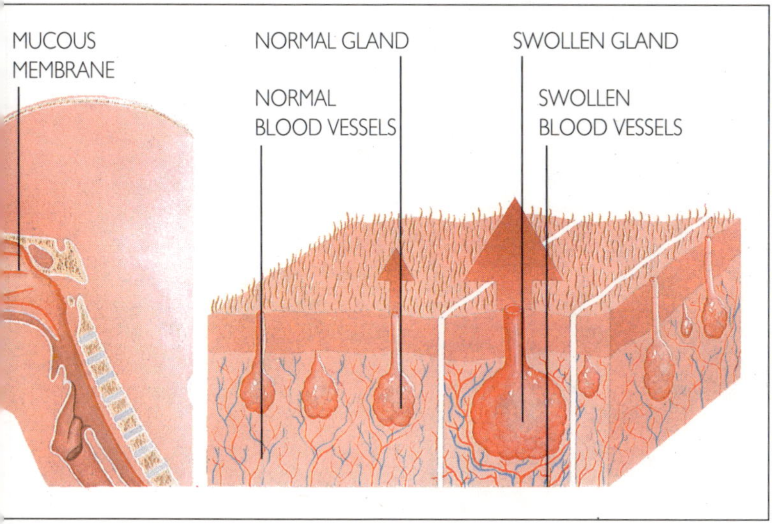

Self **Help**

NOSE BLEED

If you have a nose bleed:

- Sit and lean slightly forward, breathing through your mouth.
- Pinch the lower part of both nostrils for about 15 minutes – this should stop the bleeding.
- Don't blow your nose for about 12 hours afterwards.
- If bleeding continues for more than, say, 20 minutes, go to your doctor or nearest hospital casualty department: you may have to have your nostril packed with gauze for a few hours.

ASK THE DOCTOR

NOSE BLEED

Q I keep having nose bleeds. Can anything be done?

A You may need to have your nose cauterised. You might also have your blood tested to check that the bleeding hasn't made you anaemic.

ASK THE DOCTOR

OBESITY

Q A friend of mine who is really fat seems quite happy with her size. Am I right to be worried about her health?

A Yes, you are. If your friend is obese, she runs a serious risk of suffering from high blood pressure, diabetes or coronary artery disease. Strokes are also more common in obese people, and anyone who has osteoarthritis will find that carrying around extra weight increases the pain in areas such as the hips and knees. Obese men, incidentally, are more prone than their slimmer counterparts to cancers of the colon, rectum or prostate.

O

OBESITY

Being obese is not the same as being overweight. The term is used when a person has too much body fat and is at least 20 per cent heavier than s/he should be for his/her height and build.

CAUSES: Generally obesity is the result of eating too much, so that more calories are going into the body than are being used up by energetic exercise. Obese people's energy requirements may be less because of a slower than average metabolic rate. A tendency to obesity can be inherited; also, rarely, it can be caused by a hormonal disorder.

SYMPTOMS AND SIGNS: A vastly increased amount of actual body fat as well as an increase in weight.

TREATMENT: Regular exercise helps up to a point. The best way to lose weight, however, is totally to re-think your eating habits: a sensibly balanced slimming diet should help at the outset, but the weight will only stay off if you continue to eat properly. In extreme cases of obesity, wiring of the jaws or surgery may be considered.

In affluent societies, obesity is one of the most common nutritional disorders of recent years. It is usually caused by over eating.

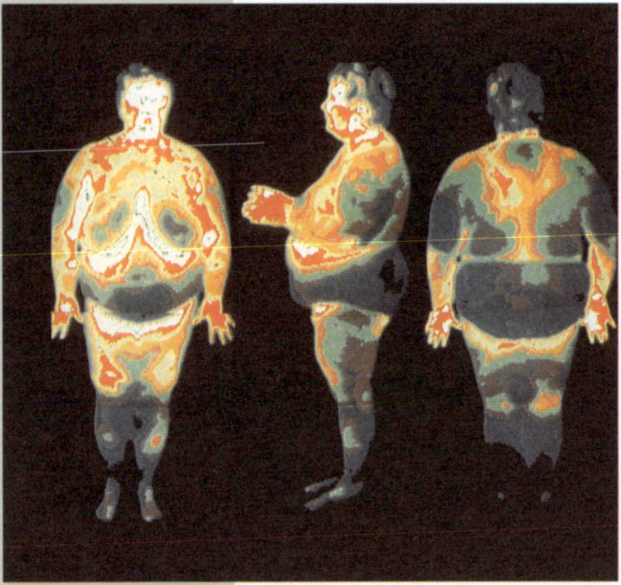

OSTEOARTHRITIS

In osteoarthritis the cartilage lining the bones at a joint becomes thin and worn out and the joint becomes painful, swollen and stiff.

CAUSES: Old age is the major cause, though other factors result in the condition being far worse in some people and in some joints than in others.

The swelling of the joints is due to a build-up of bone around the joint. When the cartilage wears down, the bones rub against each other and also become worn down; fresh bone is deposited in the area to compensate – these deposits are called osteophytes (bony outgrowths). Obesity makes the condition worse. Other factors include repeated or serious injury to a joint, congenital deformity and joints that have been subjected to unusual strain.

The tendency to suffer from severe osteoarthritis appears to be inherited to some extent and affects three times as many women as men.

SYMPTOMS AND SIGNS: Painful stiff joints, thickened by bone deposits, are the chief symptom. Although the condition doesn't usually appear until middle age, there are often indications much earlier, for instance, many younger people have one joint that aches after a long walk or heavy exercise.

Osteoarthritis is often accompanied by muscle wasting and weakness in the affected area. This occurs not because the osteoarthritis directly affects the muscles but through lack of use.

TREATMENT: There is no cure for osteoarthritis, though much can be done to alleviate the symptoms. Medication, such as simple analgesics (aspirin and paracetamol) and non-steroidal anti-inflammatory drugs (NSAIDs), may relieve the pain. Corticosteroid injections are another possibility. Stiffness may be helped by physiotherapy and exercise. The joints of obese patients will

ss-section of an elbow joint, showing how cartilage in the normal joint (left) rs down and the bones rub together, resulting in osteoarthritis (right).

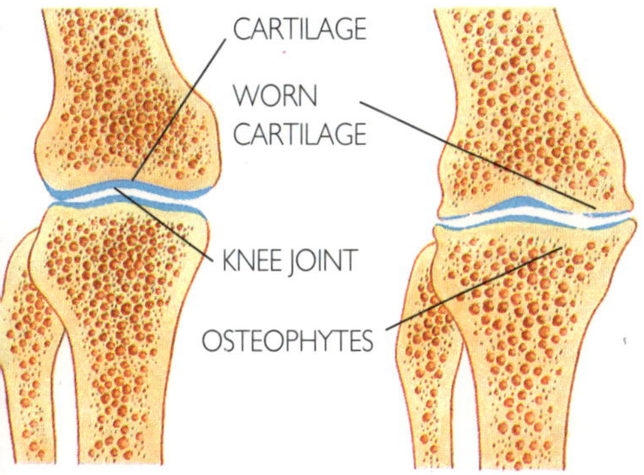

benefit from a loss of weight.

Surgery, such as joint replacement or the immobilising of a joint, may be recommended if the condition is really severe.

OSTEOMYELITIS

Osteomyelitis is an infection in a bone and its central cavity. It may be either acute or chronic: acute osteomyelitis usually occurs in children, whereas chronic osteomyelitis can affect people at any age.

Acute osteomyelitis: Boys are more commonly affected by acute osteomyelitis.

CAUSES: The bacteria that cause acute osteomyelitis are almost always *Staphylococcus aureus*. These bacteria enter the bloodstream, often via a boil, an untreated cut, or a throat infection. They usually invade only one bone, though rarely they may attack several bones. As well as infection of the bone, you may also develop septicaemia.

SYMPTOMS AND SIGNS: At first, the affected bone won't be abnormal, but it will gradually become tender, the surrounding tissue will swell and the skin above it will redden. The bone usually becomes extremely painful and your temperature may rise steeply. The pain tends to be severe. Sometimes the pain occurs almost overnight; sometimes symptoms take a week or so to develop.

TREATMENT: This is usually an intensive course of antibiotics, which will probably be given in high doses for at least a few weeks, first by injection or intravenous drip. As the infection responds, the patient can continue to take antibiotics in the form of tablets or syrup.

Meanwhile, the affected limb needs to be rested and the patient will probably be put to bed with the leg or arm raised to reduce swelling. If the infection is near a joint, that joint may need to be immobilised. Sometimes, light traction may be applied to the limb to rest it.

If a large abscess has formed, the bacteria have invaded a joint, or the infection fails to respond quickly to antibiotics, surgery is usually necessary.

Chronic osteomyelitis: This may affect any age group.

CAUSES: Chronic osteomyelitis may be caused by any illness or injury, which results in a bone becoming starved of blood and exposed to infection. Sometimes, the bacteria may be dormant for a long time and only become active when the patient's defences are low.

TREATMENT: It may be possible to bring the infection under control with powerful antibiotics over a long period of time, although the infection may flare up again as soon as the antibiotics are stopped. But the treatment for most patients is surgery, ranging from the simple removal of a piece of dead bone to a lengthy operation involving scraping out all the dead bone and infected material from the affected bone, and filling the cavities left behind with bone grafts.

ASK THE DOCTOR

OSTEOARTHRITIS

Q I am 49 and have very bad arthritis in my left hip. Would a hip replacement help me?

A It almost certainly would. Hip replacements are usually extremely successful and improvements in technology mean that they are now suitable for younger patients.

Q My mother has osteoarthritis and has difficulty performing everyday tasks. Is there anything I can buy to help her?

A There are many gadgets available to make life easier; for example, extending tongs to help pick things up from the floor or self-opening scissors with easy-to-grasp handles.

Self Help

OSTEOPOROSIS

To try to prevent osteoporosis, make sure your diet is rich in calcium: have plenty of milk and milk products, green vegetables, sardines, shellfish, and citrus fruits. It will also help if you stop smoking and cut down on your alcohol consumption.

Useful Addresses

OSTEOPOROSIS

National Osteoporosis Society
PO Box 10
Radstock
BATH BA3 3YB
0761 432472

OSTEOPOROSIS

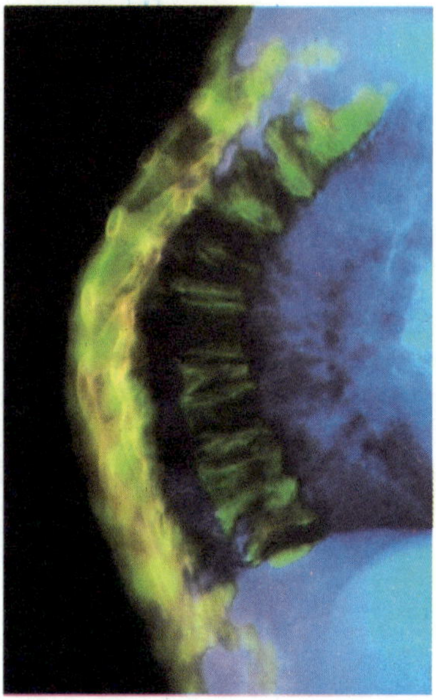

False-colour X-ray of the middle section of the spine in a woman suffering from osteoporosis.

Osteoporosis is the wasting away of bone. It is often incorrectly referred to as 'brittle bone disease', which, unlike osteoporosis, is inherited and affects children. Osteoporosis, on the other hand, is a natural part of aging, but becomes a problem more often in white people, particularly post-menopausal women.

CAUSES: The most common causes are ageing and, for women, the menopause because the ovaries no longer produce the hormone oestrogen which helps to protect bones. Other causes include disorders of other hormones, a lack of calcium, lengthy treatment with corticosteroids and prolonged immobilisation of some part of the body. In some cases, osteoporosis is hereditary; it is also more common among heavy smokers and drinkers, and people who have chronic bronchitis or emphysema.

SYMPTOMS AND SIGNS: If osteoporosis occurs in your backbone, you will have backache and you may become shorter and very round-shouldered; in severe cases, a few vertebrae may collapse altogether and cause intense, sudden pain. More often the disease is signalled by a bone fracture after a minor fall because the bone has been weakened.

TREATMENT: It is difficult to replace lost bone tissue, but further degeneration in menopausal women can be slowed down or halted with HRT (hormone replacement therapy), which compensates for the loss of oestrogen. Your doctor may make sure you are not also suffering from osteomalacia, a bone condition due to vitamin D deficiency.

OTITIS EXTERNA

Otitis externa (infection of the outer ear) can be very painful but is easily treatable.

CAUSES: Otitis externa often occurs when the ear has come into contact with contaminated water. If it is a bacterial infection, it may be a localised one such as a boil, or the outer ear can become inflamed because of a general skin disorder such as eczema. Scratching inside the ear can also cause this problem. It is essential to get treatment before the rest of the ear canal becomes affected. Do not attempt to treat yourself.

SYMPTOMS AND SIGNS: The first symptom is usually irritation, and this may be followed by pain. The ear canal may be visibly red and swollen and there may be a small area of eczema on the outer ear. There may be some discharge and, if pus blocks the outer ear, loss of hearing.

TREATMENT: Before treatment, it may help to cover the ear with a dry cotton-wool pad and take a painkiller. Your doctor may simply

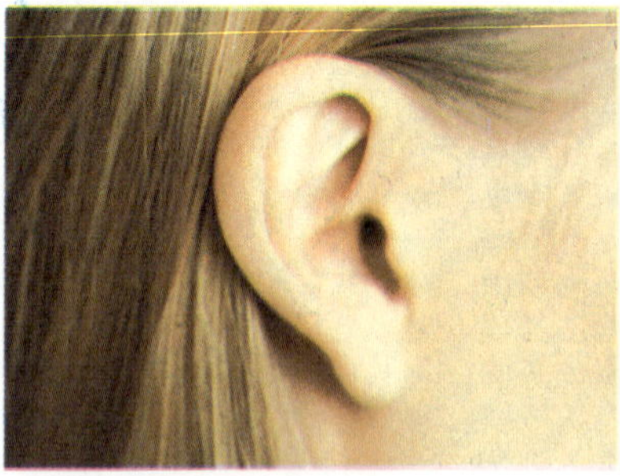

Otitis externa usually results from specific infections. It is sometimes called 'swimmer's ear'.

clean the ear. If you have a severe infection, however, s/he may prescribe antibiotics, antifungal drugs, or painkillers. It is important to have ear infections treated by your doctor because they can persist and can occasionally affect underlying cartilage and bone.

OTITIS MEDIA

Otitis media (infection of the middle ear) is a complication of other illnesses.

CAUSES: Otitis media is the result of a viral or bacterial infection in the upper respiratory tract. Fluid produced by the infection settles in the middle ear and is not properly drained away, causing a build-up of pus behind the eardrum.

SYMPTOMS AND SIGNS: The infection causes severe earache, fever and muffled hearing due to a build-up of fluids in the middle ear, which naturally only contains air. Sometimes, in untreated cases, the eardrum perforates or the condition may lead to glue ear.

TREATMENT: Antibiotics and analgesics (painkillers) are usually prescribed. Chronic cases may be treated by surgically creating an opening in the eardrum.

OUTER EAR INFECTION

see OTITIS EXTERNA

OVARIAN CANCER

Malignant growths in the ovary are fairly common, but rarely happen to any woman under the age of 50.

CAUSES: Why these growths occur is unknown. Occasionally, a long-standing ovarian cyst becomes malignant.

Pregnancy and oral contraception seem to give some protection against this condition; women who have never had children are three times more likely to develop tumours in their ovaries.

SYMPTOMS AND SIGNS: The first symptoms may be a swelling in the abdominal area with vague discomfort. Nausea, vomiting and vaginal bleeding are other common symptoms.

TREATMENT: Ovarian cancer usually requires surgery. After surgery, further treatment with anti-cancer drugs and radiotherapy may be required.

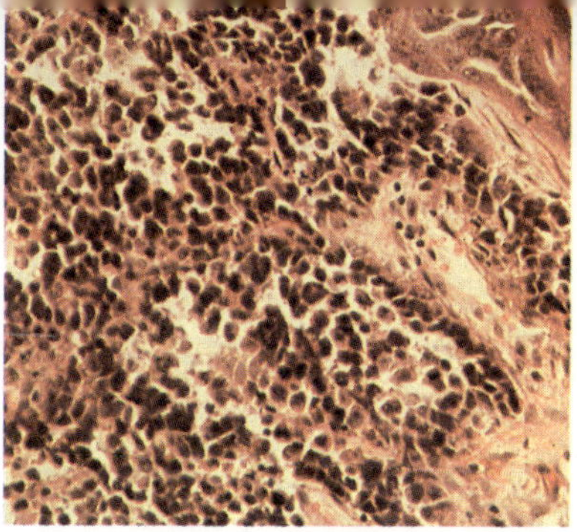

Light micrograph of a section through the ovary, showing an ovarian cancer.

OVARIAN CYST

An ovarian cyst is an abnormal swelling on the ovary, which is filled with fluid.

CAUSES: Sometimes cysts form as the result of a hormonal imbalance but in most cases, the causes are not known.

SYMPTOMS AND SIGNS: Cysts can range from the size of a small pea to the size of a football. When small, there are often no symptoms. There may be bleeding, pain during intercourse, menstrual problems and general discomfort in the area. Sometimes cysts cause excruciating abdominal pain, and there may be fever and vomiting. The most dangerous condition is when a cyst becomes twisted, causing gangrene.

TREATMENT: Many cysts require no treatment and may even go away on their own. If the cyst is large, surgery may be advised. This may simply involve the removal of the cyst or, occasionally, the complete ovary may be removed. Cysts caused by an imbalance of hormones may be treated with the appropriate hormonal drugs.

ASK THE DOCTOR

OTITIS EXTERNA

Q I've recently had an infection of the outer ear. Can I still go swimming?

A Yes, but wait until the infection has cleared up. Wear a swimming hat or ear plugs, and use your ear plugs, or a shower cap, when taking a bath or shower.

Q What is the best way to clean my ears without damaging them?

A Simply allow them to be rinsed with warm water when you are taking a bath or shower. Shake out excess water as soon as possible afterwards. Do not use cotton-wool buds in the ear canal, as you could damage the lining – thereby increasing the risk of infection.

ASK THE DOCTOR

OVARIAN CYST

Q Can a cyst turn into cancer?

A Yes it can, but only after many years and the chances are very slight.

ASK THE DOCTOR

PANCREATIC CANCER

Q I read the other day that 90 per cent of people who get cancer of the pancreas die of the disease within a year. Why is it so difficult to treat?

A If treated in the early stages, pancreatic tumours can be removed by surgery and the patient stands a good chance of being cured. But, unfortunately, the symptoms are often very vague and the condition may only be diagnosed after the cancer has spread throughout the pancreas and to other parts of the body, such as the liver.

p

PANCREATIC CANCER

Cancer of the pancreas, although still fairly rare, is on the increase. However, it is very unusual under the age of 50.

CAUSES: There seems to be a connection between pancreatic cancer and smoking. Continuous alcohol abuse, drinking large amounts of coffee and a diet rich in animal fats may also play a part.

SYMPTOMS AND SIGNS: The most common symptom is pain in the upper part of the abdomen, which often goes through the body to the middle of the back. Other symptoms include loss of appetite and jaundice.

There may also be nausea, with vomiting and diarrhoea.

TREATMENT: In the early stages, cancer of the pancreas may be successfully treated by surgical removal of part of the pancreas, together with anti-cancer drugs and radiotherapy.

If the cancer is advanced, the outlook is not hopeful. Treatment will be aimed at relieving symptoms and making the patient comfortable.

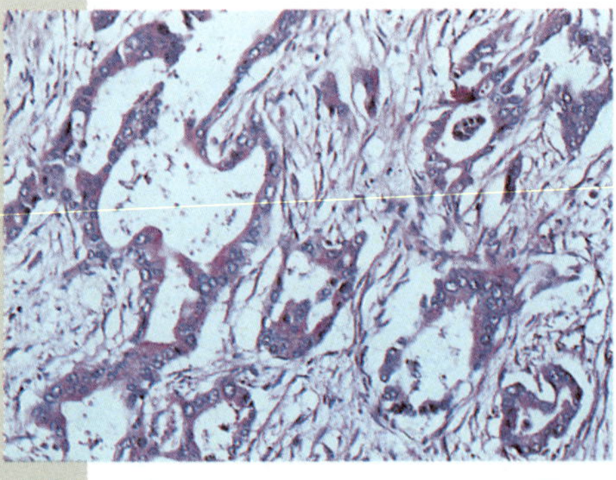

A light micrograph showing the irregularly shaped cells of pancreatic cancer. Tumours of the pancreas are not common, but can remain undetected until very advanced.

PANCREATITIS

Pancreatitis is an inflammation of the pancreas – the gland that secretes chemicals, which help in the digestion of food as well as producing insulin. It is a serious condition, which occurs in both acute and chronic forms.

CAUSES: Most cases of pancreatitis are a result either of gallstones blocking the bile duct or of continuous alcohol abuse. Less frequently, there may be other causes, such as an injury in the area or a viral illness such as mumps. Occasionally chronic pancreatitis develops after an acute attack.

SYMPTOMS AND SIGNS: In an acute attack, the symptoms usually come on very suddenly. These include a severe pain in the upper part of the abdomen, which can go right through to the middle of the back. The patient will probably be pale and sweaty, and there may be nausea and vomiting.

If the attack is relatively mild, the symptoms will probably persist for three or four days and then disappear. Sometimes, however, the condition may suddenly worsen; the patient may be confused and may even collapse.

The symptoms of chronic pancreatitis are usually similar but far less severe. Sometimes, though, there is no pain. Other signs include diabetes, loss of weight and signs that food has not been digested properly, such as greasy stools and diarrhoea.

TREATMENT: There is no specific drug to cure the inflammation.

In all cases, heavy drinkers will have to cut down on their drinking. If gallstones are present, they may need to be removed. Pain is often more bearable if the sufferer sits up in bed and hunches forward.

Most acute cases are treated in hospital. They will usually be given an intravenous drip feed as well as painkilling injections. The majority of cases will improve with rest and careful nursing.

Chronic cases are treated with painkillers, with insulin if they have developed diabetes, and with enzymes to help them digest food.

PARATYPHOID

Paratyphoid, or paratyphoid fever, is not as severe as typhoid.

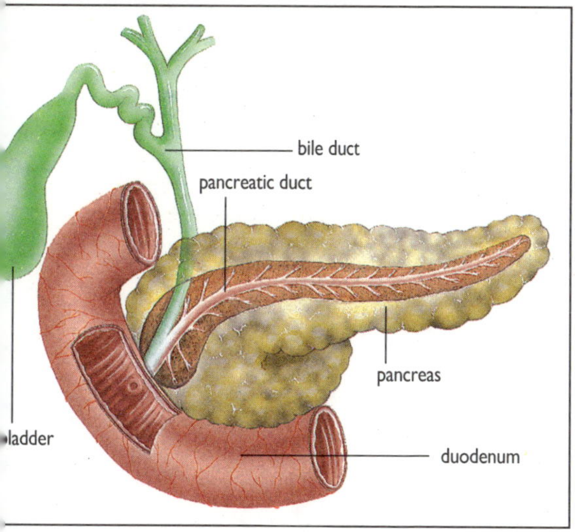

The pancreas can become inflamed if the ducts leading to the duodenum are blocked, but alcohol also causes damage, and excessive overdrinking can cause pancreatitis.

CAUSES: It is caused by the bacterium *Salmonella paratyphi*, which is contracted from the faeces of a symptomless carrier or from someone who actually has the disease.
SYMPTOMS AND SIGNS: The symptoms are similar to those of typhoid, including a rash or rose-coloured spots, severe headache, fever, stomach pains, delirium and diarrhoea.
TREATMENT: Immediate medical attention is vital, and your doctor will prescribe antibiotics to eradicate the bacteria.
See also TYPHOID.

PARKINSON'S DISEASE

Sufferers from Parkinson's disease have difficulty controlling their movements as nerve cells in the brain are destroyed.

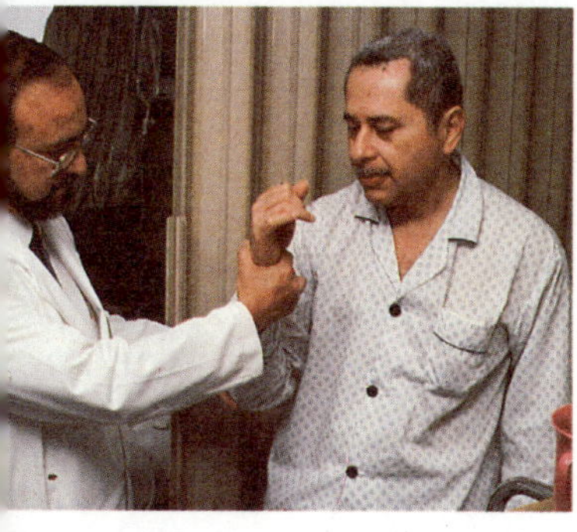

Parkinson's is a disease that affects the nervous system. It may also be called paralysis agitans. It is more common in men than women, and most commonly affects people over the age of 50.
CAUSES: Parkinson's is caused by the gradual deterioration of 'junctions' in the nervous system, called ganglia, which are located at the base of the brain. In turn, this affects muscle control and movement. The exact cause is usually unknown.
SYMPTOMS AND SIGNS: Symptoms usually develop over a long period of time; at first they are hardly perceptible. Tremors begin in a hand or limb when the muscles are at rest. The trembling gets progressively worse and spreads to both sides of the body. Walking may become stiff and unbalanced and may be so uncontrollable that it breaks into a little run. Posture is usually very stooped and stiff, simple everyday tasks become very difficult or impossible, and depression is common.
TREATMENT: In the early stages, Parkinson's is treated with physiotherapy. As the disease develops, your doctor will probably prescribe drugs which aim to minimise the symptoms, although they cannot lead to a cure. Some younger, and otherwise healthy sufferers are given the opportunity to have an operation on their brain in the hope of reducing the tremors and stiffness, but this unfortunately is often unsuccessful.

PELVIC INFLAMMATORY DISEASE

see SALPINGITIS

ASK THE DOCTOR

PARKINSON'S DISEASE

Q My mother has got Parkinson's disease. Does this mean that I'm likely to get it too?

A Although the cause of Parkinson's is unknown, there is no evidence that it is hereditary. It affects more men than women, and is largely a disease that hits elderly people. About one person in 200 has Parkinson's.

Q I am in my late thirties, and occasionally when I reach for something my hand starts to shake. Could this be a sign of Parkinson's?

A This seems unlikely, the shaking usually occurs when the muscles are at rest. You would, however, have reason to be concerned if your hand shakes when it is doing nothing. Check with your doctor to ease your mind.

Useful Addresses

PARKINSON'S DISEASE

Parkinson's Disease Society
22 Upper Woburn Place
LONDON
WC1H ORA
071 383 3513

Self **Help**

PEPTIC ULCER

- Avoid aspirin-based medicines, as they may exacerbate stomach bleeding.
- Avoid alcohol, tea and coffee and stop smoking.
- Follow a balanced diet and eat regular meals, containing high-fibre foods, which help the digestive process.

ASK THE DOCTOR

PERFORATED EAR DRUM

Q What should I do if I suspect I have a perforated ear drum?

A Cover your ear with a clean, dry cloth, take some painkillers, if necessary, and consult your doctor.

Q My child has a perforated ear drum and the doctor has advised a skin graft operation. She says, however, that this is not possible until my child is a teenager. Why can't my child have the operation now?

A It is routine procedure to delay certain operations until the part of the body being operated on is fully grown. The operation will be more effective and successful when your child is older.

PENILE WARTS

see GENITAL WARTS

PEPTIC ULCER

Any ulcer in the digestive tract is called a peptic ulcer. This term includes both stomach and duodenal ulcers. Ulcers are fairly common in middle-aged men and women. They occur when a small area of the stomach or duodenal lining loses its natural resistance to the acids and juices involved in digestion. When this happens, the juices act on that point of the lining and create a sore patch.

CAUSES: Stomach and duodenal ulcers can be triggered off for several reasons. Heavy drinkers and smokers are particularly susceptible, as are those people who eat badly and irregularly. It is also a common side effect from taking regular aspirin or non-steriodal anti-inflamatory drugs.

Peptic ulcers occur when the lining of the stomach or duodenum loses its resistance to the digestive juices, which then begin to work on the stomach itself.

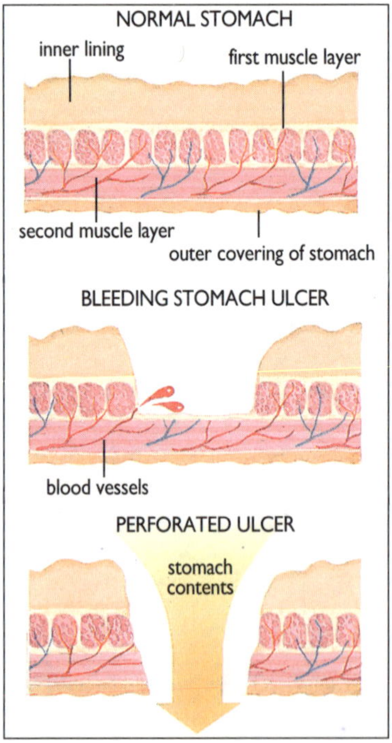

SYMPTOMS AND SIGNS: Burning pain in the upper abdomen or below the left ribs. Sometimes the pain is experienced after eating, but it can also be relieved by eating. It may come and go over long periods of time. Some sufferers may feel nauseous.

TREATMENT: The doctor may organise tests, such as barium X-rays or endoscopy, to confirm the diagnosis. The first treatment is likely to be with antacids and/or ulcer-healing drugs. The ulcer may heal in a matter of months but, in some cases, it may take years. Surgery is only required if the ulcer remains for a very long time; or if complications, such as blood in vomit or faeces, arise; or if a biopsy, taken during endoscopy, shows that the ulcer is cancerous.

PERFORATED EAR DRUM

A perforated ear drum is simply a hole in the ear drum, which can result from infection or trauma.

CAUSES: Perforation may be caused by a middle-ear infection due to a build-up of pus. This usually heals but occasionally doesn't, in which case a permanent or chronic defect remains in the ear drum. Occasionally, perforation is caused by insertion of a sharp object into the ear, a blow to the ear, pressure from flying or diving, or an exceptionally loud sudden noise such as an explosion.

SYMPTOMS AND SIGNS: Perforation can cause brief severe pain and their may be some bleeding and discharge from the ear. A chronic perforation can cause an infection in the middle ear and there may be discharge through the perforation.

If you have a permanent perforation, you will not hear so well in that ear. Just how badly the hearing is affected varies quite widely – some people have a minimal 10-20 per cent less, but it can be much more severe. A permanent perforation is usually painless – unless it becomes infected. It is important to keep water out of your ear if you have a permanent perforation, to cut

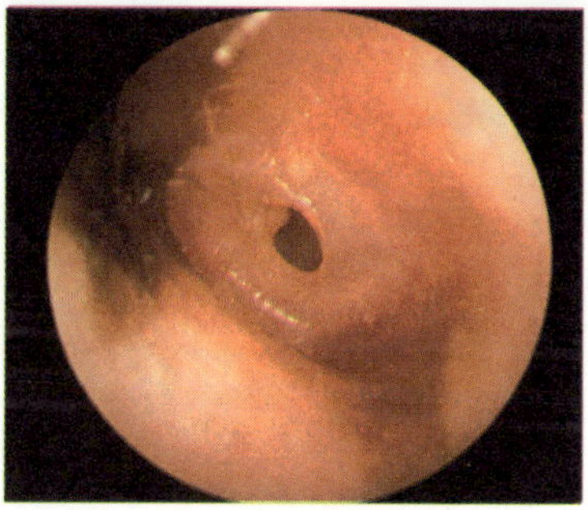

Perforated ear drums usually heal within about two weeks in children, but they may take a little longer in adults.

down on the risk of infection. Wear waterproof earplugs to swim, and do not dive.

TREATMENT: If there is an infection, the doctor will treat it with antibiotics. S/he may also need to clean out infected material from inside your ear. Sometimes the doctor may perform an operation to deliberately puncture the ear to drain the middle ear. If the perforation is not infected and there is no risk of complications, the doctor will usually advise leaving it alone, otherwise s/he may suggest an operation to repair the perforation. This involves taking a small graft of tissue and placing it over the hole in the ear drum. This usually succeeds in closing the hole and improving your hearing. It is a delicate operation, however, which does not always work perfectly and may need to be repeated.

PERIOD PROBLEMS

see AMENORRHOEA, DYSMENORRHOEA, MENORRHAGIA, PREMENSTRUAL SYNDROME

PERITONITIS

Peritonitis literally means an inflammation of the peritoneum, which is the thin membrane that lines the abdominal and pelvic cavity.

CAUSES: Peritonitis is a feared complication of acute appendicitis, and the reason why an appendicectomy is rarely delayed. It occurs when a swollen or gangrenous appendix bursts or perforates, releasing harmful bacteria into the peritoneal cavity and spreading infection through the rest of the abdomen. Peritonitis can be life-threatening and may develop very suddenly.

SYMPTOMS AND SIGNS: Severe abdominal pain, located either in one place or all over the stomach. The stomach will feel hard and tender and you may have a fever and feel nauseous.

TREATMENT: An urgent operation will probably be performed to drain the abdomen of pus, and you will be given strong antibiotics, often by an intravenous drip, to destroy the bacteria and prevent the spread of infection. You are likely to feel unwell for a number of days and will usually need to stay in hospital. See also DIVERTICULITIS, PEPTIC ULCER.

PHARYNGITIS

Pharyngitis is an inflammation of the pharynx – the passage that connects the back of the nose with the back of the mouth. There are two main forms of pharyngitis: acute and chronic.

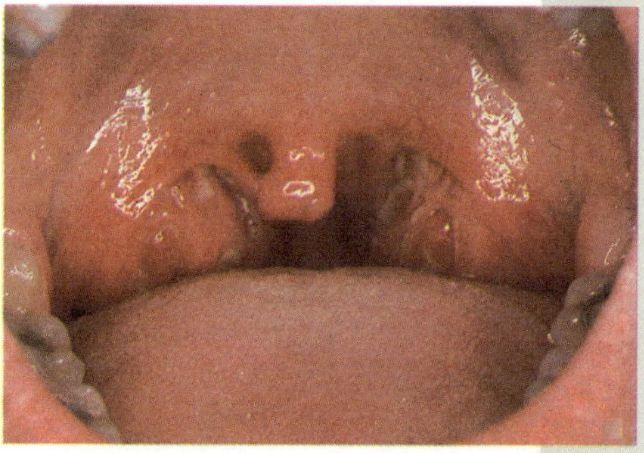

Chronic pharyngitis can be annoying, and tends to recur at times of stress.

CAUSES: Acute pharyngitis is caused by infection by viruses or bacteria, while chronic pharyngitis is caused by exposure to irritants in the air, such as pollution or smoking. Pharyngitis is a common complication of another illness, such as a cold, flu, measles or German measles.

SYMPTOMS AND SIGNS: The symptoms of acute pharyngitis are sore throat, swollen

ASK THE DOCTOR

PERITONITIS

Q I have recently been discharged from hospital after suffering from peritonitis, which was the result of a burst appendix. Will I have to change my lifestyle at all?

A If your operation went smoothly and there were no complications, it may take about three months before you are fully recovered. After that, you will be able to live life to the full again.

Self Help

PHARYNGITIS

- Gargle with warm, salty water.
- Give up smoking.
- At the first sign of an attack, drink plenty of fluid to relieve the sore throat and prevent dehydration.
- Avoid strenuous exertion – which may make the infection worse.

ASK THE DOCTOR

PHLEBITIS

Q I have been told that I am more likely to get phlebitis when I'm pregnant. Is this true, and how can I avoid it?

A During pregnancy, the pressure that the uterus exerts on the veins in the pelvis means that the circulation of the blood is impaired and pressure builds up in the veins. Hormones that the body releases during pregnancy may affect the vein wall, making it thin and more likely to become varicosed. Both these factors may lead to thrombosis and phlebitis in the legs. Take some time each day to put your feet up and relax. Avoid standing in one position for long periods and do regular calf exercises during the day.

ASK THE DOCTOR

PLEURISY

Q I recently fell off my bicycle and fell on to the handlebars. Since then I have had a pain in my chest. Could this be pleurisy?

A Although you are probably experiencing a pain similar to that in pleurisy, you are unlikely to be suffering from it. It is far more likely that you have injured your ribs, either cracking one of them or straining the muscles between them – but check with your doctor.

glands in the neck, dry cough and sometimes headache, raised temperature or chills. Chronic pharyngitis is signalled by a persistent sore, red throat. Call your doctor if you cough up green or yellow phlegm or you have a persistent high temperature. You should also consult your doctor if you have earache or develop a rash.

TREATMENT: Take painkillers, such as paracetamol, being careful not to exceed the stated dose. Pharyngitis usually clears up on its own, but your doctor may prescribe a course of antibiotics to overcome a bacterial infection. With chronic pharyngitis, try to remove the source of irritation and give up or at least cut down on smoking.

PHLEBITIS

Phlebitis is an inflammation and swelling of the walls of a vein, which can lead to clotting in that particular vein (thrombophlebitis). It most commonly occurs in the legs.

CAUSES: The inflammation may occur as a result of infection, autoimmune disease, damage to the vein or, rarely, cancer located somewhere else in the body.

SYMPTOMS AND SIGNS: The area around the vein will be painful and the skin may look red and swollen.

TREATMENT: Wear support tights if the inflammation is in your legs. Your doctor may prescribe anti-inflammatory or painkilling drugs – as tablets or creams.

Phlebitis most commonly affects the veins in the legs, causing swelling and discomfort.

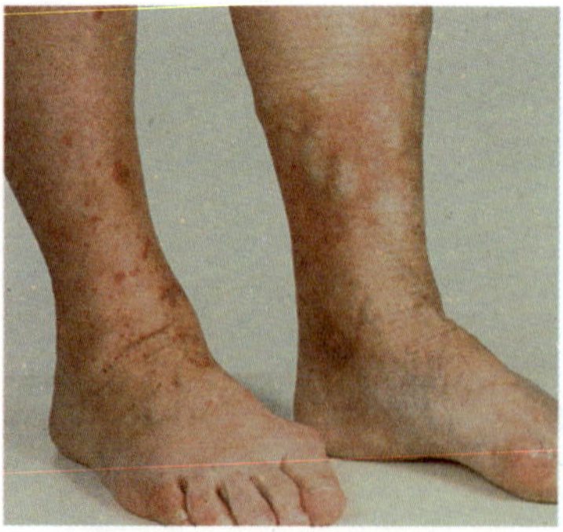

PILES

see HAEMORRHOIDS

PLEURISY

Pleurisy is an inflammation of the pleura, the thin membrane covering the lungs and lining the inside of the double-layered chest cavity. Normally, there is just a thin layer of fluid lying between and lubricating the two surfaces, enabling your lungs to move easily when you breathe. In pleurisy, the membranes thicken and the layers may rub together. There may also be a build-up of fluid between them, causing effusion, which is when a body fluid escapes from its normal area into another body cavity.

CAUSES: Pleurisy is usually caused by a small patch of pneumonia at the edge of the lung. This then spreads to cause inflammation of the pleura. Viruses may also be responsible.

SYMPTOMS AND SIGNS: The main symptom of pleurisy is pain connected with breathing. Each breath produces a sharp pain in the area where the pleurisy is located. There may be a temperature and a general feeling of being unwell.

TREATMENT: Antibiotics are given, either by injection or by mouth, to clear up the infection and painkillers to relieve the discomfort. See also PNEUMONIA.

PMT

see PREMENSTRUAL SYNDROME

PNEUMOCONIOSIS

see ASBESTOSIS

PNEUMONIA

Pneumonia is a general term for an inflammation of the lungs, usually due to infection. It may occasionally occur as a late complication of other illnesses and is still a fairly common cause of death in Britain.

CAUSES: Pneumonia is caused by many dif-

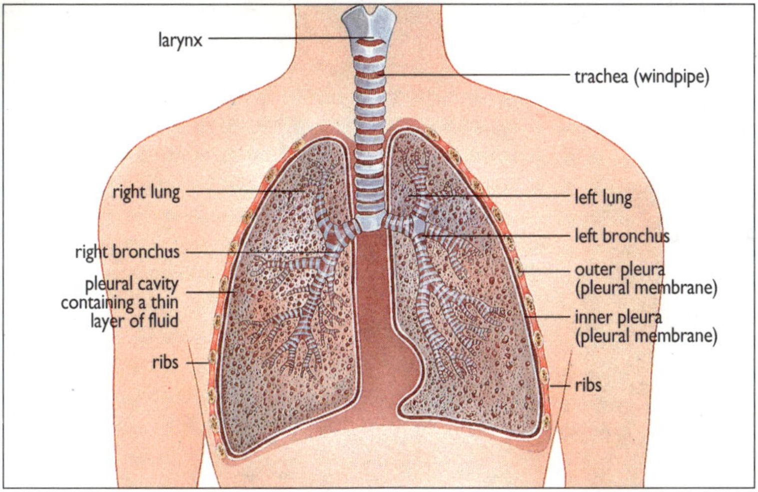

Dry pleurisy, when the pleural membranes between the lungs and the chest walls become inflamed, can be extremely painful.

ferent kinds of virus, such as chickenpox or flu, or bacterial infections, such as Legionnaires' disease. Occasionally it can result from inhalation of vomit or sputum or by chemical damage such as inhaling poisonous chlorine gas. The symptoms, treatment and the success of the treatment vary according to the original cause of the disease and the general health of the patient. Pneumonia is most prevalent among children and old people, particularly men, and among those with reduced immunity, such as alcoholics and AIDS sufferers.

There are two types of pneumonia. Bronchopneumonia is an infection of the bronchi and bronchioles (airways) and spreads to patches of tissue in one or both lungs; lobar pneumonia involves one whole lobe of the lung being affected. Lobar pneumonia is rare in developed countries. Double pneumonia simply means that the condition is present in both lungs.

Symptoms and signs: There is usually a fever, chills, coughing, shortness of breath and the patient may bring up yellow-green sputum and sometimes blood. Chest pain is usually worse when breathing in because of associated pleurisy. Pneumonia through flu can kill a frail or elderly person in 24 hours but a mild case in a healthy, young person may result in symptoms not very much worse than a common cold.

Pneumonia may develop into pleural effusion (fluid around the lung), emphysema (pus around the lung) and, in rare cases, an abscess in the lung.

Treatment: The doctor will examine your chest and may recommend a chest X-ray. Samples of blood and sputum may be sent for analysis. Some cases require hospitalisation. Drugs prescribed are usually antibiotics for a bacterial pneumonia, as well as aspirin or paracetamol to reduce fever, depending on the nature of the organism causing the problem. In severe cases, artificial ventilation and oxygen therapy may be required.

See also PLEURISY.

Light micrograph of a section of the lung infected with pneumonia. In rare cases, pneumonia results from a complication of flu, and can be fatal.

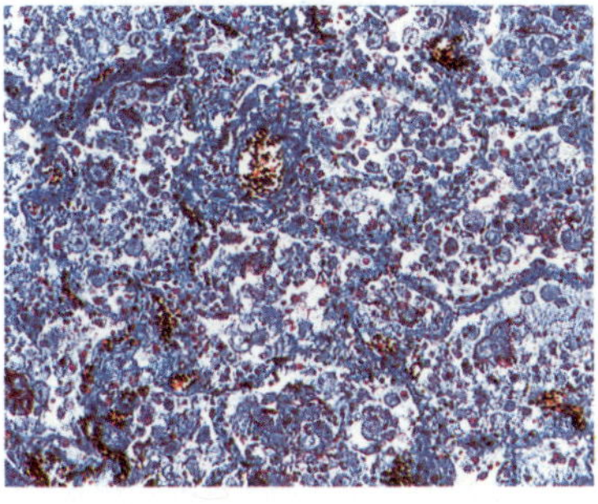

ASK THE DOCTOR

PNEUMONIA

Q How long does it take to recover from a bout of pneumonia?

A In most cases, about two weeks.

Q Why do people die from pneumonia?

A People who have a lung disorder, such as emphysema, or whose defences have been weakened by some other chronic illness, may not respond to treatment and they can die as a result of respiratory failure.

Body contour maps, such as this, can be used to measure the degree of spinal deformity caused by polio.

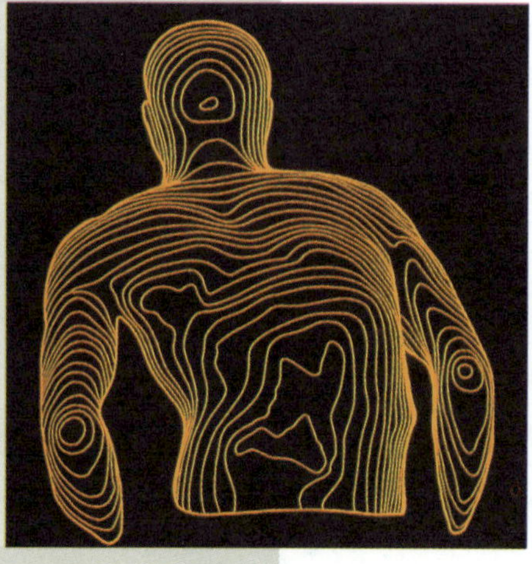

POLIOMYELITIS

Poliomyelitis – polio for short – is an infectious disease, which attacks nerve cells in the spinal cord, leaving some victims paralysed. It used to be a major cause of death. It is now rare in developed countries, due to widespread immunisation programmes (in Britain since 1956) and high standards of hygiene. Most people who contract the disease today are those who have not been immunised against it.

Young children are most likely to suffer from the disease, and it is also known as infantile paralysis. Babies are less likely to be affected because they may still have some immunity passed on from their mothers.

CAUSES: Occasionally a person may catch polio through inhaling particles of the virus, but the disease is usually spread by direct contact. The virus is generally taken into the body via the mouth, either through contaminated food or water or by being transferred from the hands.

Once someone has polio, s/he excretes the virus in his/her faeces, so poor public sanitation or lack of care in personal hygiene can help to spread the infection to food and drink. Flies can also carry the polio virus from excreta to food. In underdeveloped countries, human faeces are sometimes used to fertilise ground where food crops are growing, and this practice can transmit the virus to large numbers of people.

SYMPTOMS AND SIGNS: Damage can result in paralysis of the muscles. With disuse, the muscles waste away. If contracted early in life, before the bones have finished growing, the disease may lead to skeletal deformities.

The incubation period varies but is usually 10-12 days. First symptoms are similar to an attack of flu. These may last for a few days before disappearing. In most cases, this is all that happens and the disease may pass away without the patient realising s/he has the disease. About one-third of sufferers find that the symptoms worsen after three to five days. The headache and fever become more severe, vomiting increases, and the patient complains of extreme pain and stiffness in the neck. These symptoms result from the virus attacking the meninges – the covering of the brain and spinal cord. The back may also feel stiff, and sometimes the patient becomes hypersensitive to light. The polio patient remains alert and awake; patients with other types of meningitis become drowsy or even lose consciousness.

This phase of the illness may last up to a week. Paralysis often occurs, sometimes within hours, sometimes gradually, usually affecting the legs and lower part of the trunk. Once paralysis has occurred (about 7-10 days after the onset of the illness), it is likely to get worse for up to 48 hours, after which there will be no further deterioration.

The extent of paralysis can be as mild as a limb becoming floppy and useless over a few days and recovering within a few months. When more limbs are involved, it will take the patient longer to recover.

Sometimes the diaphragm and the other muscles controlling breathing are affected and the patient will need a tracheotomy (surgical creation of a windpipe by inserting a breathing tube) and artificial breathing support. Occasionally paralysis can affect the throat muscles concerned with swallowing. This can be very serious as there is a risk of the patient inhaling food and drink into his/her lungs.

TREATMENT: The doctor may collect a throat swab and a sample of faeces, or s/he may perform a lumbar puncture to remove some cerebrospinal fluid. These will be analysed to confirm the causative virus. Once a paralytic stage has been reached, diagnosis can be made on symptoms alone.

Self **Help**

POLIOMYELITIS

Vaccination is widely available and it is the only way to prevent catching the disease. If you are going abroad, consult your doctor to make sure your vaccination is up to date. In Britain the vaccine is usually taken orally, on a sugar lump. It is given during infancy at three, five and seven months, with a booster dose at the age of five.

There is no effective drug treatment for polio. It is important for the patient to rest. Sometimes the limbs may be placed in splints so that the muscles are completely rested. If paralysis does occur, careful nursing and physiotherapy are required.

POST VIRAL SYNDROME

see MYALGIC ENCEPHALOMYELITIS

PREMATURE EJACULATION

Premature ejaculation is when a man ejaculates his semen either before or soon after entering his partner during sexual intercourse. It happens to most men at some point, but is more common in very young men and can have a demoralising effect on both partners.

CAUSES: The reason is usually because the man is worried about how he is going to 'perform'. Premature ejaculation can also happen if a man tries to make love too hurriedly, if he's over-stressed, or if he's hyped up.

SYMPTOMS AND SIGNS: Ejaculating before, or very soon after, penetration.

TREATMENT: It's not usually a lasting problem and, in most cases, just trying to forget about it and even laughing it off can do the trick. Constantly dreading it might happen can become a self-fulfilling prophecy. If it does become a long-term problem, though, do go to your doctor: it's possible s/he may suggest sexual counselling. There are several simple and effective techniques for delaying ejaculation.

Premature ejaculation can be demoralising for the couple but, with reassurance, it need not be a long-lived problem.

PREMENSTRUAL SYNDROME

Premenstrual syndrome (PMS), also known as premenstrual tension, is the term given to the emotional and physical symptoms that affect women in the days leading up to their monthly period. In its worst form, it is more common in women who tend to suffer from depression.

CAUSES: No one is quite sure what causes premenstrual syndrome, though many doctors believe it is due to the various hormonal changes that occur in a woman's body around this time.

SYMPTOMS AND SIGNS: You can become depressed and tired, irritable, clumsy, aggressive and tearful. Your breasts may be tender and feel heavy, your tummy bloated and your ankles swollen; you may also put on weight because of fluid retention. Other symptoms include backache, headache and pain in your lower abdomen. The problems usually occur a few days before bleeding, but they can start up to two weeks before and continue during the the period itself.

TREATMENT: Different women find that different things help: for some, cutting out salt, caffeine and chocolate works wonders; others swear by oil of evening primrose. There are various preparations you can buy at the chemist which might work for you, but if PMS becomes insufferable, go to your doctor who may prescribe diuretic drugs to help with the fluid retention, and hormone-based pills or tranquillisers to combat the other symptoms. Vitamin B6 (pyridoxine) also helps some sufferers.

ASK THE DOCTOR

PREMATURE EJACULATION

Q My boyfriend suffers from premature ejaculation. What can I do to reassure him?

A The best way for you to help him, and give him confidence, is to be as generally loving as possible and place no emphasis at all on the problem. If you indicate that it is nothing out of the ordinary, it will probably not be a problem for long.

ASK THE DOCTOR

PREMENSTRUAL SYNDROME

Q Sometimes I get PMS so badly that I can't work properly and I snap at my husband so much that he loses patience with me. Is this normal?

A Unfortunately it is. Some women do have PMS extremely badly and may need to take a few days off work each month, though this is rare. Husbands and partners need to understand what is happening in your body and make allowances, but PMS is not a ticket to behave as badly as you like and have everyone forgive you!

A prolapsed uterus occurs when the muscles that support it become slack.

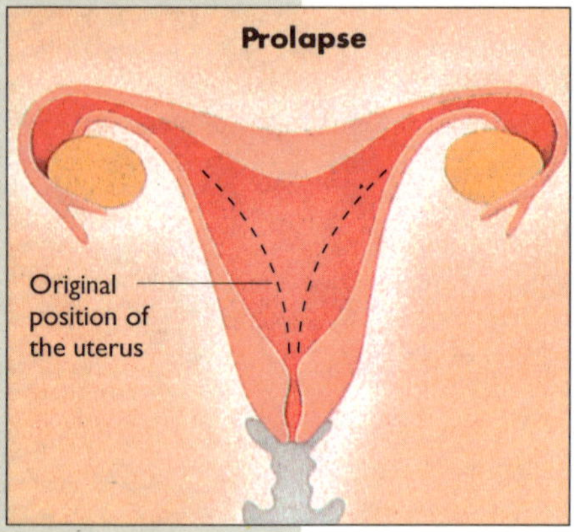

PROLAPSE

Prolapse (the displacement of all or part of an organ from its original position) most commonly affects the uterus and vagina.

Causes: The uterus is normally held in position by a series of muscles, ligaments and connective tissues. These are usually stretched during childbirth, and will slacken naturally as the woman gets older. When these slacken, there is a danger of uterine prolapse. The condition is most common among middle-aged women who have had children, although it can also occur in women who haven't had children.

Both obesity and retroversion of the uterus increase the chance of prolapse occurring.

Symptoms and signs: There are often no symptoms. Sometimes there may be a dragging feeling and backache. Prolapse of the uterus always involves some vaginal muscle relaxation, but the vagina may relax without affecting the uterus. In severe cases, the uterus can be seen outside the vulva.

In first-degree prolapse, the neck of the uterus (cervix) moves down slightly into the vagina. In second-degree prolapse, the cervix is visible outside the body on straining but retracts on relaxation. In third-degree prolapse, also called procidentia, the uterus is clearly visible outside the body. The surface of the uterus and the inverted vaginal wall will dry out and be replaced by thick white tissue. Soreness, ulceration and infection can occur in severe cases.

A patient suffering from any of these problems will probably have trouble passing both urine and faeces.

Treatment: Exercise of the pelvic floor muscles can help mild cases of prolapse. In other cases, ligaments may be tightened and some vaginal repair work may be done surgically. If the prolapse is severe, it will be necessary to perform a vaginal hysterectomy, which is the removal of the uterus through the vagina. Sometimes surgery can be avoided by the insertion of a plastic ring-shaped pessary to support the uterus. The plastic rings must be regularly replaced by a doctor.

Self **Help**

PROLAPSE

Exercising your pelvic floor muscles (the muscles you use to stop the flow of urine mid-stream) for a few minutes every day can reduce the risk of prolapse. It is especially important to do this after childbirth. If you are overweight, go on a diet. Eat a high-fibre diet, so you can open your bowels without straining.

PROLAPSED DISC

see SLIPPED DISC

PROSTATE ENLARGEMENT

The medical name for prostate enlargement is benign prostatic hypertrophy – or BPH for short. It is by far the most common prostate problem; in Britain more than 50 per cent of men over 65 have enlarged prostates, a figure that rises to nearly 100 per cent in men over 80.

Causes: The prostate is a male sex gland about the size of a horse chestnut. It is made up of a cluster of little glands which surround the urethra at the point where it leaves the bladder.

Over the years, harmless nodules develop in the tissues. These accumulate and gradually enlarge the gland. This is a normal part of the ageing process.

It's usually only when the gland gets so large that it interferes with the bladder and the urethra that problems arise. As the gland enlarges, it narrows the diameter of the urethra and interferes with the flow of urine.

Symptoms and signs: The most common symptom is the frequency with which the patient has to urinate – two or three times at night as well as constantly during the day.

It may be difficult to start urinating, and often the stream is narrower and less powerful than it was. It may be difficult to stop urinating once the process has started, and there may be a tendency to dribble. After urinating, there is often a feeling that the bladder isn't quite empty.

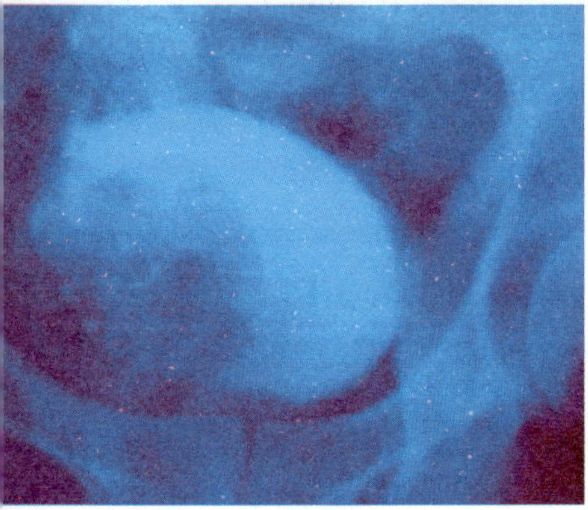

An enlarged prostate gland, which appears to be filling the bladder.

Straining may cause some blood to appear in the urine.

As the condition progresses, it can become very painful, cystitis may develop and, in time, the flow of urine may be reduced to a few drops at a time or stop altogether (a condition known as retention).

TREATMENT: Mild cases need no treatment. If the symptoms are severe, they need to be treated immediately.

Antibiotics may be prescribed to cure cystitis and a catheter will relieve retention. If the patient is in good health, the usual treatment is to remove the prostate, or part of it, by surgery – an operation known as a prostatectomy. If the patient is too ill to be operated on, a permanent catheter may be the only answer. Drugs are currently being developed that can shrink an enlarged prostate gland.

PROSTATIC CANCER

Cancer of the prostate is one of the most common cancers in British men, with about 10,000 new cases diagnosed every year. The condition occasionally strikes young men but is more usually a disease of the elderly.

CAUSES: The exact causes of cancerous growths in the prostate are not known, but the male hormone testosterone seems to be involved.

SYMPTOMS AND SIGNS: The symptoms of cancer of the prostate are very similar to those of an enlarged prostate: difficulties with urinating, cystitis and, if the urethra gets blocked, urinary retention.

In some advanced cases, there may be pain in the bones, indicating that the cancer has spread from its original site.

TREATMENT: A course of antibiotics may be prescribed to cure any associated cystitis and a catheter will relieve retention. Surgery, radiotherapy or hormone therapy may be prescribed. Fortunately, cancer of the prostate is a slow growing form of cancer and, if caught in the early stages, treatment will usually keep it under control for many years.

See also PROSTATE ENLARGEMENT.

PSORIASIS

Psoriasis is one of the most common skin disorders, affecting one person in 30. It usually starts between the ages of 14 and 24 and is life-long – except for a minority of sufferers who experience only a few isolated attacks.

CAUSES: The exact cause of psoriasis remains a mystery, although some cases may be triggered by a viral infection, immunisation or a period of extreme stress. Normally, skin cells produced in the deepest layers migrate upwards and, when they reach the topmost layer, they come away as microscopic flakes. In an area of skin affected by psoriasis, this happens 10 times more rapidly than usual and the skin becomes 'heaped up'. As it is forming so quickly, it does not even possess the normal structures which bind the layers of skin together – so it flakes off.

Psoriasis has a hereditary component although some people can pass on the disease even if they haven't actually shown the symptoms themselves. Stress often brings on an attack of psoriasis. Young people may start their first attack six or eight weeks after a severe sore throat or tonsillitis.

Occasionally, a patch of psoriasis occurs in

ASK THE DOCTOR

PROSTATE ENLARGEMENT

Q I am about to have a prostatectomy. Will this put an end to my sex life?

A Probably not. Many men continue to enjoy sexual intercourse when they've had a prostatectomy. But you will be sterile. After the operation, semen is ejected into the bladder during orgasm instead of through the penis, and is emptied later with the urine.

ASK THE DOCTOR

PROSTATIC CANCER

Q My husband has recently had an operation for cancer of the prostate and has been told by his doctor that his chances of a complete cure are very high. Is this true?

A There are about 10,000 cases of prostatic cancer diagnosed every year, yet fewer than 1,500 deaths each year from this disease. If your husband's cancer was caught in the early stages, his chances of successful treatment are extremely high indeed.

Psoriasis can occur all over the body, including the palms of the hands, although the knees, elbows, back, trunk and scalp are the most common sites.

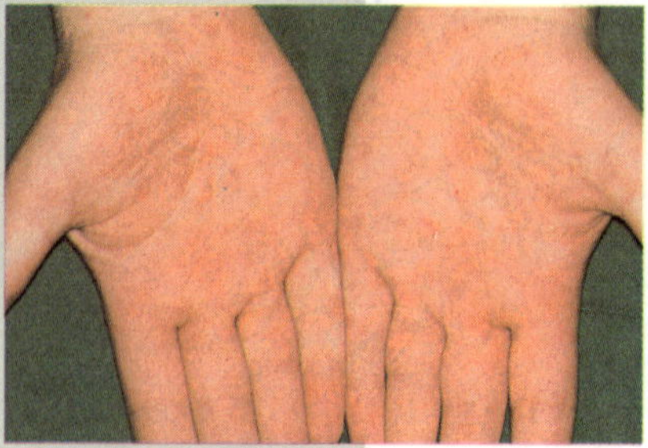

an area of skin which has been damaged by a cut, scratch or abrasion. Although the skin heals, psoriasis appears in the scar. In women, the condition may clear up in pregnancy – but unfortunately it often reappears again after the birth of the baby.

Symptoms and signs: There are several different types of psoriasis rash. The most common one is deep red or purple, it makes the skin thick and is covered with a silvery scale. It can affect any area of the body, although it rarely attacks the face.

Treatment: Your doctor will prescribe appropriate creams, lotions and shampoos. Steroid creams, containing cortisone, are sometimes prescribed for psoriasis. However, it is not advisable to use these in the long term. PUVA is a relatively new form of treatment, involving phototherapy. Other drugs used for severe cases include cyclosporin and methotrexate.

PUBIC LICE

Pubic lice (*Phthirus pubis*), also known as crabs, are small, blood-sucking lice with crab-like claws which cling persistently to the pubic hair.

Causes: Pubic lice usually spread by sexual contact with somebody who already has them.

Pubic lice cling to the pubic hair with their long, powerful, clawed legs. Infestation is fairly common – there are about 10,000 cases reported every year in the UK.

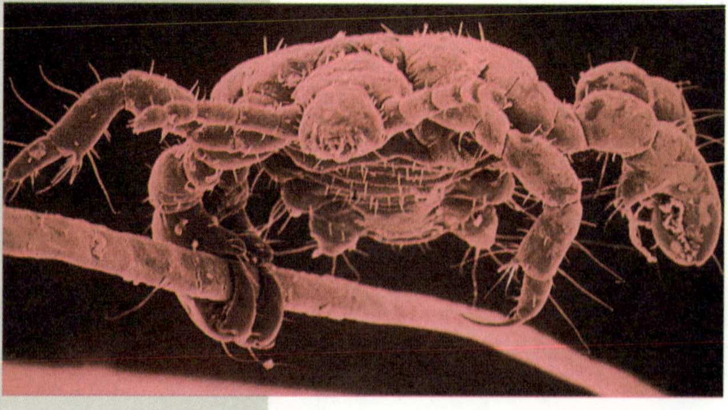

Symptoms and signs: Itching in the pubic region, particularly at night. It takes several weeks for the lice to breed, so it may be a while before you realise you have caught them. Both the lice and their eggs (nits) will be visible to the naked eye. The lice are yellowish-brown in colour and about the size of a pinhead and will cling to the root of the pubic hairs. The pale, shiny eggs are so firmly attached to the hairs that ordinary washing will not dislodge them

Treatment: A genito-urinary (GU) clinic or your doctor will prescribe a special cream to kill the lice and their eggs. However, it is important that your partner is informed and treated, as lice are easily passed on. The doctor may also check that no other sexually transmitted disease is involved.

PULLED MUSCLE

see STRAIN

r

RABIES

Rabies is a viral infection which attacks the nervous system and brain tissue. Once symptoms occur, death is usually inevitable. Britain has been rabies free since the early 20th century.

Causes: Rabies is carried by mammals and is transferred by means of a bite, or a lick to an open wound. Although the disease can be transmitted by contact with any rabid animal, a dog bite is the most common source of infection. The virus embeds itself in local tissue and attacks nearby nerve-endings. It then travels along the nerve pathways to the brain.

Symptoms and signs: These manifest themselves from between nine days and several months after contact. The usual period is from four to eight weeks. Early symptoms are mild fever, headache, fatigue and loss of appetite, followed by numbness or 'pins and

Strict regulations and quarantine laws are aimed at preventing the spread of rabies to the UK.

needles' around the site of infection. These are followed by characteristic fits and spasms, which result in total exhaustion and the sufferer lapses into a coma before death. In about 20 per cent of cases, the disease causes progressive paralysis before death.

Treatment: Prompt and thorough cleansing of the wound with antiseptic followed by an immune serum injection and a course of rabies vaccine injections is effective in 80-90 per cent of cases. Once symptoms develop, treatment – which involves putting the sufferer on a ventilator and maintaining the heartbeat and other vital functions – has been known to save life, in a very few cases.

RAYNAUD'S DISEASE

This complaint affects the blood vessels in the hands and feet, more commonly in young women. The small arteries, which supply the fingers and toes with blood, suddenly contract.

Causes: There are two types of Raynaud's – primary, where the cause is unknown and secondary, where an underlying disease interferes with peripheral circulation – eg scleroderma, rheumatoid arthritis.

Symptoms and signs: The fingers and toes turn white when they get very cold. As the circulation improves, the digits turn blue and then flush red before returning to their normal colour. Your fingers and toes may tingle, feel numb or very hot and painful. In particularly bad cases, the blood flow doesn't return and the fingers or toes may become ulcerated and even gangrenous.

Treatment: Drugs that widen the blood vessels may be prescribed. Very occasionally, an operation may help.

RETINAL DETACHMENT

The retina is the delicate membrane at the back of the eye on to which the lens focuses light from the objects a person sees. The patterns of light and colour are converted into nerve implulses which are sent up the optic nerve to be interpreted by the brain.

Causes: Retinal detachment may be due to trauma, for example a blow to an eye, but often occurs spontaneously. There also appears to be a link between very severe short-sightedness and the tendency for the retina to become detached.

Symptoms and signs: Although it isn't painful, a detached retina results in partial loss of sight.

Treatment: Surgery is needed to reattach the retina, and, if there is an obvious cause, such as a cyst, that will have to be treated to ensure that the problem does not recur.

One method of repairing the retina is to burn around the tear, so sealing it and fixing it back in place. This is sometimes done by pointing a laser beam through the pupil of the eye and aiming it at the retina. Another method is to seal and reattach the retina by freezing it with an ice probe.

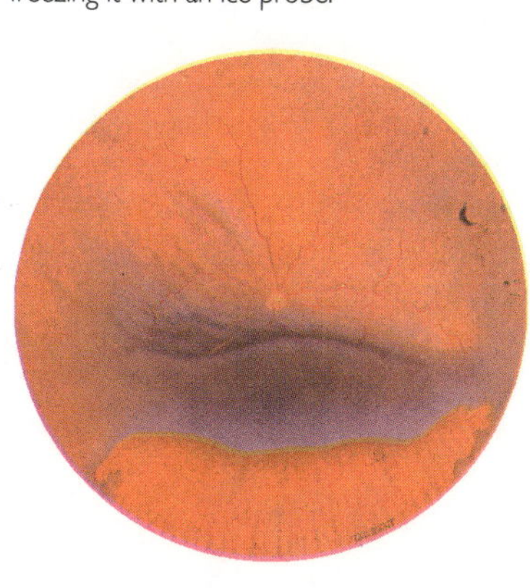

Self **Help**

RABIES

Prevention always being better than cure, arrange to be vaccinated against rabies before visiting countries where contact with rabid animals is likely.

Avoid touching or stroking all strange animals, including pets but especially strays, and keep clear of those that are behaving oddly, for example, dogs that stumble, bark frenziedly and salivate excessively.

If you are bitten by a warm-blooded animal when abroad, always seek medical attention at once.

Self **Help**

RAYNAUD'S DISEASE

If you suffer from Raynaud's disease – stop smoking immediately as this will only constrict your blood vessels even more. Don't let your hands or feet get cold in the first place. Avoid picking up frozen foods and wear gloves outdoors.

Retinal detachment is quite common among short-sighted people and may be associated with trauma. Accidents during contact sports, such as boxing and rugby, can also cause retinal detachment.

ASK THE DOCTOR

RHEUMATIC FEVER

Q Does everyone who suffers from rheumatic fever get heart trouble?

A No, if you are treated with antibiotics at an early stage, risk is reduced.

RHEUMATIC FEVER

Rheumatic fever is a disease of children that causes inflammation of the joints and may lead to problems with the heart.

CAUSES: Rheumatic fever, now rare in most developed countries, usually follows a throat infection caused by streptococcus bacteria. However, only a small proportion of the people suffering from this particular throat infection will actually get rheumatic fever.

SYMPTOMS AND SIGNS: There are a variety of different signs, including general illness, fever and loss of appetite. There may also be painful swelling of one or more of the larger joints, such as the hip or knee.

Rheumatic fever may also affect the skin. A rash may appear on the trunk or limbs and hard nodules sometimes appear under the skin, often over bony areas, such as wrists, knees and elbows.

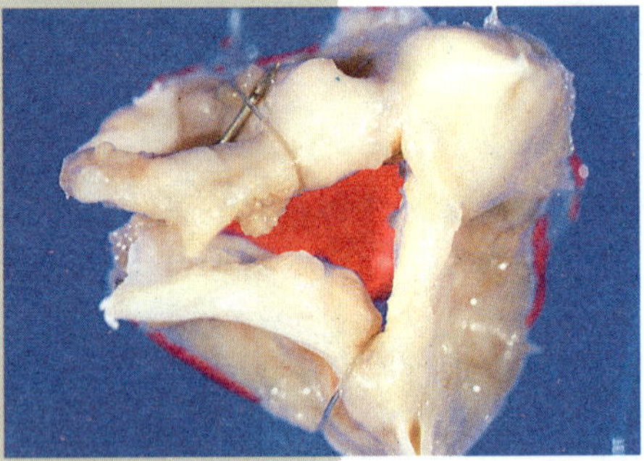

Rheumatic fever can damage the heart, causing thickening and scarring of the heart valves.

One of the most worrying things about rheumatic fever is its effect on the heart. The bacteria can affect the heart in several ways, the most common and serious being a thickening of the heart valves. This is not always noticeable at the time of the disease, but it is progressive and permanent and may lead to heart problems much later in life.

Rheumatic fever can also affect the nervous system and some children may suffer from St Vitus Dance, whereby their limbs may move in an irregular and uncontrollable fashion.

TREATMENT: Penicillin is used immediately to kill the streptococci bacteria and other drugs are used to control the pain in the joints and minimise inflammation of the heart. It may take up to six weeks to recover fully, although rheumatic fever does recur and a patient may be required to take antibiotics until s/he is 18 years old to prevent further damage to the heart. If any heart valves are damaged as a result of rheumatic fever, heart surgery may be necessary and antibiotics must always be given before any surgery including dental procedures and insertion of urinary catheter as a precaution.

RHEUMATOID ARTHRITIS

Rheumatoid arthritis is a disease which affects the cartilage lining of the joints. Women are three times as likely to be affected as men, and the condition first occurs most often between the ages of 30-50, although no age group is immune. The severity of rheumatoid arthritis varies considerably: it can be mild and short-lived or cause multiple joint deformities and considerable handicap. The disease usually begins slowly and affects a large number of joints from the outset, but sometimes it only affects one joint for months or even years, before spreading to others. In very rare cases, the symptoms begin abruptly, virtually overnight.

CAUSES: The cause of rheumatoid arthritis is not known, although it is thought to be an autoimmune disease. Diet is also thought to be a contributory factor in some cases; there may also be hereditary factors.

SYMPTOMS AND SIGNS: In the early stages your joints and muscles may feel stiff in the morning – usually in the fingers and toes, although wrists, elbows, shoulders, ankles, knees, hips and even the neck can be affected too. Rheumatoid arthritis may be preceded by slight loss of weight, tiredness or a feeling of being generally unwell but it will probably be the pain or stiffness in the joints which prompts you to go to the doctor.

As the disease progresses, some physical disability is likely and joints look very swollen and mishapen, particularly the finger joints.

TREATMENT: If you suffer from mild arthritis, you will probably be given some sensible advice about the importance of rest when the joints are acutely inflamed. But for those with arthritis that becomes increasingly severe over a period of months, the disease is normally treated with aspirin, anti-inflammatory drugs, steroid hormones or gold

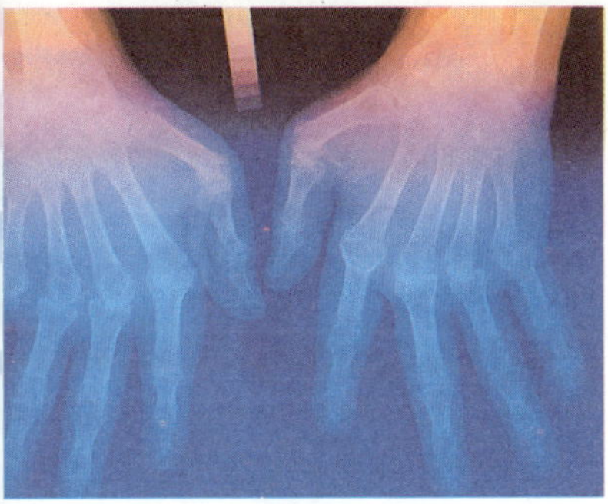

Rheumatoid arthritis typically affects joints symmetrically, for example, the fingers, wrists, feet, hips and shoulders.

compounds and other powerful drugs. Surgeons can replace damaged joints, such as the hip or knee, with man-made substitutes. Operations on the joints or on tendons may help to alleviate pain and stiffness.

RHINITIS

Rhinitis is an inflammation of the lining of the nose, caused either by a cold or by an allergy. Hay fever affects people who are allergic to dust in the air and pollens of certain grasses, trees and other plants.

Causes: Hay fever occurs when the lining of the nose gradually becomes 'sensitised' to a substance in the pollen, which is known as the 'allergen'. With repeated exposure to the allergen in the pollen, the body's immune response comes into play – producing antibodies which attach themselves to 'mast' cells in the nasal lining. These release chemicals (including one called histamine) which cause the familiar symptoms of hay fever. The more you are exposed to the pollen (or allergen), the more antibodies are built up, and the more histamine is released. Your reaction may therefore become progressively worse. Allergy to dust is actually a reaction to protein in faeces of the dust mites.

Symptoms and signs: When the small blood vessels in the nose dilate, excessive amounts of mucus are produced, the nose becomes blocked and itches maddeningly. The reaction is fast – within five to 15 minutes of pollen entering the nose or eyes, the hay fever symptoms will appear.

Bright light becomes a source of irritation and you may suffer from a mild headache, or pain over the sinuses. Irritation of the windpipe and the flow of the mucus into the back of the throat causes many people to develop an irritating cough. Without treatment the symptoms can last for several hours, and may even go on for two to three days depending on the weather, producing fatigue, irritability or even depression.

Treatment: There are many 'decongestant' nose drops and sprays available that may temporarily relieve some of the symptoms of hay fever. But relief is generally only short-lived and you should not rely on them too heavily, as they tend to make the symptoms worse in the long run. Your doctor may recommend antihistamine drugs. These drugs are most effective if you suffer from mild symptoms. Unfortunately, antihistamines do have certain undesirable side effects – drowsiness and dryness of the mouth, for example. Other treatments for rhinitis are steroid drugs in the form of nasal sprays. Desensitising the mast cells in the nose by a course of injections is an alternative treatment, which stops them reacting to the pollen in the first place. However, this is not effective in everyone and can cause dangerous side effects.

See also COMMON COLD.

Hay fever caused by an allergy to pollen is usually seasonal, but the symptoms occur all year if the sufferer is allergic to house dust, moulds or pets.

RINGWORM

Most commonly contracted in childhood, ringworm has nothing to do with worms, but is a fungal infection which attacks the scalp, feet (athlete's foot) and groin. It is so named

Useful Addresses

RHEUMATOID ARTHRITIS

The Arthritis and Rheumatism Council
41 Eagle Street
LONDON WC1R 4AR
071 405 8572

ASK THE DOCTOR

RUBELLA

Q Can I get rubella a second time?

A No, an infection of rubella itself gives immunity. Once contracted, rubella rarely strikes again. A second attack casts doubt on the first diagnosis.

Q If I contract rubella while I am pregnant, is damage to my child inevitable?

A No, but if you suspect you have been in contact with a rubella sufferer or you show signs of having the infection yourself, you should see your doctor immediately. You will be offered an immunoglobulin injection which should prevent you passing on any infection to the foetus.

Useful Addresses

RUBELLA

Child 2000
(formerly The National Rubella Council)
311 Gray's Inn Road
LONDON WC1X 8PT
071 837 0623

SENSE
The National Deaf/Blind and Rubella Association
311 Gray's Inn Road
LONDON WC1X 8PT
071 278 1000

because sometimes – but by no means always – the eruptions on the surface of the skin, usually the scalp, resulting from infection form a circle.

CAUSES: Ringworm is contagious and is passed on via physical contact from one person to another and by contact with objects which have come into contact with the affected area of the sufferer's body. The fungus fastens on to dead skin tissue then embeds itself into the living tissue beneath.

SYMPTOMS AND SIGNS: Ringworm of the scalp develops as red, itchy patches which heal then move outwards in the characteristic ring, leaving behind grey, scaly skin. This spreading causes the hairs to break near the root, leaving circles of stubble. As the infection progresses over the head, a mottled appearance results.

TREATMENT: If the infection is mild, a proprietary anti-fungal cream, which can be bought at any chemist, will be effective. However, it is better to seek medical attention whatever the severity of the infection, as the doctor will also be able to advise on personal hygiene as a preventative measure to further infection. This usually takes the form of scrupulous cleanliness of the hair and body, and not sharing brushes, combs and hats, even with other members of the family.

In severe cases, or where the cream proves ineffective, an antifungal drug, such as terbinafine, may be prescribed to be taken by mouth.

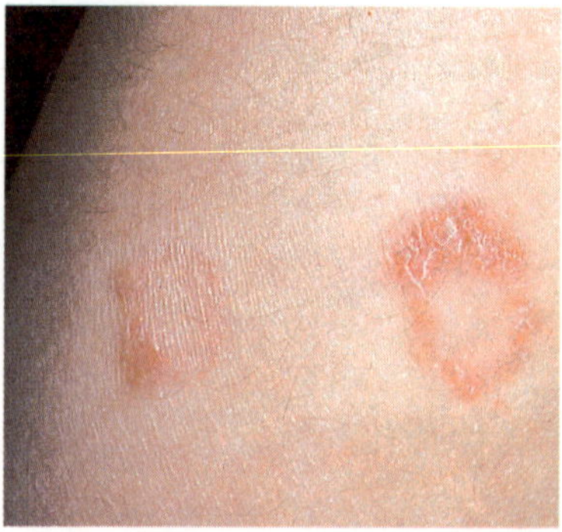

Ringworm is the common name for certain types of fungal skin infections that can form characteristic rings, leaving the skin in the centre unaffected.

See also ATHLETE'S FOOT.

ROUNDWORM

Cylindrical-shaped worms, or nematodes, which inhabit human and animal intestines. Roundworm is dangerous in small children if left untreated. Contact with infected dog faeces may lead to toxocariasis, a roundworm infection, which can affect the sight.

CAUSES: Worms are contracted through poor hygiene (not washing hands after a visit to the lavatory), contact with animal excrement or consumption of contaminated food.

SYMPTOMS AND SIGNS: Usually there are no symptoms unless the worms are visible in faeces.

TREATMENT: Most infestations can be cured with anthelmintic drugs, which paralyse or kill the worms, thus preventing them gripping the intestine walls and allowing them to pass out with the bowel movement.

RUBELLA

This is often called German Measles, although it bears little resemblance to the measles virus. Rubella usually affects children between the ages of six and 12. Adults can also be infected and the symptoms are more marked, but not serious, unless the sufferer is a pregnant woman, in which case the health of her unborn child is threatened. The earlier the stage of pregnancy, the greater the damage the virus can cause to the foetus – most commonly deafness, heart disease, mental handicap, eye disorders and cerebral palsy. The risk is greatest during the first four months of foetal development. After six months, the foetus is fully formed and the risk of damage diminishes. Of those children who are affected by the virus before birth, about 20 per cent die in infancy.

Rubella infection can be prevented by early vaccination. Formerly given to girls at the age of 12 or around the onset of puberty, immunisation is now offered to all babies via a triple injection for mumps, measles and rubella (MMR) at around 15 months. Should a woman be contemplating pregnancy, she should have her rubella status established and be immunised if necessary.

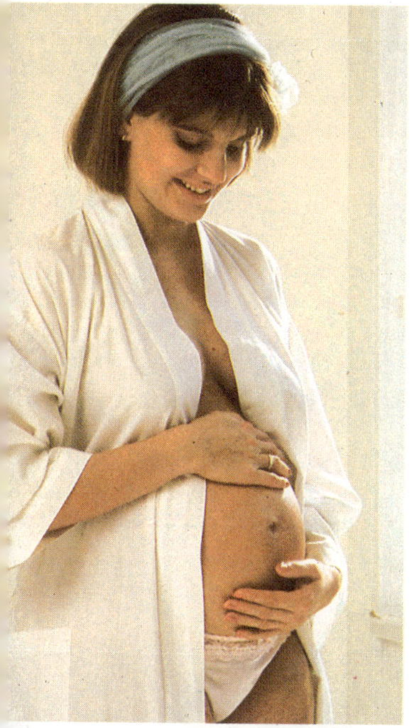

The rubella vaccination provides effective immunity against the illness, reducing the risk of infection during pregnancy.

CAUSES: The rubella virus lodges in the nasal passages of the sufferer and is passed on to others by the inhalation of tiny airborne droplets. A pregnant woman passes on the infection to the foetus through the bloodstream via the placenta.

SYMPTOMS AND SIGNS: The virus takes two to three weeks to incubate. Meanwhile, the sufferer is infectious, although there are no visible signs. The first symptoms are a runny nose and sometimes inflamed eyes, then the appearance of a rash of fine pink dots on the face and neck which spreads over the body, arms and legs. Swelling of the lymph glands at the back of the neck and, less commonly, in the armpits and the groin follows together with a mild rise in temperature, which is rarely more than 38°C (100°F). The symptoms of illness last about four or five days.

TREATMENT: Viral infections do not respond to any known drug. Paracetamol may be given to help bring down the temperature, otherwise the patient should be kept as comfortable as possible. A child need not be confined to bed unless s/he is feeling particularly unwell. Isolation is not necessary as the infectious period will have occurred before symptoms developed.

S

SALMONELLA

Salmonella is the most common form of food poisoning. It is caused by a bacteria that can infect meat, poultry and eggs.

CAUSES: Salmonella food poisoning is caused by the salmonella bacteria, which readily infects cattle and poultry. The animals rarely suffer symptoms and so the disease remains undiagnosed on the farm. Unfortunately, contaminated meat is usually indistinguishable from uninfected meat.

SYMPTOMS AND SIGNS: Diarrhoea, vomiting and sometimes headaches and stomach pains. The symptoms vary according to the severity of the poisoning and usually pass after two or three days.

TREATMENT: If you suspect you are suffering from food poisoning, see your doctor. Samples of faeces and vomit, as well as any suspect food left behind may be sent to the laboratory for confirmation, and to help identify the source. Many people treat themselves by resting for a day or two and drinking plenty of liquids to replace the fluids lost through the diarrhoea or sickness. It is advisable to stay off solid foods for a day or two.

However, if the symptoms are severe or last more than three days, or if young babies or elderly people are infected, a doctor should always be consulted.

ASK THE DOCTOR
SALMONELLA

Q How do the salmonella bacteria actually infect eggs?

A The bacteria originate in the hen's or duck's ovaries or may occur as a result of faecal contamination via the egg shell.

Self **Help**
SALMONELLA

- The bacteria will be killed at a temperature of about 60°C so always cook or reheat meat thoroughly.
- Freezing does not kill the bacteria, it merely prevents them breeding. Make sure that all frozen meat is properly defrosted, then cook it thoroughly.
- Never let raw foods come into contact with cooked meats.
- Salmonella can also be carried in eggs. Cook all eggs thoroughly and avoid foods that use uncooked eggs, such as home-made mayonnaise.
- Wash your hands after using the lavatory and always before handling food.

SALPINGITIS

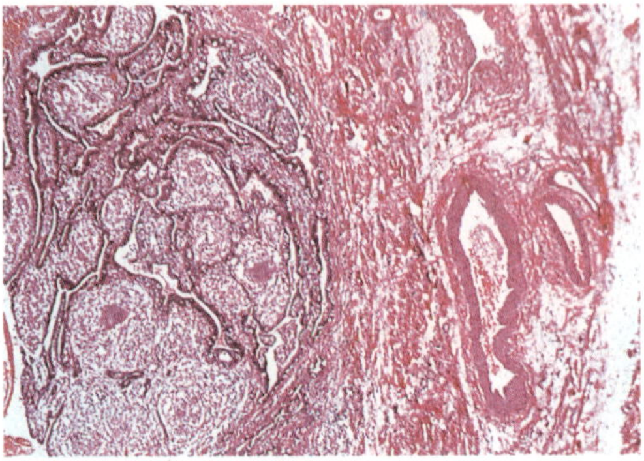

Tuberculous salpingitis, which affects the fallopian tubes, can lead to an ectopic pregnancy.

This is an inflammation of a fallopian tube.

CAUSE: The inflammation is usually caused by an infection, which is often sexually transmitted, the most common being chlamydia. Salpingitis may also occur after a miscarriage, abortion or childbirth. Gonorrhoea, peritonitis and tuberculosis are less common causes.

SYMPTOMS AND SIGNS: The abdomen will feel very sore and tender to touch and there may be an unpleasant vaginal discharge.

TREATMENT: Treatment usually includes painkillers and antibiotics to deal with the infection. If the infection doesn't clear up quickly, the damaged tube may need to be removed.

SCABIES

This is a skin infestation caused by a mite. It is most common in young adults and children.

CAUSE: It is highly contagious in close quarters. Scabies occurs when the female itch mite, a disc-shaped creature, burrows into your skin and lays her eggs. After a few weeks, you may develop an allergy to the mites and your skin will be intensely itchy.

SYMPTOMS AND SIGNS: This itching is the main symptom of scabies and it becomes much worse at night. The burrows made by the itch mites are usually between the fingers, on the front of the wrists, on the genitals, or in the armpit or groin. These little tunnels are often difficult to find, though you may see small raised pimples and patches of crusty skin at the point of entrance. If several members of a family develop an itchy skin rash one after the other the cause may well be scabies, but as skin rashes can be due to many other causes you should visit a doctor to find out what's wrong.

TREATMENT: There are several insecticides that can destroy the itch mite; they are available as creams or lotions. All members of the family must be examined carefully and treated at the same time. After a hot bath, the ointment or cream has to be rubbed well into the skin over the whole body from the neck downwards. This is then left in place for 24 hours before being washed off. After treatment, freshly washed clothes and bedclothes should be used. Normal washing and ironing should kill off any mites that are left in clothes and bedding.

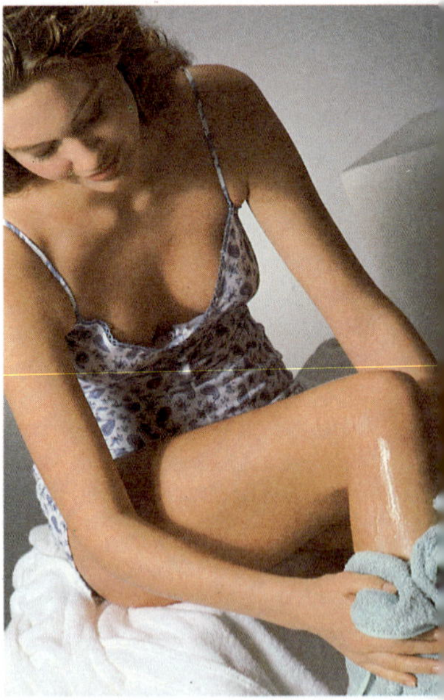

To treat scabies, lotion containing insecticide should be rubbed into the skin after a bath.

ASK THE DOCTOR

SCABIES

Q Two of my children have got scabies. I was advised that the whole family should be treated, but none of them shows any symptoms. Do I need to bother?

A The rash itself may not develop for over a week after the mite infection, so it would be advisable to treat the whole family and any of your children's friends who have been in close contact with them. This may seem like an inconvenience, but it should help prevent anyone from re-infecting your children once they are cured.

SCARLET FEVER

Scarlet fever is an infectious bacterial disease, which is more common in childhood. It is also known by the name of scarlatina.

CAUSES: Scarlet fever is caused by a strain of streptococcus bacteria. It is spread in droplets coughed or breathed into the air by an infected person. The infectious stage lasts for about 10 days.

SYMPTOMS AND SIGNS: The symptoms usually appear two to four days after contact with the bacterium. The first signs are a sore throat with fever and headache. There may also be vomiting.

Two days later, a rash of tiny red spots appears on the neck and chest. This soon spreads over the whole body except for the face. At this stage, the face is typically flushed, with a white ring around the mouth.

The tongue is often coated white with tiny red spots – known as a strawberry tongue. This coating will peel off in a couple of days, leaving the tongue a bright red colour.

The rash usually lasts four to five days When it fades, the skin starts to peel.

TREATMENT: If you suspect scarlet fever, call the doctor who will usually prescribe antibiotics. Although antibiotics won't alter the course of the disease, they will help to ward off dangerous complications. Common complications of scarlet fever include rheumatic fever and inflammation of the kidneys and middle ear.

The patient should be kept in bed and given plenty to drink. Paracetamol will relieve the headache and help control fever.

If the temperature goes above 39.4°C (103°F), strip the patient and sponge down the body with tepid water.

To prevent the infection spreading further, keep the patient in quarantine for 10 days. Inform close contacts and, in the case of a child, the school.

SCHIZOPHRENIA

The word schizophrenia actually means 'split mind', but it does not indicate a dual personality. It is the overall term for a mental illness in which the sufferer is severely disturbed in his/her thinking and behaviour. Symptoms usually appear between the ages of 18 and 30 and affect men and women equally.

CAUSES: No one is sure what causes schizophrenia, but chemical disorders of the brain and inheritance are thought to be major factors.

Stress can cause and aggravate symptoms.

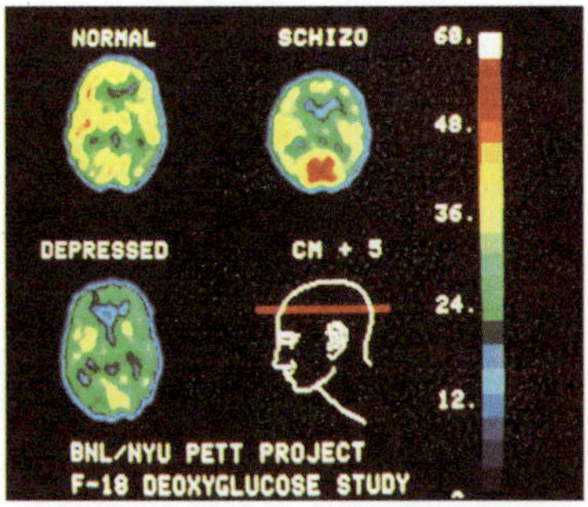

People aged 15-30, who live in inner city areas, are more likely to suffer from schizophrenia than others.

SYMPTOMS AND SIGNS: When it is stress-related, schizophrenia can start suddenly. Otherwise it usually develops slowly over months or even years. Typically, sufferers gradually become more and more withdrawn and less in touch with reality, often having hallucinations, 'hearing voices', and referring to themselves as 'he' or 'she'.

With paranoid schizophrenia, sufferers feel everyone is getting at them or listening to their thoughts, or they can become intensely jealous. With catatonic schizophrenia – a rare illness – they may have bouts of constantly repeating the same movement, or of adopting a rigid posture for long periods.

Nearly all schizophrenics have trouble concentrating, and their thought processes become jumbled up. This means they often make no sense when talking, but they themselves think they are completely lucid. It is impossible to make any emotional impact on them: their reactions are often utterly irrational, such as laughing insanely when being told something very sad.

ASK THE DOCTOR

SCARLET FEVER

Q My son has already had scarlet fever. Now his best friend has gone down with it. Can my son get it again?

A Yes he can, but he probably won't. People have been known to get scarlet fever more than once, but this is unusual.

ASK THE DOCTOR

SCHIZOPHRENIA

Q Is it possible to care for a schizophrenic at home?

A It depends on how badly s/he affects other members of the family. Although a sufferer should always be referred for medical help in the first instance, s/he may well be able to live at home once the symptoms are controlled. However, schizophrenics can be very difficult to live with, though not dangerous, and relatives may need guidance as to how to cope. It is, for example, no use trying to persuade a schizophrenic that his/her hallucinations are not real, since this will only cause further upset. It is important to make sure s/he takes any medication regularly to try to avoid a relapse.

Useful Addresses

SCHIZOPHRENIA

MIND (National Association for Mental Health)
22 Harley Street
LONDON WIN 2ED
071 637 0741

The National Schizophrenia Fellowship
28 Castle Street
KINGSTON UPON THAMES
Surrey KTI 1SS
081 547 3937

SANE (Schizophrenia and National Emergency)
5th Floor
120 Regent Street
LONDON WIR 5FE
071 494 4840

TREATMENT: Anyone who has symptoms that point to schizophrenia should be taken to a doctor. Most sufferers are treated with drugs, sometimes in hospital to start with, until major symptoms are controlled; afterwards they might benefit from psychotherapy.

Some people recover completely; others may have relapses or just become tolerably 'eccentric'. A few suffer permanent mental damage and have to be kept in hospital permanently, but there is a growing school of thought that the more often patients are returned to the community, the higher their chance of recovery.

See also MANIC DEPRESSION.

SCIATICA

Sciatica – one of the most common accompaniments to back trouble – is a severe pain that shoots along the sciatic nerve, affecting all or part of the buttock, thigh, calf and foot area.

CAUSES: Pressure on a spinal root of the sciatic nerve, often caused by a slipped disc or facet joint injury/displacement. It can be brought on by lifting something heavy, by sitting awkwardly or by straightening up after bending. Any condition that results in pressure on the sciatic nerve, such as a tumour, abscess, blood clot or spasm in a nearby muscle, may cause this type of pain.

Sciatica usually affects the buttock and thigh, but it can also be felt in the foot.

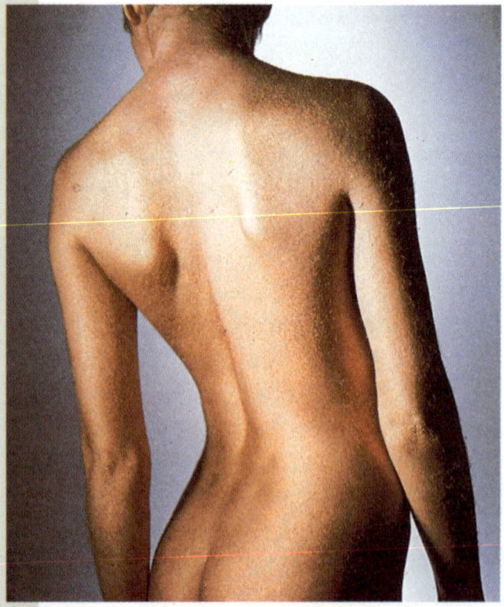

SYMPTOMS AND SIGNS: You will suffer mild or intense pain in the buttock, thigh, calf or foot, or in all of these areas. If the pressure on the nerve is severe, you may also find the areas feel numb and/or weak. The numbness, however, is not always accompanied by back pain and this can lead to sciatica being mistaken for a pulled muscle.

If you experience numbness, pins and needles and loss of bladder control along with sciatica, the nerve pressure could be bad enough to cause permanent damage and it is therefore very important that you see a doctor immediately.

TREATMENT: The best remedy is bed rest and painkillers. The pain should ease and finally disappear in a few days, but it could go on for a few weeks.

ASK THE DOCTOR

SCIATICA

Q Once I've had sciatica, can I get it again?

A Yes, unfortunately you can: it is a condition that often recurs.

SEBACEOUS CYST

This is a large, smooth nodule under the skin. It may also be called a wen.

CAUSES: When sebum cannot escape from a sebaceous gland because it is blocked, the gland swells and is filled with trapped material. This then becomes a cyst.

SYMPTOMS AND SIGNS: The cyst may grow very large (sometimes as big as a tennis ball) and, if it becomes infected, it may be quite painful. Cysts are usually located around the neck, face, genitals and scalp.

TREATMENT: Infected or large cysts can easily be removed surgically under local anaesthetic.

SENILE DEMENTIA

see ALZHEIMER'S DISEASE

SEPTICAEMIA

Septicaemia, commonly known as blood poisoning, occurs when bacterial toxins get into

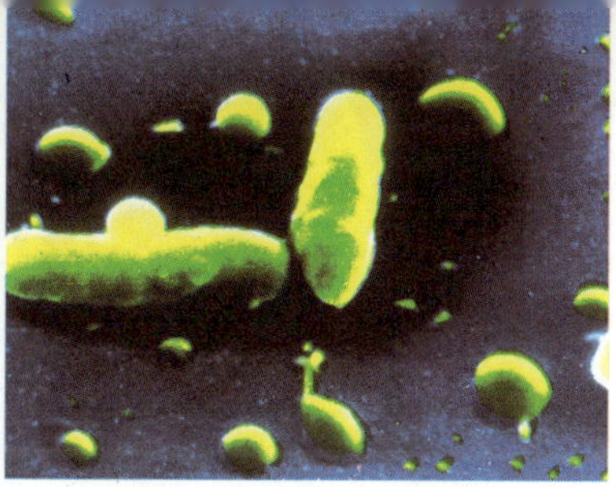

When bacteria escape from an infected part of the body, they can spread, resulting in septicaemia.

the blood and multiply. It can be a very serious condition.

CAUSES: If you are suffering from any infection, such as pneumonia, meningitis, a urinary tract infection or an abscess, the bacteria in your body may escape into your blood system. When these bacteria start to multiply in large numbers within the bloodstream, this is called septicaemia. This is far more likely to happen if your body's immune system is not working as efficiently as it should. Drug addicts are particularly prone to septicaemia if they use dirty needles.

SYMPTOMS AND SIGNS: You will usually have a high temperature, a headache and feel confused. In extreme cases, if there are a lot of bacteria in your blood, you may suffer from septic shock, which causes a dramatic fall in blood pressure. This can be dangerous.

TREATMENT: Treatment should begin as soon as possible. You will almost certainly be admitted to hospital, where you will be attached to a drip to replenish body fluids lost with extra sweating. You will also be given antibiotics. The source of the original infection must be identified and your doctor may decide to remove any infected material surgically. Although this can be a life-threatening complaint, if it is caught early enough you will usually make a full recovery.

SEXUALLY TRANSMITTED DISEASES

see AIDS, THRUSH, CHLAMYDIA, GENITAL HERPES, GENITAL WARTS, GONORRHOEA, NSU, SYPHILIS, TRICHOMONIASIS

SHINGLES

Shingles – medical name herpes zoster – is a virus that affects the nerves supplying certain areas of skin. The disease causes a great deal of pain and a rash along the path of the nerve.

CAUSES: The chickenpox virus causes shingles. After a bout of chickenpox, the virus can lie dormant for many years in nerve endings. It is activated by physical or emotional stress, usually after the age of 50 when the immune mechanism begins to get less efficient.

SYMPTOMS AND SIGNS: The first sign of shingles is extremely sensitive areas of skin followed by knife-like pain. Then itchy blisters appear on the skin over the affected nerves. These become yellow and crusty. When the crusts fall off, they leave scars similar to those of chickenpox. The rash of blisters usually lasts about a week, but the pain may persist for months or even years. The virus can affect almost any part of the body but usually develops on one side of the trunk over the ribs, or one side of the neck and arm, or the face. If it is on the face you may experience temporary paralysis of the face muscles. If the virus reaches the eyes, it can cause corneal damage.

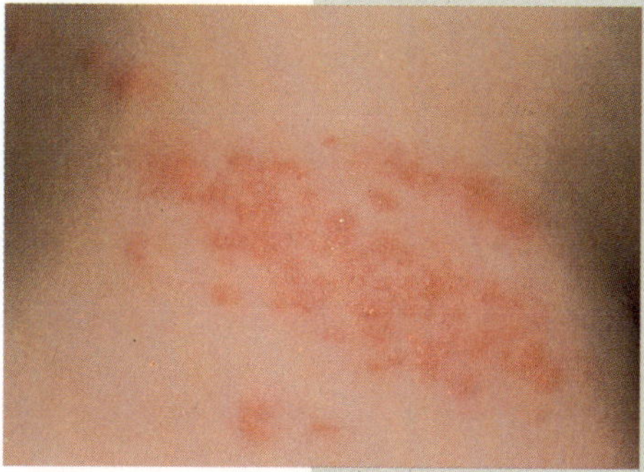

Every year in Britain, one person in 350 suffers an attack of shingles, or herpes zoster.

TREATMENT: See your doctor immediately you suspect you have shingles, especially if your face is affected, because damage to the eyes is potentially serious. Anti-viral drugs can limit the damage to the nerves, but once shingles has set in, it is difficult to treat – which is why it's important to see your doctor as soon as you can. Painkillers may give some relief from the pain, but if it is severe and long lasting it is sometimes treated with injections of local anaesthetics or, in extreme cases, surgery to cut out the affected nerves.

See also CHICKENPOX.

ASK THE DOCTOR

SHINGLES

Q If I have had shingles, can it recur?

A It is unlikely that you will suffer from shingles again as the first attack usually brings immunity from further outbreaks.

ASK THE DOCTOR

SHOCK

Q My aunt fainted when she heard that her husband had been killed. Was this shock?

A No, not clinical shock. What your aunt suffered was emotional shock, the symptoms of which are very similar, although less severe, and fortunately short-lived. Doctors refer to shock as a physical condition due to lack of blood to the vital organs.

Q Can people die of shock?

A Yes, if the heart or brain are deprived of oxygen for more than a few minutes, this can be fatal. However, if you mean emotional shock, it is unlikely to cause any long-lasting effects, unless the person already suffers from another serious condition, such as heart disease.

People who are involved in road traffic accidents are likely to suffer from shock.

SHOCK

Shock is caused by a reduced circulation of blood to the body's vital organs, usually due to severe bleeding, heart attack, animal bite or serious burn. In every case, the body's reaction is to narrow the blood vessels to try to maintain the pressure of blood to the brain and other vital organs. If the blood or fluid loss is severe, the vessels may not be able to constrict enough to maintain blood pressure, so not enough blood and oxygen reach the vital organs. A severe emotional shock can bring on the same symptoms, but this is not the same as clinical shock, and the symptoms will clear very rapidly if the person sits down quietly and puts his/her head between the legs.

CAUSES: Any serious accident or illness can lead to shock. Severe loss of fluid caused by burns, vomiting or diarrhoea can also lead to shock. Internal bleeding can also result in shock.

SYMPTOMS AND SIGNS: The usual symptoms are rapid, shallow breathing, with pale, clammy cold skin and a rapid, weak pulse. Vision may also be blurred and there may be nausea or vomiting, or the sufferer may complain of thirst. The person may also seem unnaturally quiet and react slowly. Speech may be slurred, and the sufferer may seem restless, and yawn or sigh repeatedly. Unconsciousness may follow.

TREATMENT: Shock is serious and needs urgent treatment. Call your doctor as soon as you can, but do not leave the patient unattended.

Reassure and comfort the sufferer. Do not try to move him/her, but administer treatment on the spot and deal with any obvious injury, such as burns or bleeding, first. If the sufferer has any broken bones, try to immobilise him/her. Keep the person warm, but do not give a hot-water bottle or move him/her close to a fire as this will increase flow of blood to the skin, away from the vital organs. Cover the person with a blanket. Make sure that clothes are not restricting breathing, so loosen any tight garments. If the sufferer is thirsty, moisten the lips with water, but do not offer a drink, as this may delay any medical treatment. If the person becomes unconscious, put him/her into the recovery position. If s/he stops breathing and the heart stops, administer cardio-pulmonary resuscitation (chest compression). The sufferer should be taken to hospital by ambulance.

SHORT SIGHT

see MYOPIA

SINUSITIS

This is literally inflammation and swelling of the mucous membrane lining the sinuses, the bone cavities leading from the nose.

CAUSES: The sinuses usually contain nothing but air, but if there is a great deal of catarrh in the nose, the holes connecting the sinuses to it can get blocked and filled with mucus, which may then become infected. This condition is called sinusitis.

Some people are more prone to sinusitis than others. This is often because they tend to get a lot of catarrh – perhaps because of a nasal allergy – or it may be that the holes draining the sinuses are smaller than usual and so more liable to get blocked. Chronic rhinitis or a cold may also bring on sinusitis.

SYMPTOMS AND SIGNS: Characteristic symptoms are constant pain over the infected sinus, either in a cheekbone or in the forehead, or sometimes both if more than one sinus is infected. Your face will feel full and heavy, and the pain is usually worse when you bend forward. In the area over the infected sinus, the face is very tender to touch, but not usually swollen. Your nose is usually – but not always – full of catarrh, and if the sinus has started to drain, the patient

An inhalation may help to moisten the nasal secretions caused by sinusitis.

may notice thick yellow or green catarrh emerging from the nostril on the same side as the infection.

Treatment: Nasal decongestant sprays may be useful, but if the symptoms persist, you should see your doctor who may prescribe decongestants in tablet form. If the sinuses are badly infected, antibiotics should help to clear this up, but they can't clear the mucus out of the sinuses.

Sometimes the sinus infection is very severe or persistent or it recurs fairly frequently in spite of treatment with antibiotics and decongestants. In these cases, your doctor may recommend that you have the infected material drained away under local anaesthetic. Occasionally, the entire lining of a sinus may be removed surgically to prevent recurrent infections. The lining replaces itself in time, and the new lining doesn't produce mucus so readily.

See also COMMON COLD, RHINITIS.

SKIN CANCER

Skin cancer is one of the most common forms of cancer. There are three main forms of skin tumour: malignant melanoma, rodent ulcer (basal cell carcinoma), and squamous cell carcinoma.

Causes: The main cause of skin cancer is excessive exposure to sunlight. Fair-skinned people are most at risk. The incidence of squamous cell carcinoma is higher in people who work with certain chemicals such as coal, paraffin and arsenic.

Symptoms and signs: Squamous cell carcinoma: This starts as a firm, painless lump, which gradually enlarges into a growth resembling a wart or ulcer. The most common sites are the back of the hands, the lips and the ears.

Rodent ulcer: Another name for this type of skin tumour is basal cell carcinoma. This starts as a small pearl-like, waxy pimple, which grows gradually into a button-like tumour – or sometimes into a globular mass. Ulcers form on the growth. This scabs over and breaks down again. The most common sites are the face, neck and nose.

Malignant melanoma: This form of cancer involves abnormal growth in the pigment containing cells of the skin. The site is often an existing mole, which becomes malignant. Signs to look out for are: a new pigmented growth and moles that change colour or grow larger. The area may bleed, develop a black edge, scab over or itch. Malignant melanomas can develop anywhere on the body, including the eyes and under the nails.

Treatment: The sooner the skin cancer is treated, the better the chances of a cure. Treatment may be by surgery, radiotherapy, cryosurgery or anti-cancer drugs. After treatment, skin grafts may be needed to cover unsightly scars.

One of the most common forms of cancer – of the skin – is indicated here by excess melanin (red).

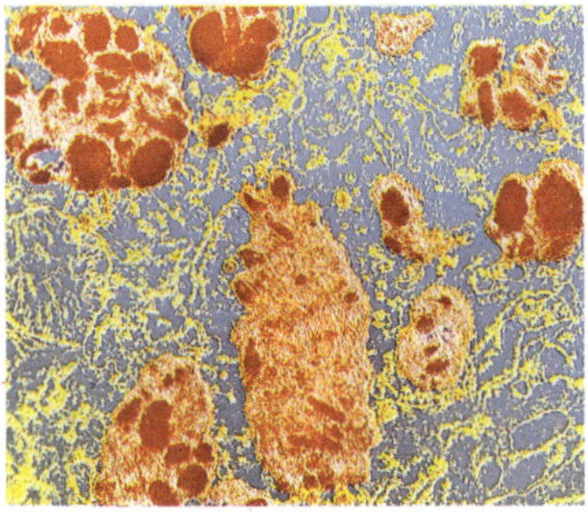

Self Help

SINUSITIS

If the symptoms are mild, steam inhalations may help to drain your sinuses. Use a bowl of boiling water with some menthol or another proprietary inhalant in it, and put a towel over your head. Breathe in the steam – this will thin the mucus in the nose and encourage the sinuses to drain.

Self Help

SKIN CANCER

All signs point to the sun as the most likely cause of skin cancer, so it makes sense to avoid excess exposure to the sun, to protect your head with a hat and to use a good sun screening cream that filters out harmful rays.

If you notice a growth on the skin, however small, or see changes in a mole, have it checked by a doctor.

Self Help
SLIPPED DISC

- Rest on a flat, firm bed. If your bed is rather saggy, place a thin foam mattress on the floor.
- Relieve the pain slightly with a heat lamp or hot-water bottle.
- Take painkillers in recommended doses.

SLIPPED DISC

A slipped disc – more correctly called a prolapsed disc – can cause severe pain. One or more discs in the spine may rupture and the soft central material protrudes out to press on a nerve.

CAUSES: Each vertebra in the spine is cushioned from the next by a disc, which consists of a fibrous outer layer inside which is a jelly-like substance. Parts of the jelly-like centre can be squeezed out of place if the outer layer is damaged, either through degeneration of the spine (usually through the ageing process) or by straining the back in some way, often through lifting heavy loads. Some of the soft centre is pushed through the fibrous outer layer and presses on a nerve, which is extremely painful. Most cases occur in the lower back, although this injury can occur in the neck.

SYMPTOMS AND SIGNS: A prolapsed disc can cause severe shooting pains in the lower back or legs, or in the shoulder and upper arm. It often develops after an awkward movement, or lifting something heavy, although it may sometimes occur after a seemingly trivial movement such as turning over in bed. It can cause sciatica in one of the legs. The acute pain is sometimes accompanied by numbness or a tingling sensation in the arms or the legs, rather like pins and needles. In some cases, the numbness can be permanent or muscle, bladder or bowel function may be disrupted.

TREATMENT: Bed rest, in which you lie flat on a firm mattress for at least a few days, is usually the first treatment. You will probably be given painkillers and muscle relaxants, too. This may then be followed by a course of special exercises. If bed rest is not successful, surgery may be needed to treat a prolapsed disc but an injection of an enzyme made from the papaya fruit is gaining popularity among orthopaedic surgeons. The process known as chemonucleolysis uses this enzyme to break down the protruding jelly-like substance of the disc.

A false-colour image of a slipped disc, causing intense pain and loss of nerve function.

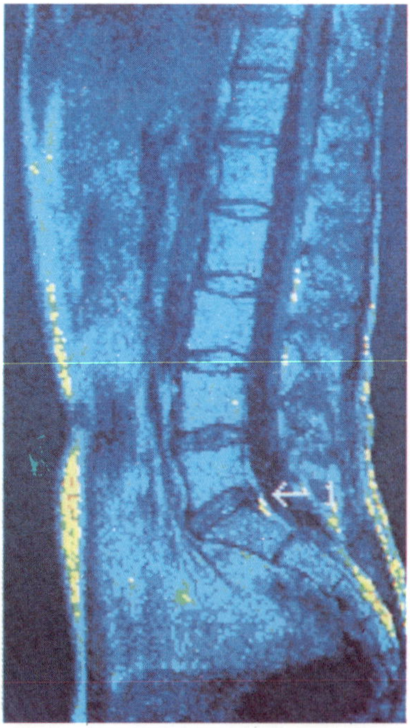

WARNING

If your pain is accompanied by numbness, pins and needles, weakness or loss of bladder or bowel control, you must see a doctor immediately. These are warning signs of pressure on a spinal nerve which, if left untreated, could cause permanent damage.

SORE THROAT

Usually harmless, sore throats are an extremely common symptom of several illnesses.

CAUSES: A sore throat may be the first sign of flu, a cold, pharyngitis, laryngitis or tonsillitis, as well as several common childhood illnesses, such as chickenpox, measles and mumps.

SYMPTOMS AND SIGNS: If you are suffering from a sore throat, it will feel rough and

Self Help
SORE THROAT

Before reaching for the aspirin bottle, you could try gargling with salt water to relieve the symptoms.

painful, especially when you swallow.

TREATMENT: Adults may take aspirin or paracetamol to relieve the symptoms. Children should only be given paracetamol. If your throat is still sore after a couple of days, and especially if it is accompanied by a rash, you should consult your doctor. If the cause is bacterial, s/he may prescribe antibiotics.

See also FLU, COMMON COLD, LARYNGITIS, PHARYNGITIS, TONSILLITIS, CHICKENPOX, GERMAN MEASLES, MUMPS.

SPASTIC COLON

see IRRITABLE BOWEL SYNDROME

SPINA BIFIDA

This is a congenital disorder in which one or more of the vertebrae fails to develop properly, leaving the spinal cord exposed and unprotected. It is most common in the lower spine. The severity of the condition depends on the amount of tissue exposed.

CAUSES: The cause of spina bifida is unknown, but it does have a higher incidence among those born to very young or relatively old mothers. If a woman has already had one spina bifida child, she is 10 times more likely than average to give birth to another.

SYMPTOMS AND SIGNS: These vary widely according to the severity of the condition. At its least serious, the condition is only noticeable from a small dimple or a tuft of hair on the spine lying over the area of the problem. This may pass unnoticed. At its worst, the child may suffer severe paralysis of the lower limbs and complications that can result in brain damage.

Spinal nerves in the lower back control the muscles in the legs, bladder and bowels so in addition to the paralysis there can be some incontinence. There may be a large reddish-purple membrane covering a gap in the spine, which can easily be damaged and become infected. In some cases, this infection can lead to meningitis. Hydrocephalus ('water on the brain') and bladder infections are the additional risks.

A young girl suffering from spina bifida learns to walk on crutches.

TREATMENT: There is no cure for spina bifida. Any paralysis is usually permanent and surgery is often carried out soon after birth to repair the membrane on the back and prevent infection.

Children with spina bifida should have special care and through physiotherapy, they can learn to gain maximum mobility with the aid of wheelchairs and other walking aids. Antibiotics may be administered to reduce the risk of urinary and other infections and the child must be watched for signs of meningitis and hydrocephalus.

Operations are possible as the child grows older to correct deformities of the legs and aid bladder control, though this is often learned naturally.

SPINAL CORD INJURY

Spinal cord injury is when the spinal cord is compressed, torn or severed.

CAUSES: It is usually caused through an accident, when the spine can be fractured, dislocated or crushed.

Useful Addresses

SPINA BIFIDA

Association of Spina Bifida and Hydrocephalus
42 Park Road
PETERBOROUGH PE1 2UQ
0733 555988

Scottish Spina Bifida Association
190 Queensferry Road
EDINBURGH EH4 2BW
031 332 0743

Useful Addresses

SPONDYLITIS

Back Pain Association
31 Park Road
TEDDINGTON
Middlesex TW11 OAB
081 977 5474/5

Self Help

SPONDYLOSIS

- Take painkillers, such as aspirin or paracetamol.
- Apply heat to the affected area. Use a hot-water bottle wrapped in a towel or an electrically heated pad.
- Rest in bed during severe bouts of pain: lie as flat as possible on your back on a firm mattress, using only one pillow under your head.
- If the pain remains bad for three to four days, consult a doctor.
- Take regular exercise to keep your spine and your abdominal and neck muscles strong. This is essential to provide good support for your back and neck. Ask your doctor or physiotherapist to recommend suitable exercises.

Symptoms and signs: If you experience severe back or neck pain after a fall or a blow to the spine, you may have injured it in a way that puts your spinal cord at risk. The pain may be worse when you move or your limbs may feel weak. The spinal cord carries messages between the brain and the limbs: if it is injured, it may be difficult to control your limbs and movement. There may be numbness or tingling in your limbs, or even paralysis. Loss of bladder or bowel control are other warning signs.

Treatment: If you think that someone may have injured his/her spinal cord, do not move him/her, as you may cause further damage. It isn't always possible to tell whether there is any injury, so call for an ambulance or doctor straight away if you have any doubts. Fractures of the spine can often be successfully treated – sometimes just with bed rest, and more usually by surgery. If nerves in the spinal cord are damaged, however, they cannot be repaired, although the condition may sometimes improve during the first year after injury, as other nerves take over the function of the damaged ones.

SPONDYLITIS

Spondylitis is an inflammation of the joints between the spinal vertebrae. It is generally caused by osteoarthritis or rheumatoid arthritis. Some cases are due to ankylosing spondylitis, in which the inflammation can lead to the fusion of vertebrae that results in a rigid, stooped posture. Very rarely, spondylitis can be caused by a bacterial infection that has spread from somewhere else in the body.

SPONDYLOSIS

Spondylosis, which is a form of osteoarthritis, is the degeneration of the intervertebral discs, which results in the spaces between the vertebrae narrowing and the spine becoming stiff, hard and inflexible.

Causes: Ageing is the most usual cause of spondylosis. It is common in people over 40 when the discs begin to dry out and become thinner.

Symptoms and signs: You may get pain in the affected part of your back. It often occurs in the neck (cervical spondylosis). When the spinal column begins to stiffen, it can result in considerable strain on the surrounding muscles and ligaments, often resulting in further pain. Bony outgrowths sometimes develop on the vertebrae, which can press painfully on the nerves. Spondylosis gives middle aged or elderly people general backache, which seems to worsen during cold weather and after strenuous activity.

Treatment: Try self help at first (see opposite) but if the symptoms persist, see your doctor who may recommend X-rays and specialised treatments including heat treatment, physiotherapy to improve flexibility of the spine, and painkillers.

See also OSTEOARTHRITIS.

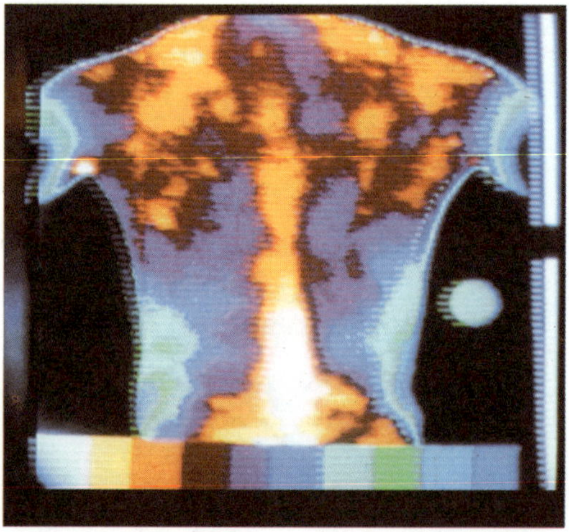

Thermogram of the back of a man suffering from ankylosing spondylitis, which shows an abnormal distribution of temperature (hot = yellow, cold = blue).

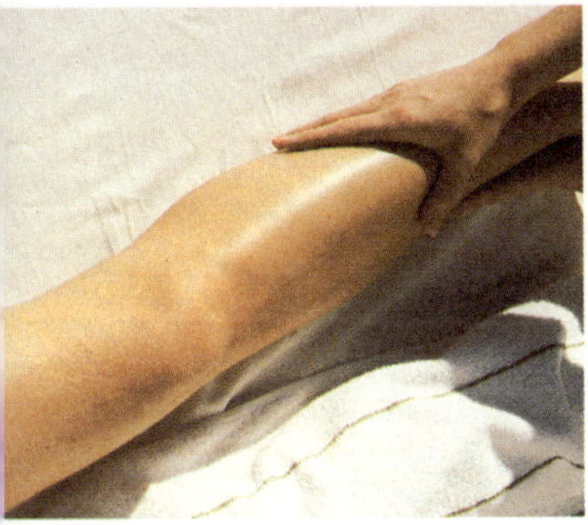

A sprain may be confused with a fracture. If the pain and swelling are still present after three or four days, you should have an X-ray.

SPRAIN

A sprain is a common injury caused by over-stretching a ligament.

CAUSES: A sprain is caused by a sudden or violent pull on the ligaments that support a joint. The most commonly sprained joint is the ankle. Ankle sprains usually occur as a result of a fall, which causes you to turn over on the outside of your foot with your body weight exerted on the ankle and the joint wrenched beyond its normal range.

SYMPTOMS AND SIGNS: Painful swelling, tenderness and bruising. The joint cannot be moved without causing additional pain. There may also be an involuntary contraction (spasm) of the surrounding muscles. If ligaments are badly damaged, the joint may feel unstable.

TREATMENT: Apply a cold compress or an ice-pack to reduce the pain and swelling, and wrap the joint in a bandage. Rest the affected joint in a raised position until the swelling subsides. Exercise the joint gently after 48 hours, but do not put full force through it for several days.

A more serious sprain is often indistinguishable from a fracture, so if the swelling has not gone down within three or four days or it remains very painful, an X-ray may be necessary to ensure that one of the bones is not fractured.

See also FRACTURES.

SQUINT

Squint, or strabismus, is the most common form of eye complaint in children.

CAUSES: Many young babies have a squint where one eye points in a different direction because the mechanism that controls the movement of their eyes has not yet developed. A squint that develops later on is often caused by a breakdown in this mechanism.

Squints also develop when a young child is very long-sighted and attempts to correct this by using his/her near focusing muscles to see near objects more clearly. This may cause the eyes to turn in so that the child appears to be cross-eyed. Sometimes, the eye muscles are not strong enough to hold both eyes in alignment.

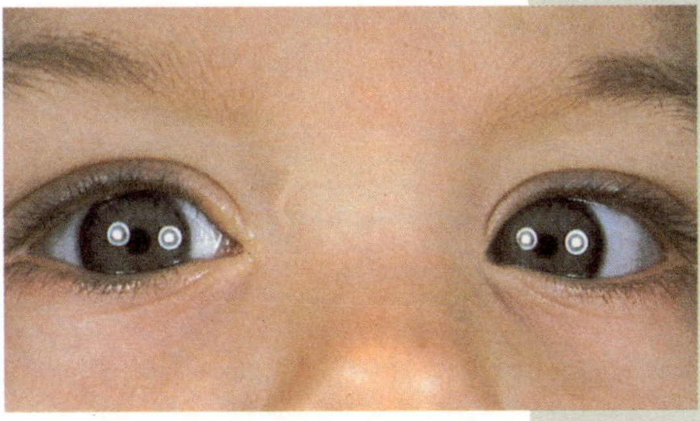

If a squint has not corrected itself by the age of six months, specialist help should be sought as soon as possible to help realign the eyes.

SYMPTOMS AND SIGNS: The child's eyes look in slightly different directions.

TREATMENT: Specialist treatment must be sought immediately if any signs of a squint are evident in children over six months old. If a squint is left unchecked, it may develop into a lazy eye and gradually lose its ability to see. Any treatment – usually corrective exercises or glasses – must be done before the child is seven years old. Occasionally, one of the eyes may have to be covered with a patch for a few hours each day, to encourage the return of normal vision to the lazy eye. A few children need surgery to realign the eyes.

ASK THE DOCTOR

SPRAIN

Q What is the treatment for a severe sprain?

A The damaged joint may be placed in plaster for several weeks. Occasionally, surgery may be required to repair badly torn ligaments.

ASK THE DOCTOR

SQUINT

Q Can an adult develop a squint?

A Yes, but it is very rare and usually has some underlying cause. It may be a disorder of the brain, of the nerves controlling the eyes, or of the eye muscles themselves. It may also be a symptom of some other illness, such as stroke, diabetes or hyperthyroidism.

Self **Help**

STINGS

People who know they are hypersensitive to wasp or bee stings can get an emergency kit for the self-injection of adrenaline: they should carry it around with them always, but especially at vulnerable times, such as during the summer.

ASK THE DOCTOR

STOMACH CANCER

Q Isn't there some way of screening for stomach cancer?

A Yes there is. Early tumours can be spotted by a gastroscopy – the insertion of a narrow viewing tube down the oesophagus into the stomach. There is a mass screening programme in Japan where stomach cancer is a big problem. This has been very successful at catching the tumours before they have spread.
In the UK, anyone with persistent symptoms of a peptic ulcer will be gastroscoped to exclude stomach cancer.

STAMMERING

see STUTTERING

STINGS

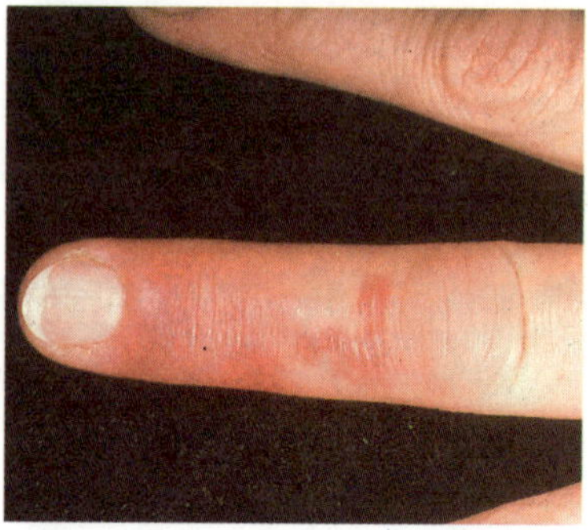

The pain and swelling from a wasp sting will generally subside within about 48 hours.

Most people will suffer from stings at some time in their lives.
CAUSES: The most common types of sting are from wasps and bees.
SYMPTOMS AND SIGNS: Your skin will become red, swollen and painful, but should be back to normal in a couple of days.

Roughly one person in 200 is allergic to insect venom, suffering a bad itchy rash, dizziness, wheezing, vomiting and swelling of the throat and face; sometimes s/he may also have difficulty breathing and may even collapse.
TREATMENT: If a bee has left its sting in your skin, gently scrape it away with a knife blade or your fingernail – don't use tweezers or squeeze the skin with your fingers as this will inject more venom. Afterwards, wash the skin with soap and water and put a wad of cold, damp cotton wool or something similar on it; calamine lotion or an antihistamine cream may relieve itching and you might need to take painkillers.

If you are stung in the mouth or throat, immediately suck some ice cubes if you can and go straight to your doctor or local hospital casualty department, as in severe cases swelling can dangerously obstruct breathing.

If anyone suffers the symptoms of an allergic reaction, it is essential that s/he gets medical treatment urgently: the initial treatment is an injection of adrenaline; later, a technique called hyposensitisation which reduces sensitivity to bee or wasp venom may also be recommended. In very severe cases of allergic reaction, resuscitation could be necessary.

STITCH

A stitch often happens after you've been running a lot, especially if you are tense, or if you've suddenly started taking exercise you're not used to. A stitch is also more likely if you exercise within one hour of eating.
CAUSES: The exact cause is unknown. It may be due to a spasm in the diaphragm muscle.

A stitch is particularly common while running. Reduce pain by bending forwards and taking a few deep breaths.

Cancer of the stomach causes around 13,000 deaths each year in the UK.

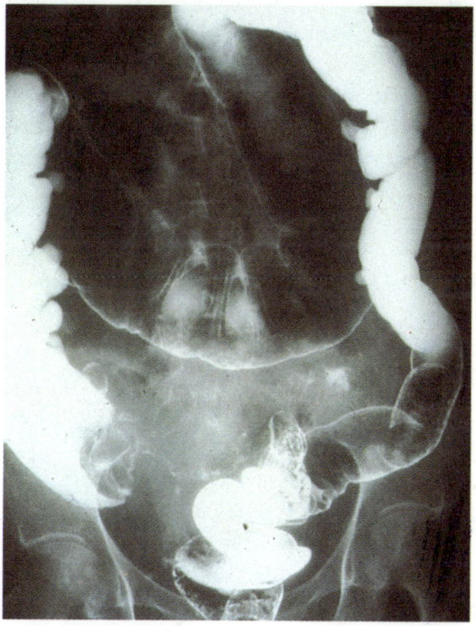

SYMPTOMS AND SIGNS: A sharp pain in the side.

TREATMENT: A stitch usually eases off in a few minutes once you stop still. If you keep running, the pain may be reduced by taking a few deep breaths and bending forward, or leaning away from the side that hurts.

STOMACH CANCER

Stomach cancer is a malignant tumour in the stomach lining. This form of cancer has decreased dramatically over the last 50 years.

CAUSES: People who are most likely to get stomach cancer are typically over the age of 40, male with blood group A and smokers. People with pernicious anaemia or a history of gastric ulcers are also more susceptible.

The incidence of stomach cancer varies greatly over the world, which suggests that diet may be a factor in its development. For example, people living in Japan are four times more likely to develop this disease than people living in the UK.

SYMPTOMS AND SIGNS: Often none in the early stages, or there may be vague symptoms of indigestion. Later on, there may be swelling and pain in the upper abdomen, appetite and weight loss, anaemia, nausea, vomiting and bleeding from the stomach, which can cause blood in vomit, and black, tarry faeces.

TREATMENT: Surgery is the usual treatment if the tumour is caught in the early stages before it has spread beyond the stomach lining. This involves the removal of the stomach – known as a gastrectomy. Where surgery is not possible because the tumour has spread, anti-cancer drugs may prolong life.

STRAIN

A strain occurs when a muscle or tendon has been pulled too far.

CAUSES: If a muscle or tendon is violently stretched during exercise, its fibres may be torn.

SYMPTOMS AND SIGNS: A pulled muscle or tendon will be painful, swollen and tender. Bleeding in the damaged area may cause a bruise to appear over the next few days.

TREATMENT: Apply an ice pack to reduce pain and swelling. Rest the injured part for at

ASK THE DOCTOR

STRAIN

Q I do a lot of strenuous sport. How can I avoid pulling a muscle or tendon?

A The risk of strain can be reduced by doing warm-up exercises before beginning any sporting activity. These increase the natural elasticity of soft tissues. You should also do cooling-down exercises after any sport.

A pulled muscle or tendon is a common complaint among athletes, especially after violent or strenuous exercise.

Self **Help**

STROKE

To guard against a stroke:

- Stop smoking.
- Reduce the amount of fat in your diet.
- Take regular exercise.
- Have your blood pressure checked regularly.

ASK THE DOCTOR

STUTTERING

Q When I listen to my friend stuttering, I often supply the word I think she's trying to say, but someone told me this is just rude. Who's right?

A Well, it's not exactly rude to 'speak' for your friend, but it could be aggravating her condition by making her feel even more frustrated. Best, perhaps, to ask her how she feels.

Useful Addresses

STUTTERING

Association for Stammerers
St Margaret's House
21 Old Ford Road
LONDON E2 9PL
081 983 1003

Association for Research into Stammering in Childhood
10 Fallowfield
STANMORE
Middlesex HA7 3DF
081 954 5377

least 48 hours. If the strain is in one of the limbs, keep it elevated.

Bandaging or strapping the injury will give it support. However, do not bandage the limb too tightly or the swelling may obstruct the circulation.

STROKE

Stroke is damage to the brain, due to a breakdown of normal blood supply. Strokes are uncommon in people under 60.

CAUSES: Strokes usually occur when the blood supply to the brain is impaired, by an embolus or thrombosis (types of clot). Another cause is a burst blood vessel in the brain, resulting in internal haemorrhage, which is how approximately 25 per cent of strokes happen. Untreated high blood pressure increases your risk of a stroke.

SYMPTOMS AND SIGNS: The symptoms of a stroke depend on the severity of the damage and the part of the brain that has been affected. If you have a stroke, you may wake up with impaired speech or movement of part of the body. You may also find that one of your limbs is heavy and awkward, or that the whole of one side of the body is useless. Sometimes loss of consciousness occurs, as well as numbness, weakness, confusion and dizziness.

False-colour X-ray of the head, revealing a ruptured aneurysm (red), which is a major cause of stroke.

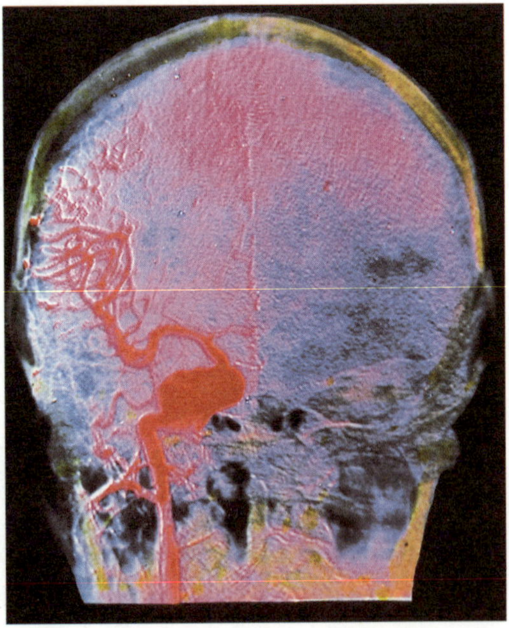

TREATMENT: Your doctor may prescribe a drug, such as aspirin, to help stop your blood clotting unnecessarily, and to disperse clots that have already appeared. Surgery is an option in some cases and almost all sufferers will benefit from physiotherapy. If you smoke, you will be advised to stop immediately and your doctor may prescribe pills to keep your blood pressure down.

STUTTERING

Stuttering, also known as stammering, is a speech disorder more common in twins and people who are left-handed; men are more often affected than women. It generally begins in childhood before the age of eight, and very small children can suffer from temporary stuttering.

SYMPTOMS AND SIGNS: Symptoms include hesitating over words or not being able to speak them properly; repeating words, and prolonging a vowel or consonant for an unusually long time. Some stutterers are worse when anxious, some when they're relaxed; a few also have nervous tics and tremors.

CAUSES: Some people think stuttering is caused by a form of brain damage, others that the cause is psychological. Some children can begin stuttering simply by copying another stutterer for effect and then being unable to stop. The problem often runs in families.

TREATMENT: Speech therapy can usually help.

Stuttering may be helped by singing, especially in the company of other people.

STYE

A stye is a small, painful swelling, which occurs along the upper or lower eyelid.

CAUSES: Styes are caused by an infection in one of the small oil-secreting glands at the base of the eyelashes. Sometimes more than one stye may appear.

SYMPTOMS AND SIGNS: Sore, itchy eyes. A stye will develop a head of whitish pus and looks like a boil.

TREATMENT: Hot compresses help to alleviate the pain and to burst the stye, allowing the pus to be discharged. A clean face cloth soaked in hot water and then wrung out is usually sufficient. Alternatively, use a solution of boric acid, which is available from the chemist, or your doctor may prescribe an antibiotic ointment, especially if the stye keeps on reappearing.

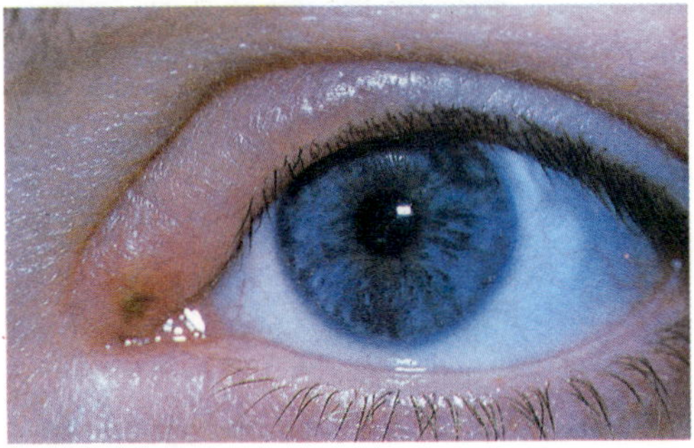

The most common place for a stye to form is near the inner corner of the eye.

SUNBURN

Sunburn is inflammation of the skin which results from overexposure to sunlight.

CAUSES: In sunburn, overexposure to the ultraviolet rays of the sun destroys the top layer of skin cells and damages tiny blood vessels underneath them. Overexposure to a sun lamp has the same effect.

Not all the sun's rays cause burning. Ultraviolet B (UVB) rays are the ones that are responsible. These rays can penetrate cloud to a certain extent, which is why you can still get sunburnt on an overcast day.

Fair-skinned people tend to be most at risk. Melanin, the pigment in the skin responsible for a suntan, gives some protection, but cannot protect the skin if you attempt to get your tan too quickly.

SYMPTOMS AND SIGNS: The symptoms are much as other burns: sore, reddened skin, often with blisters. After a few days, the dead cells will peel away.

There may also be the symptoms of sunstroke; faintness, dizziness and, in extreme cases, high fever.

TREATMENT: Try to avoid getting burnt in the first place (See Self Help). If the sunburn is fairly mild, give the patient paracetamol or aspirin (not for children) to relieve the pain. Calamine lotion or a sunburn cream will help soothe the skin. If the sunburn is severe, contact your doctor. S/he may prescribe a corticosteroid cream to help relieve the symptoms.

See also SUNSTROKE.

ASK THE DOCTOR

SUNBURN

Q Can some drugs make you more sensitive to sunlight?

A Yes, there are drugs that increase sensitivity in some people: for example, oxytetracycline and the oral contraceptive Pill, to name but two.

Self **Help**

SUNBURN

To avoid getting sunburnt:

- Don't overexpose yourself when the sun is at its hottest.
- If your skin isn't used to strong sunlight, break it in gently: about half an hour the first day, and an hour the next would be about right for people with medium complexions. People with very fair skins should take it more gently and those with darker skins can probably stand the sun for longer without suffering any ill-effects.
- Use a good sunscreening cream and shade those areas that are most exposed to the sun.

Sunstroke usually occurs when a person is unaccustomed to a hot climate and stays out in the sun too long.

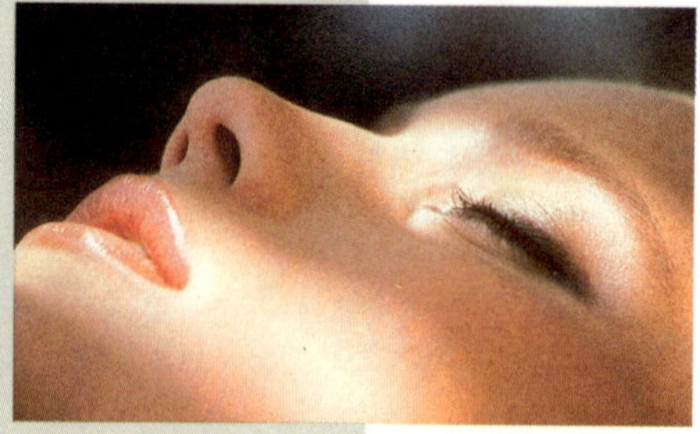

ASK THE DOCTOR

SUNSTROKE

Q Is there any difference between heatstroke and sunstroke?

A No, they are basically the same, except that heatstroke is a reaction to excessive heat rather than the sun's rays. Working in an extremely hot environment out of the sun can produce the same symptoms.

Self **Help**

SYPHILIS

Condoms provide some, but not complete, protection. Because promiscuous people are more at risk, the best way to avoid possible infection is to have a monogamous relationship.

SUNSTROKE

Sunstroke (heatstroke) results when the body becomes dangerously overheated – a condition that can be fatal if not treated promptly.

CAUSES: Overexposure to hot sunlight can result in sunstroke. Two main things happen: excessive sweating causes the body to become dehydrated and the mechanisms with which the body regulates its temperature to break down.

Victims are usually people who are not acclimatised to hot weather. Babies and old people at most at risk. Other factors that increase susceptibility include: overeating, drinking too much alcohol, overstrenuous exercise, and wearing clothing that is too warm for the weather conditions.

SYMPTOMS AND SIGNS: The first signs of impending heatstroke are often those of heat exhaustion. The person turns pale, the skin is cold and clammy. Other symptoms include profuse sweating, weakness, exhaustion, dizziness, headache, rapid pulse and vomiting. When heatstroke develops, the sweating usually slows down, and may stop altogether. The skin will become hot, dry and flushed, the pulse rapid and weak. Other symptoms include headache, weakness and nausea. The temperature may rise to 40°C (104°F) and, finally, the victim may become unconscious.

TREATMENT: This is an emergency, consult a doctor immediately.

Heat exhaustion: The aim is to cool the patient and replace fluids. Lie the patient down in a cool place and remove any warm clothing. Check the temperature and pulse. Fluids should be sipped frequently until the patient is obviously better. While most people will recover with this treatment, it is nonetheless important to call a doctor in case heatstroke develops.

Heatstroke While waiting for the doctor, take the following action:

- Lie the patient down in a cool place. Remove clothing and wrap the patient in sheets or towels which have been soaked in cold water.
- Check the temperature and pulse every five minutes.
- Fan the patient continuously; if you have an electric fan, this is ideal.
- If the patient is conscious, give frequent sips of water.
- When the temperature drops to 38°C (101°F), remove the wet sheets and replace with dry ones.

SYPHILIS

Syphilis is a sexually transmitted disease, now much rarer than it used to be before penicillin was discovered. Almost all sufferers are men, most of them homosexual. There are a very few cases of congenital syphilis, which occurs when a baby's mother has the disease during pregnancy.

CAUSES: You can catch syphilis by having intimate body contact with someone who is infected: this includes oral and anal intercourse, kissing and, in rare cases, touching an infected person with an unnoticed scratch on the hand.

SYMPTOMS AND SIGNS: The disease typically goes through several stages. The first stage

Circular skin lesions in secondary syphilis. Syphilis is treated with antibiotics.

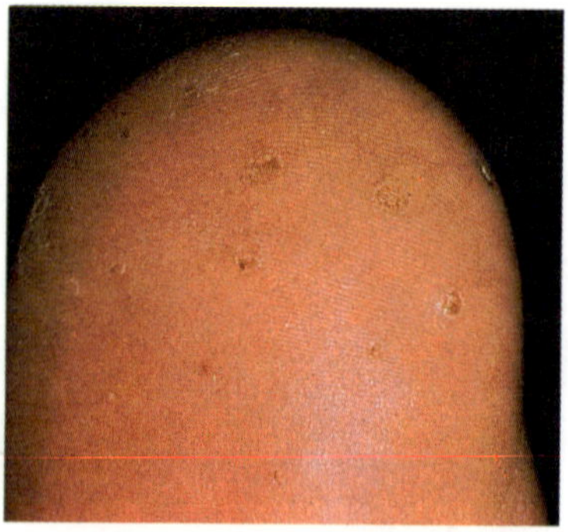

happens three or four weeks after contact: a highly infectious, tiny painless sore with a hard base develops where the infection has entered the body, usually on the penis, anus or vulva, but sometimes on the throat or lips, and very occasionally on the fingers. Because the sore is inconspicuous and heals on its own in four to eight weeks, people often don't seek medical help and the second stage of the disease can start a few weeks later, when a non-itchy rash appears: in white people, this rash consists of crops of pinkish, pale red round spots; while in black people, the rash is pigmented, and appears darker than normal skin. Sometimes, the rash is localised, but usually it appears all over the body, including the soles and palms; this can last a short time or for months, and there may also be a painless swelling in the lymph glands or moist wart-like lumps around the anus or in the armpits. Other symptoms may include loss of appetite, headache, aches and pains, fever and tiredness; meningitis may develop, hair may fall out in clumps, and very infectious thickened grey or pink patches may appear on moist areas of skin. Left untreated, the person may otherwise remain healthy, though a few sufferers will develop tertiary syphilis many years later, which can cause permanent damage to various parts of the body.

TREATMENT: A course of penicillin-based antibiotics is usually effective.

t

TB

see TUBERCULOSIS

TENDINITIS

Tendinitis is an inflammation of a tendon. The fibrous tissue of the tendon becomes inflamed and tender.

CAUSES: It is usually the result of an injury.

SYMPTOMS AND SIGNS: Tendinitis is usually very painful and may restrict certain movements. It most commonly occurs in the tendons around the shoulders, knees and elbows, but it can happen to any tendon.

TREATMENT: Rest the area as much as possible – a strapping may help. If the pain persists, see your doctor. S/he may prescribe painkillers or anti-inflammatory drugs, or occasionally give a corticosteroid injection.

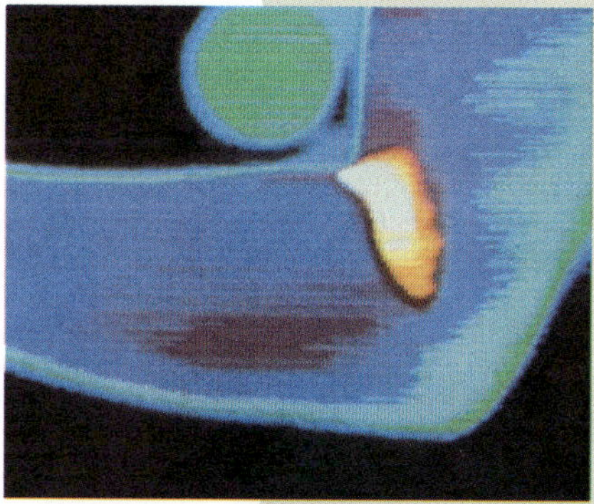

Tendinitis often results from an injury and causes pain and swelling in the affected area.

TENNIS ELBOW

The proper name for this complaint is lateral epicondylitis.

CAUSES: Tennis elbow is caused by an inflammation of the bony area where the tendon that joins the muscles of the forearm joins the humerus (the upper arm bone). Most people know tennis elbow as a racquet sport injury, but tennis and squash are not the only causes. More commonly, it occurs as a result of a repetitive movement, which involves the forearm muscles, and a tight grip – for example, painting ceilings or gardening.

SYMPTOMS AND SIGNS: The pain and tenderness are located on the outside of the

Tennis elbow is often caused by gripping a racquet incorrectly. It can also be caused by activities such as gardening.

elbow and sometimes in the forearm.

TREATMENT: As well as taking painkillers, soothing the pain with an ice-pack and possibly strapping up the injury, you should also try to get to the root of the problem. If the injury is a result of a racquet sport, take a rest from that particular game and analyse your racquet technique. It could be that you are hitting the ball incorrectly, your grip is wrong, or your racquet is too heavy. Ask a professional coach for advice.

TESTICULAR CANCER

Testicular cancer is a malignant tumour of the testicle. It is a fairly rare complaint.

CAUSES: The causes of testicular cancer are not known. The risk is higher in men who have had a problem with undescended testicles, and most cases occur in young to middle-aged men. This form of cancer very seldom occurs before puberty or in old age.

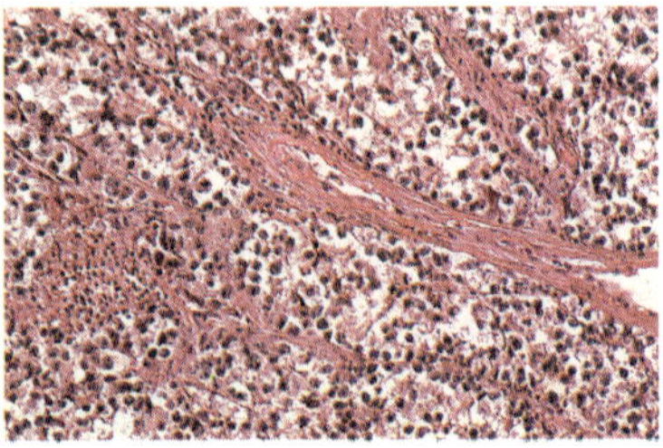

A section through a tumour in a human testicle. Testicular cancer is very rare before puberty.

SYMPTOMS AND SIGNS: The first sign is a painless swelling of one testicle. Occasionally there may be pain and inflammation.

TREATMENT: Unfortunately, the cancer cannot be diagnosed without removing the testicle – an operation referred to as orchidectomy. The doctor will, however, go to great lengths to exclude any other causes of the swelling. If the testicular tissue shows signs of cancer, there will be additional tests to see if the cancer has spread further. Surgery may be followed by radiotherapy and anti-cancer drugs. The outlook following the operation is extremely good – over 95 per cent of patients are completely cured if the disease is caught in the early stages. Even if it is discovered later, the cure rate is high.

To make sure that any abnormalities are detected at an early stage, men should examine their testicles regularly to check for lumps. Care should be taken to feel the entire surface of both testicles.

TETANUS

Tetanus, or 'lockjaw' as it is sometimes called, is a serious, potentially fatal, disease that affects the central nervous system. Fortunately, it is not common in the developed world, where immunisation is extremely effective, but there are about half a million cases a year worldwide, mostly in developing countries.

CAUSES: Tetanus is caused by infection of a wound by the bacterium *Clostridium tetani.* These bacteria live in the soil and animal manure and can also be found in the human intestine, where they live harmlessly. Any cut, particularly one caused by a dirty nail, broken glass, a garden plant or barbed wire, can become infected with the bacteria. The spores of the bacteria enter the wound and multiply in the bloodstream. They also thrive in dead skin or muscles and can survive low-oxygen conditions. The toxins the bacteria produce attack the spinal column and affect the nerves that control muscular activity.

SYMPTOMS AND SIGNS: The first symptoms usually appear six to ten days after the injury, although they can take several months. The head muscles are usually affected first, the jaw becomes stiff (trismus), and the sufferer has difficulty opening his/her mouth, leading to the common name of lockjaw. Gradually other muscles in the face and neck are affected. The lips become tense and drawn back over the teeth, causing a fixed, humourless smile. There may also be a general stiffness of the abdominal and spinal muscles. If the muscles of the throat are affected, the sufferer may have difficulty swallowing. About half the people who catch tetanus suffer even more severe symptoms with spasms in the chest muscles that can cause suffocation. The

ASK THE DOCTOR

TESTICULAR CANCER

Q Does treatment for testicular cancer make a man sterile?

A If the remaining testicle is healthy, treatment with anti-cancer drugs and radiotherapy does not usually cause sterility.

Self **Help**

TETANUS

In western countries, tetanus has almost been eradicated because of successful immunisation programmes. Ensure that all your family are vaccinated against the disease, and that they have regular booster shots every 10 years.

Make sure all wounds, even small ones, are scrupulously clean and always use an antiseptic.

See your doctor about any wound that has dirt ingrained in it, or for a deep puncture wound or animal bite.

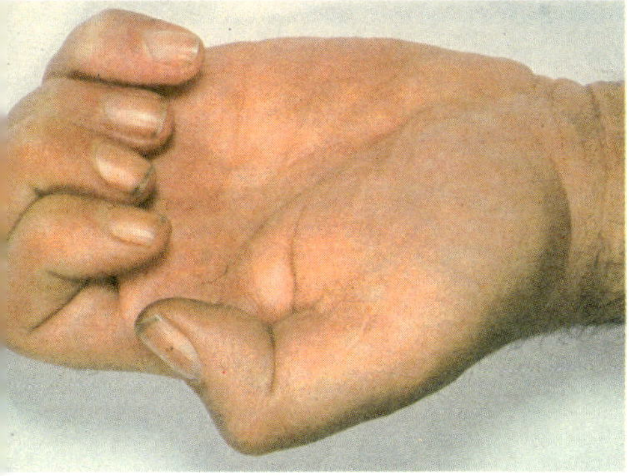

Tetanus can cause the contraction of muscles. In the UK, tetanus is controlled by regular vaccination.

muscles in the back and neck can also go into spasm, causing the back to arch and the head to be forced back. In some cases, the spasms are so severe that they can cause fractured bones. The heart may be affected and there may also be a slight fever, profuse sweating and a weak pulse. It is therefore essential that, if you suspect tetanus, you call your doctor straight away.

TREATMENT: Call your doctor immediately you suspect tetanus. As soon as a diagnosis has been made, the sufferer will be given injections of antitoxin, and tranquillisers to control the muscle spasms. Strong painkillers may also be administered. S/he will probably be moved to a hospital in case of complications. In severe cases, when the sufferer is having difficulty breathing, a surgeon may insert a tube into the sufferer's windpipe (tracheotomy) to enable him/her to breathe or use an artificial ventilator. If his/her heart is affected, drugs will be used to stabilise the condition and circulation problems overcome using a drip. Given prompt treatment, 90 per cent of people make a full recovery within two to three weeks.

THREADWORM

Threadworm is common in children living in temperate areas. An estimated 20 per cent of children in Britain are affected at any one time.

CAUSES: Female worms that inhabit the intestines emerge from the anus, where they lay their eggs. The resultant itching and scratching is the direct cause of reinfestation through the mouth (usually from sucking fingers) and onward into the intestine.

SYMPTOMS AND SIGNS: Some 1cm (⅓ inch) long and visible to the eye, worms may be seen in the faeces or at the opening of the anus, from where samples may be taken for analysis and identification.

TREATMENT: Drugs, available on prescription, are usually effective. It is advisable if all members of the sufferer's family are treated, to ensure complete eradication. Ointment may also be prescribed for anal itching, to break the itch/scratch cycle.

See also ROUNDWORM.

THROAT CANCER

The term throat cancer covers three distinct types of cancer, depending on where the tumour develops in the throat. Cancer of the larynx (voice box) occurs at the bottom of the throat; cancer of the nasopharynx occurs at the top, behind the nose; and cancer of the pharynx involves the central section, starting behind the mouth.

CAUSES: While the exact causes of throat cancer are not known, there seems to be a strong connection between its development and heavy cigarette smoking. High alcohol consumption also seems to be implicated in cancers of the larynx and pharynx.

Apart from cancers of the nasopharynx, which are most common in the 40-45 age group, throat cancers usually occur in the elderly and are particularly prevalent in 60- and 70-year-olds. All forms are more common in men.

SYMPTOMS AND SIGNS: Nearly all patients experience persistent pain, discomfort or irritation in the throat. There may also be general symptoms such as lack of appetite,

ASK THE DOCTOR

TETANUS

Q I was vaccinated against tetanus as a child. Am I still protected?

A Not necessarily. Tetanus vaccinations need to be renewed every 10 years. Your doctor will be able to give you these simple injections in his/her surgery. A course consists of three intramuscular injections – the second one a month after the first, and the final one within the year.

Q My child has a nasty cut on his leg. Could he get tetanus?

A No, providing he has been vaccinated. In the UK, children are routinely given the DPT vaccination against diphtheria, pertussis and tetanus during their first year of life. Your child should have a booster injection before he goes to school, and another when he is about 10. After that, he should renew his protection every 10 years.

Q Does the tetanus vaccination kill the tetanus bacteria?

A No, the vaccination works against the toxin that the bacteria produce, rather than against the bacteria. This is because it is the toxin that causes the problems.

weight loss and an overall feeling of ill-health. Most symptoms, however, depend on the precise site of the tumour.

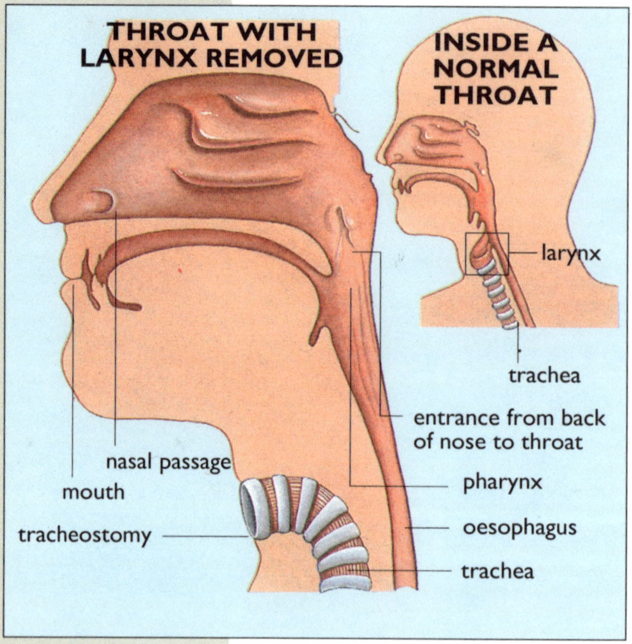

Small tumours on the larynx are often removed by laser surgery. In severe cases, the whole larynx is removed.

ASK THE DOCTOR

THROAT CANCER

Q How does a laryngectomy affect speech?

A After the operation, the patient can no longer speak in the normal fashion. It is possible to use an electronic larynx, which is held against the throat. An alternative is to learn a new way of talking called oesophageal speech. This takes many hours of practice with a speech therapist.

Cancer of the larynx: There is usually persistent hoarseness, and later swallowing and breathing may be difficult. The glands in the throat may swell and become painful, and occasionally the sufferer coughs up blood.

Cancer of the nasopharynx: There are not always symptoms in the early stages. Symptoms may include frequent nose bleeds, bad breath, difficulty in breathing and swallowing, and a pain in the throat, which may spread to the whole of one side of the face.

Cancer of the pharynx: Swallowing is usually difficult, the throat sore and, frequently, there is pain in the ears. The sufferer may cough up blood.

TREATMENT: As with most cancers, the chances of cure depend on early treatment, before the cancer spreads.

Cancer of the larynx Small tumours are usually treated with laser surgery or radiotherapy. Larger tumours may require partial or total laryngectomy, sometimes combined with anti-cancer drugs and radiotherapy.

Cancer of the nasopharynx: Radiotherapy is the usual treatment.

Cancer of the pharynx: The growth may be removed surgically or treated with radiotherapy. Anti-cancer drugs may also be given.

THROMBOSIS

The formation of a thrombus (blood clot).

CAUSES: Normally, when the wall of a blood vessel is damaged, the blood clots. If clotting occurs when the blood vessel isn't damaged, this is considered abnormal. It becomes dangerous when the thrombus blocks an artery, preventing blood and therefore oxygen getting through to where they are needed. If the clot is in the artery leading to the heart, the condition is called coronary thrombosis (heart attack); if it affects an artery which leads to the brain, cerebral thrombosis (stroke) results. Blood clots may occur in almost any part of the body. Thrombosis is more likely to happen if you have been immobile for a long period. Often

Only one branch of this abdominal aorta is visible, as a clot (or thrombus) has blocked the left-hand fork.

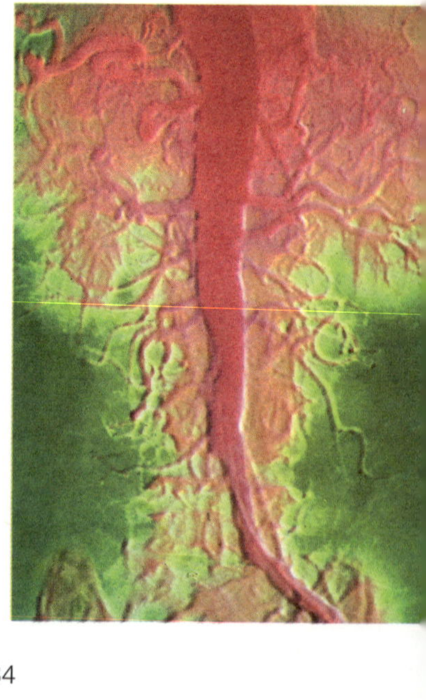

there is no obvious cause, in which case it is assumed that some underlying factor has gone unnoticed, such as some minor damage to a vein. Taking the Pill causes a slightly increased risk of abnormal clotting and therefore of thrombosis.

Symptoms and signs: A thrombus (blood clot) may not cause any symptoms until the part of the body supplied by that vessel begins to malfunction. Thrombosis in a vein may cause pain and swelling in the tissues that drain blood into that vein, due to a build-up of fluid in them.

Treatment: Your doctor may prescribe drugs to dissolve blood clots, anti-inflammatory drugs or drugs to thin the blood.

See also DEEP-VEIN THROMBOSIS, STROKE, HEART ATTACK.

THRUSH

The proper name for thrush is candidiasis. It is a fungal infection that affects mucous membranes – particularly the vagina – inside the mouth or moist skin. Both babies and adults can get thrush.

Causes: It is caused by a yeast-like fungus called *Candida albicans*, which often lives quite harmlessly on the skin or in the vagina. This fungus starts to multiply when your resistance is low, or you have been on a course of antibiotics, which has killed the harmless bacteria that normally live in these areas and suppress fungal growth.

Oral contraceptives, diabetes and hormonal changes in pregnancy may all encourage the growth of this fungus.

Thrush can also be a sexually transmitted infection, which affects more women than men. Penile thrush is fairly rare, but more common in men who haven't been circumcised. Babies sometimes get thrush in the mouth and around the nappy area.

The skin at the base of one of the nails may also become infected with thrush, causing swelling and soreness that may last for weeks. Too much moisture is often responsible for this condition, which tends to develop in people who have their hands in water a great deal, such as bar workers and hairdressers.

Symptoms and signs: Thrush may cause a white, creamy discharge from the vagina, making it itch and causing slight discomfort when passing urine. In men, the head of the penis may become swollen.

Oral thrush produces sore, creamy patches inside the mouth. Thrush in babies may infect the nappy area, causing the skin to look red and itch.

Treatment: Your doctor will probably prescribe an anti-fungal cream and/or pessaries to treat vaginal thrush. To prevent infection, your doctor may recommend that your partner is also treated with anti-fungal cream. Mouth infection is usually treated with anti-fungal drops or lozenges.

TINNITUS

This is an annoying ringing or high-pitched buzzing in the ear, which is particularly noticeable when the sufferer is trying to concentrate.

Causes: You are quite likely to suffer from transient tinnitus if you have been to a very loud rock concert or have been exposed to any other loud noise. Although the tinnitus will usually disappear, there may be a permanent loss of hearing if you suffer from noise-induced tinnitus regularly. It can also be the result of an ear complaint or simply because of a build-up of ear wax. A head injury or a reaction to certain drugs may also bring on tinnitus. It is much less likely that your tinnitus is a result of an aneurysm or tumour constricting the blood vessels in the brain, although this is a possibility.

Symptoms and signs: Sometimes, the ringing in your ears will be more or less constant, although you may not always be fully aware of it. Some people find the noise intolerable, whereas others simply learn to live with it.

Treatment: If there is an underlying problem that is causing your tinnitus, it will be treated separately – for example, wax may be syringed out of your ears. Long-term sufferers use other

Self **Help**

THRUSH

Women who use oral contraceptives and suffer repeatedly from vaginal thrush should consult their doctor. It could be that a change to a different method of contraception may be advisable.

If you are susceptible to thrush infection of the nails, make sure you keep your hands as dry as possible by wearing rubber gloves when putting your hands in water, and drying them thoroughly after washing.

VAGINAL THRUSH:

- Don't sit in hot baths.
- Don't sit on the edge of your chair at work, sit well back on your chair to let the vaginal orifice breathe.
- Don't drink alcohol, or eat chocolates or sweets.
- Avoid tight clothing and nylon underwear.
- Maintain a high level of personal cleanliness.
- Don't swim regularly in chlorinated water.

Self **Help**

TONSILLITIS

If your child suffers from tronsillitis:

- Keep the child indoors.
- Offer plenty of fluids and paracetamol to reduce fever and ease pain.
- Allow him/her to eat cooling desserts if s/he finds it helps, while a cooling fan may help reduce temperature.
- As tonsillitis is highly contagious, keep him/her away from other children until s/he is better.

ASK THE DOCTOR

TOXIC SHOCK SYNDROME

Q Should I stop using tampons to avoid this disease?

A The number of women who have suffered from this condition is very small and millions of women continue to use tampons with no adverse effect. It is important to change tampons regularly. The disease seems to develop suddenly on the fourth day of a period so, if you are concerned, use an external form of sanitary pad during the later stages of your period.

noises, such as music, to block out the tinnitus. Some find that it helps to listen to a specially prepared, random collection of sounds on a tape when they are trying to fall asleep.

TONSILLITIS

Tonsillitis is an inflammation of the tonsils due to infection. It is a common childhood complaint.

CAUSES: Tonsils are there to protect the upper respiratory tract from infection by trapping and destroying micro-organisms. Sometimes they too become infected by the

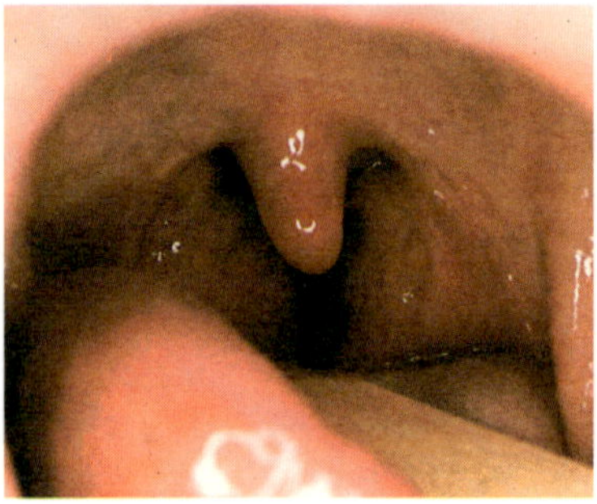

Examination of the throat will soon lead to a diagnosis of tonsillitis.

micro-organisms. Tonsillitis is most common in children under nine, although it occasionally occurs in adolescents and young adults. When it does occur in adulthood, the symptoms are usually more severe.

SYMPTOMS AND SIGNS: The throat becomes sore and inflamed and there is often difficulty in swallowing. There may also be other symptoms such as fever, headache, earache and swollen neck glands. There may be temporary deafness. If symptoms persist for more than 24 hours, or if there is pus visible on the tonsils, consult your doctor.

TREATMENT: If the infection is thought to be bacterial, the doctor will prescribe a course of antibiotics. If the child suffers from repeated severe sore throats, his/her tonsils may have to be surgically removed (tonsillectomy), though this operation is now viewed by doctors as a last resort.

TOOTH ABSCESS

see DENTAL ABSCESS

TOXIC SHOCK SYNDROME

Toxic shock syndrome is a rare and relatively new disease, which affects mostly women, usually during the course of a period.

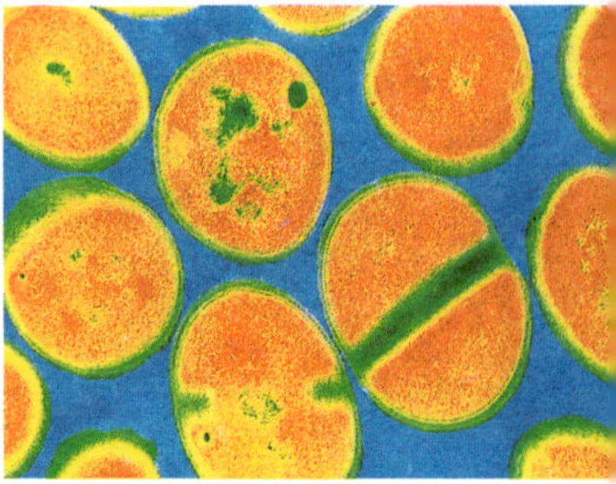

A colony of Staphylococcus aureus, *the toxin that causes toxic shock syndrome.*

CAUSES: Toxic shock syndrome is caused by a toxin produced by the bacterium *Staphylococcus aureus.* It has been suggested that the use of tampons during periods may be a contributory factor, especially if a tampon is left in by mistake for a few days. This syndrome has also occurred after minor skin surgery, due to contamination of the wound.

SYMPTOMS AND SIGNS: High fever, low blood pressure, a skin rash on the palms, soles and fingers (the skin usually peels off after about two weeks). Other symptoms can include aching muscles, abdominal pain, diarrhoea and nausea. It can lead to kidney and liver failure.

TREATMENT: Treatment is with antibiotic drugs to kill the bacteria. Intravenous fluid replacement is often given to maintain normal blood pressure until the infection is under control. Other problems that may arise are treated as they occur. Most sufferers recover fully after about 10 days. However, the mortality rate is about two or three per cent and is mainly due to liver, kidney and lung complications.

TRAVEL SICKNESS

Travel sickness is a condition that some people suffer from when they're in a moving car, or on a ship or aircraft.

CAUSES: The physical cause is that the balance of the inner ear is disturbed by repeated, pronounced movement. People can also suffer when the atmosphere inside the car is stuffy or fume-laden; if they've eaten a lot just before the journey; if they're worried about repeating previous attacks; or if they focus on something nearby such as a book or map.

Because someone complaining of travel sickness can sometimes have his/her mind taken off it, or even feel sick before a journey, the cause is often thought to be psychological and, while this might well be true in some cases, it doesn't explain why babies and animals can also suffer.

SYMPTOMS AND SIGNS: Symptoms can range from mild discomfort and a headache to excessive sweating, nausea and vomiting.

TREATMENT: You can buy various preparations over the counter at the chemist to try to prevent the condition, though if you're driving, remember that some tablets may make you feel drowsy and increase the effect of any alcohol you drink.

Motion sickness can make it difficult to travel by plane, car or boat.

TRICHOMONIASIS

Trichomoniasis is usually sexually transmitted. If you have it, be sure to tell your partner.

Trichomoniasis is a genital infection, most common in women. Sometimes it is transmitted from a mother to her baby during childbirth.

CAUSES: The infection is usually sexually transmitted but you can also catch it indirectly, perhaps from an infected towel.

SYMPTOMS AND SIGNS: A woman's vagina and vulva may become painfully inflamed, and there is often a heavy, yellowish frothy discharge which smells very unpleasant; the organism that causes trichomoniasis can stay in the vagina for years without causing any symptoms. Men hardly ever have symptoms, although a few might notice some urethral discomfort and discharge.

TREATMENT: If you suspect you might have trichomoniasis, go to your doctor or local GU (genito-urinary) clinic: diagnosis will be made from a sample of the discharge or from a swab taken from your urethra. You will be prescribed antibiotics, which should clear up the condition quite quickly.

Self Help

TRAVEL SICKNESS

It's best to be somewhere in the middle of a ship or aeroplane, because that's where the see-saw motion will be least violent. On a ship, concentrate on horizon, but not through a porthole as you'll find the conflict of sensation between a horizontal deck and a moving horizon makes the sickness worse. In an aeroplane, adjust your seat to the upright position and tilt your head back to minimise the disturbance to your ears; in a car, use a headrest if possible. Eating little and often is better than going without food altogether.

ASK THE DOCTOR

TRICHOMONIASIS

Q Should I tell my boyfriend that I have trichomoniasis?

A Yes. He should also be examined and treated, to prevent re-infection.

Self Help

TUBERCULOSIS

If you are diagnosed as having TB, it is important to complete the long course of antibiotics prescribed, even if you feel better quickly. Eat a sensible and healthy diet and take plenty of rest. Do not attempt to return to your normal routine until advised to do so by a doctor.
It is important to be vaccinated against the disease. A BCG vaccination is routinely administered in Britain at about the age of 13, to people whose tuberculin test shows no natural immunity. Vaccination in the upper arm leaves a small pustule, which gradually recedes to form a scar. Even if you have been vaccinated, consult your doctor if you have been in contact with TB.

Useful Addresses

TUBERCULOSIS

British Thoracic Society
1 St. Andrew's Place
Regent's Park
LONDON NW1 4LB
071 486 7766

The Chest, Heart and Stroke Association
CHSA House
White Cross Street
LONDON EC1Y 8JJ
Tel. 071 490 7999

TUBERCULOSIS

Tuberculosis (TB) is a bacterial disease, which is best known for attacking the lungs, although it can affect other parts of the body.
CAUSES: TB is caused by a bacterium called *Mycobacterium tuberculosis*. The TB germ cannot divide more quickly than once a day, whereas many bacteria divide once every 10 or 20 minutes. This slow multiplication of the germ means the illness tends to come on slowly and last for a considerable time; treatment must be continued for at least four months.

TB is usually transmitted from person to person through the air. A common source of infection is close contact with someone who has lung TB and is coughing up sputum full of TB bacteria. This can lead to infection, not only in those with no immunity but also in those whose antibodies cannot cope with large numbers of inhaled bacteria. This is why the disease is more prevalent in overcrowded conditions.

SYMPTOMS AND SIGNS: Symptoms may be rather vague at first. The patient may complain of a poor appetite, loss of weight and feeling generally under the weather. After a while, a fever may develop which is usually worse at night.

If TB is in the lungs, a cough develops which gradually worsens, and sputum starts being produced. Even at this stage, many patients do not go to the doctor unless they begin to cough up blood – and this is something that may never happen, even in an advanced case. This coughing is caused by the lung being damaged by a small abscess, known as a tubercle.

Lung tuberculosis is diagnosed with a chest X-ray, sputum analysis and skin tests. Lungs can develop cavities and old areas of infection may show up as shadow on an X-ray. Occasionally, bronchoscopy and biopsy (the removal and examination of a piece of tissue) may be necessary. TB in other parts of the body can go undetected because the symptoms are not specific – for example, a few swollen lymph glands.

False-colour X-ray of someone's chest who is suffering from tuberculosis. The right lung (left) is more heavily affected than the left.

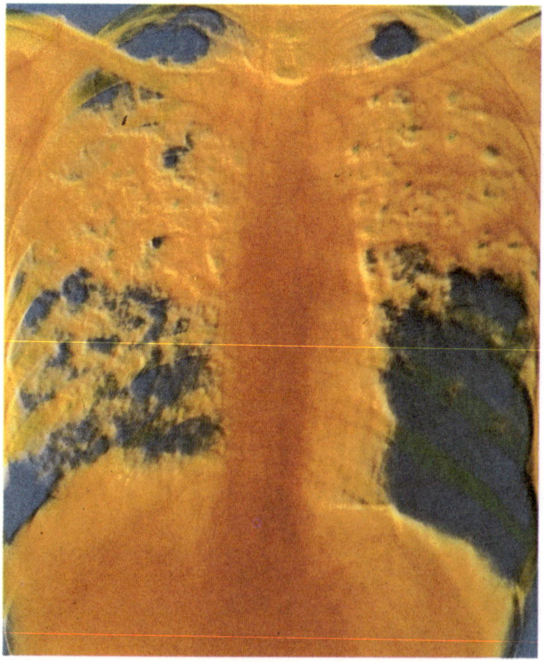

TREATMENT: Patients may be admitted to hospital. A course of antibiotics is started. Sometimes, if the patient is very ill, treatment may be started before the diagnosis has been confirmed. Only patients who have TB of the lung and are coughing up infected sputum are infectious. Close contacts of the sufferer will be invited to be examined, X-rayed and given a tuberculin test. Once treatment is underway, the patient will soon stop being infectious; providing s/he takes the antibiotics regularly.

TYPHOID

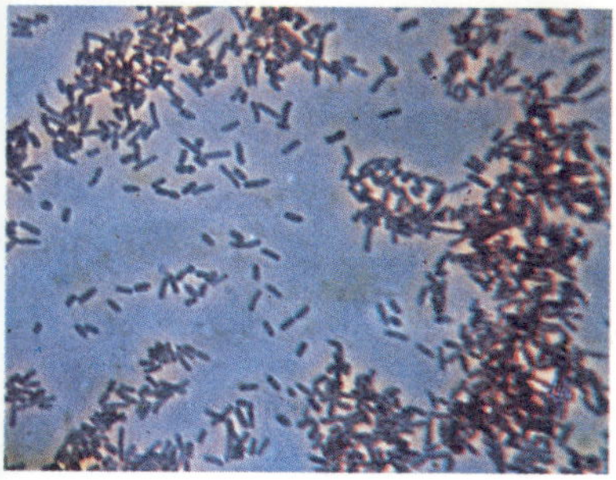

The typhoid bacteria, Salmonella typhosa, *which spreads through contaminated food and water.*

Typhoid is a contagious disease that spreads under insanitary conditions. It is very rare in the developed world.

CAUSES: Typhoid spreads through water from contaminated sewage systems and food that has been contaminated by flies, which spread the disease from infected faeces. Typhoid can also be carried by people who do not present any symptoms, but who infect others through handling food.

SYMPTOMS AND SIGNS: At first, the disease resembles flu but is far worse. There is a very high temperature (about 40°C/104°F), weakness and delirium. The patient may initially be constipated, but this will gradually change to diarrhoea. A pink rash on the abdomen may appear, but this fades as the disease progresses.

TREATMENT: If you have suspected typhoid in Britain, you will be kept in isolation in hospital. The doctor will confirm diagnosis by taking a sample of blood, faeces or urine for laboratory analysis. A course of antibiotics will be prescribed and after three or four weeks, you will be allowed home. If you are diagnosed swiftly and obtain treatment, you are unlikely to suffer from further complications. However, if you are severely ill there may be complications, and you may need a supplementary treatment with corticosteroid drugs. If you develop severe intestinal bleeding or peritonitis, surgery will be necessary.

U

ULCER

see CORNEAL ULCER, PEPTIC ULCER

ULCERATED CORNEA

see CORNEAL ULCER

ULCERATIVE COLITIS

Sometimes called inflammatory bowel disease, ulcerative colitis is a chronic inflammation of the rectum and large bowel (colon). The mucus lining of the bowel becomes damaged and, in extreme cases, the complaint can be life-threatening. Once contracted, the condition persists for life.

CAUSES: The precise cause of the inflammation is not yet known, although research suggests there may be some inborn deficiency in the patient's bowel, so the normal protection against certain germs is lost. Studies have been made – largely inconclusive – into the theory that the disease is the result of a slow-growing virus.

SYMPTOMS AND SIGNS: The onset of diarrhoea mixed with mucus and blood (from the damaged lining of the colon) is one of the first symptoms. The sufferer may also experience gripping abdominal pains, although these do not always occur. Usually, the symptoms last several days or even weeks, then disappear to recur at a later date. A severe attack can make a person very ill indeed, as bouts of diarrhoea can occur many times a day with resulting dehydration and loss of vital salts from the body.

TREATMENT: Once diagnosed, mild attacks can be effectively controlled with steroid drugs administered directly to the bowel by enema or suppository. Further treatment with drugs maintains freedom from symptoms, but these may have to be taken indefinitely. Long-term ulcerative colitis increases

Self **Help**

TYPHOID

Before going abroad to anywhere outside Europe, such as North America, Australia or New Zealand, consult a travel clinic about vaccinations well in advance. Often a typhoid vaccination will be recommended. You must have two injections, about 10-28 days apart. There will be a swelling around the area injected for a few days afterwards and it may ache and feel sore. Some people develop mild flu-like symptoms for a few days after vaccination. Protection starts immediately after the second injection, but you will require a booster injection against typhoid three years later if you are going abroad again.

Useful Addresses

TYPHOID

London School of Tropical Medicine
Keppel Street
LONDON WC1E 7HT
071 636 8636

Helpline
071 636 7921

Useful Addresses

ULCERATIVE COLITIS

Ileostomy Association of
Great Britain and Ireland
Amblehurst House
Black Scotch Lane
MANSFIELD
Notts NG18 4PF
0623 28099

National Association for
Colitis and Crohn's Disease
98a London Road
ST ALBANS
Herts AL1 1NX
0727 44296

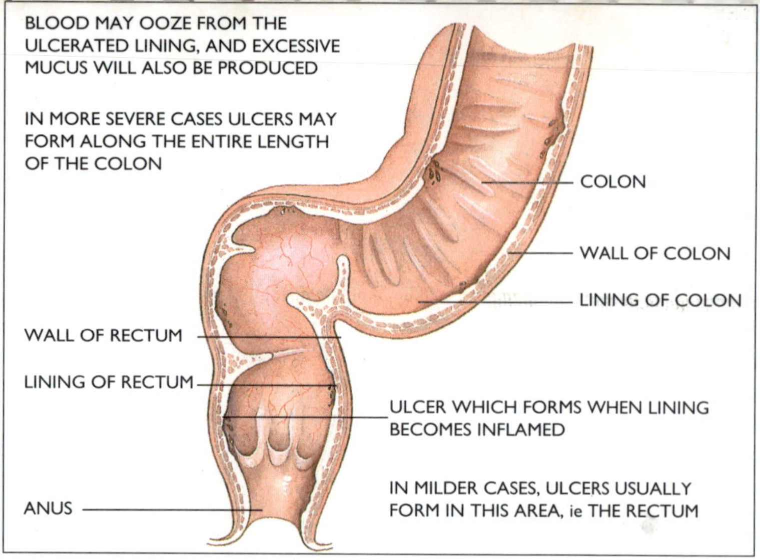

Cross-section of the colon, showing where ulcerative colitis is likely to occur.

the chances of bowel cancer. This and very severe attacks may only be relieved by surgery, where the colon is removed.

URTICARIA

see HIVES

UTERINE CANCER

Uterine cancer is a malignant growth in the lining of the uterus (the endometrium).

CAUSES: Uterine cancer is more common in women who are childless, post-menopausal, who have a late menopause or who have a history of irregular periods. The long-term taking of oestrogen hormones, without progesterone, increases the risk. The use of oral contraceptives lowers the chances of uterine cancer developing.

SYMPTOMS AND SIGNS: The main symptom is unexpected vaginal bleeding. There may be bleeding after sexual intercourse, and periods may be especially heavy. Sometimes the bleeding is in the form of an offensive-smelling brown discharge.

TREATMENT: Any unexpected bleeding should be reported immediately to your doctor. Remember, these symptoms do not necessarily mean the presence of cancer – many other benign conditions have similar bleeding patterns.

If cancer is diagnosed, you will usually need a hysterectomy. Sometimes the lymph nodes in the abdomen and pelvis are also removed. If the cancer has spread, radiotherapy and anti-cancer drugs may also be used.

ASK THE DOCTOR

UTERINE CANCER

Q Will I find sexual intercourse as pleasurable after I've had a hysterectomy?

A Yes you will. There is absolutely no need to worry about this.

v

VAGINISMUS

Vaginismus is a tensing of the muscles around the entrance to the vagina, making penetration difficult or impossible.

CAUSES: Fear is the major cause, and this can be due to several factors. A woman who has not yet had sex may have had trouble trying to insert a tampon or even her fingers and so be worried that penetration during intercourse will be painful; she might have undergone a traumatic experience like rape or sexual abuse; or be suffering from vaginitis (inflammation of the vagina), which has made intercourse painful in the past. A restrictive upbringing or lack of sex education could also be a contributing factor, as could tension in her relationship with her partner.

Symptoms and signs: As soon as penetration is attempted, the woman's pelvic floor muscles tighten, closing the vaginal entrance.

Treatment: This condition can be cured, with medical help. A doctor will examine the woman to make sure there is no physical abnormality causing the pain; s/he will also rule out the possibility of an infection. If vaginismus is diagnosed, the doctor may talk to the woman about her relationship in general and usually she will be shown how gently to introduce a series of graded dilators into her vagina, relaxing and tightening her vaginal muscles while the dilator is inside her. The first of these will be as narrow as a pencil and they will graduate until she is comfortable with one the size of an average erect penis. Nearly always, sexual intercourse is no longer a problem after this treatment.

See also DYSPAREUNIA.

VARICOSE VEINS

Enlarged or twisted veins that lie just under the skin.

Causes: As the blood circulates around the body, it has to travel up the veins in the legs and then passes through connecting veins back to the heart. Muscles in the legs contract, pumping the blood upwards. To stop it flowing back, due to the effect of gravity, there are valves in the leg veins. When these valves become damaged, the distribution of blood becomes uneven and it begins to collect in pools, causing the lumpy effect of varicose veins.

Obese people are more likely to get varicose veins, as are pregnant women and women who have reached the menopause. Those who spend a lot of time on their feet are also more likely to get the condition. They are hereditary and quite common.

Symptoms and signs: Varicose veins usually occur on the backs of the calves and inside the thighs. They are blue, raised and slightly bumpy. They may ache and often become worse prior to menstruation.

Treatment: If you suffer from varicose veins, you may only need to wear support stockings to relieve the ache. Make sure you don't spend long periods of time standing still, try to sit with you feet up and take regular walks. If your varicose veins are particularly bad, your doctor may recommend a therapy called sclerotherapy, which shrinks the damaged veins and diverts the blood to a healthy vein. In rare cases varicose veins are operated on and the whole vein may be extracted.

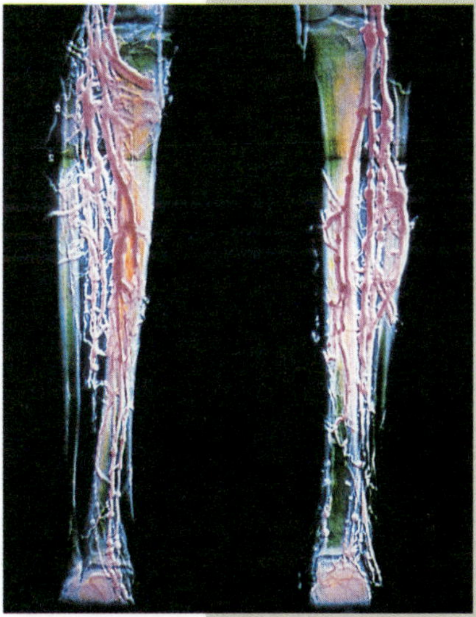

About 15 per cent of adults develop varicose veins. Varicose veins are seen on this false-colour venogram as knots of colour.

VERRUCA

Verrucas (plantar warts) are warts on the sole of the foot. They may occur singly or in clusters, and may be painful.

Causes: All warts are caused by a virus. They are usually caught from contaminated floors, at communal showers or swimming pools, for example.

Symptoms and signs: The first sign is probably a small white or flesh-coloured growth on the sole of the foot. It will be hard and horny. Inside, it will resemble tiny black splinters, caused by small blood vessels just under the surface of the skin.

Treatment: Many verrucas disappear without any treatment, leaving you immune to future infection. Some, however, may need a little encouragement. Corrosive paints can be bought from chemists and these destroy the infected tissue. If your wart still persists, consult your doctor. S/he may prescribe a gel to apply each day with an abraser to remove the dead skin over the wart. Occasionally, freezing treatment or a laser is used to remove the verruca.

See also WARTS.

ASK THE DOCTOR

VAGINISMUS

Q I have plucked up my courage to visit the doctor about my fear of penetration, but I'm worried that I will close up when he tries to examine me. What will happen if I do?

A Don't worry, your doctor will be quite prepared for this. If he cannot carry out an examination, even with the help of lubricating jelly, he may suggest it is done under anaesthetic.

ASK THE DOCTOR

WHITLOW

Q Why are people who put their hands in water frequently prone to whitlows?

A Because the natural protective oils are washed out of the skin, allowing bacteria or viruses to get into the pores very easily.

ASK THE DOCTOR

WHOOPING COUGH

Q Why does whooping cough come in epidemics?

A Every three to four years a new strain of bacteria evolves against which the population has less immunity. Also, the number of cases is linked to the number of babies immunised.

VERTIGO

Vertigo is the sensation that everything is spinning. It may be associated with nausea, vomiting and loss of balance.

CAUSES: Vertigo is usually caused by a transient viral infection in the semicircular canals of the inner ear (labyrinthitis), or a disturbance in the nerves that lead to them. It can also be caused by fairground rides and some sporting activities, such as sailing. In most cases it is only a temporary condition. It is only rarely caused by a significant underlying disorder. Vertigo can also be the symptom of Ménière's disease (a disease of the inner ear). Elderly people suffering from atherosclerosis sometimes experience bouts of vertigo and it can also be caused by psychological conditions.

SYMPTOMS AND SIGNS: A spinning feeling, nausea and loss of balance.

TREATMENT: If possible, lie down until the dizziness and nausea pass. If the symptoms persist, see your doctor. S/he may prescribe antihistamines to control symptoms or prevent recurrent attacks.

Vertigo is commonly experienced at the top of high buildings, on bridges and see-through walkways.

w

WARTS

Warts are harmless growths on the skin or mucous membrane. They can grow up to 6mm (⅜ inch) in diameter. They often have a rough, cauliflower-like surface and may have small, black splinter-like dots.

CAUSES: All warts are caused by a virus. The virus is contagious and is spread by touch or through contact with a wart's shed skin.

SYMPTOMS AND SIGNS: The first sign of a wart is usually a small, horny lump, often on the hands, face, scalp or knees, although they can grow on any part of the body.

TREATMENT: Warts are harmless and will probably disappear on their own in time. However, you can remove them. Proprietary brands of wart removers are available from most chemists and, with repeated applications, should remove even the most stubborn warts. Never use such treatment on your face or genitals. See your doctor if you have warts in these areas or if warts in other areas refuse to budge, even after several weeks of self-treatment. S/he may use laser treatment or cryosurgery (using liquid nitrogen to freeze the wart).

See also GENITAL WARTS, VERRUCA.

WATER RETENTION

see FLUID RETENTION.

WHITLOW

A pus-filled abscess or boil on the fingertip, usually next to the nail.

CAUSES: Whitlows can be caused by a virus or by a bacterium that enters the body through a cut. They particularly tend to occur on people who spend a lot of time with their hands in water.

SYMPTOMS AND SIGNS: The finger around the nail swells and is painful to touch. A blister of pus may develop alongside the nail. In

a more serious infection, the symptoms are similar but more pronounced and often the skin around the nail is also affected.

TREATMENT: Whitlows caused by bacterial infection can be treated with antibiotics and, if necessary, by lancing. A viral infection is treated with special antiviral drugs.

WHOOPING COUGH

Whooping cough is a bacterial infection of the respiratory system that usually affects children. Being extremely contagious, the disease spreads quickly, often reaching epidemic proportions every three or four years. It can be dangerous to small babies and may cause death due to lung congestion or pneumonia. Whooping cough can be prevented by immunisation in infancy, in the form of the 'triple vaccine' – diphtheria, tetanus and whooping cough.

CAUSES: Infection comes from airborne bacteria, *Bordetella pertussis*, after close contact with a sufferer. The bacteria invade the nasal passages, respiratory tract and lungs, which produce a thick, sticky mucus in an effort to combat the invasion.

SYMPTOMS AND SIGNS: The incubation period is from one to three weeks, when the sufferer will exhibit signs of the common cold. At this point, the sufferer is most contagious. A cough develops as the lungs become congested. This can last from two to 10 weeks and infection can be identified by the characteristic 'whoop' sound as the sufferer coughs to try to eject the mucus from the lungs. Coughing fits can occur up to 40 times a day and are 'paroxysmal' – violent and often leading to momentary loss of breath and vomiting. Babies who cannot cough up this mucus are most at risk at this time.

TREATMENT: If the disease is identified early enough, antibiotics can be given which should make the symptoms less severe. They will not prevent the infection from taking its course. After the disease has established itself, drugs are primarily to stop the infection passing to others. The sufferer should be kept as warm and as comfortable as possible – especially during coughing fits – and fed small meals to prevent vomiting. Keep away from tobacco smoke and draughts which can provoke coughing. Serious cases are admitted to hospital, where oxygen is administered to help breathing.

Z

ZOONOSIS

Diseases that can be transmitted from animals to humans are known medically as zoonoses.

CAUSES: Zoonoses are most commonly caught from pets or via animals used as food sources. Pet bites or contact with animal faeces present particular risks. Insufficiently cooked chicken or, more rarely, eggs can result in salmonella infections. In rare cases, zoonoses can be caught through bites from scavengers, such as rats, that transmit the disease leptospirosis.

SYMPTOMS AND SIGNS: Fungal infections will appear as a rash, or areas of reddened skin which may blister. Mites caught from pets will cause severe itching. Salmonella poisoning induces headache, severe vomiting and diarrhoea, and sometimes fever.

TREATMENT: Treatments vary according to the type of zoonosis which has been contracted.

One of the most common zoonoses is toxocariasis, which is transmitted by small worms that live in a dog's intestines and can cause blindness.

Self **Help**

ZOONOSIS

The most common cause of zoonosis in developed countries is food poisoning due to poor food hygiene. Make sure that kitchen surfaces and implements are clean, and that raw and cooked meats are not stored together. Check sell-by dates in shop-brought products, particularly poultry.

PICTURE ACKNOWLEDGEMENTS

All situation pictures are posed by models.
The publishers would like to thank the following picture agencies and libraries:

Front cover Tony Stone Worldwide; Lorna Ainger; Art Directions; Clive Barda/London; Bubbles; Camera Press; Robert Harding; Image Bank; Mondadori; National Medical Slide Bank; Science Photo Library; Winsor Fox Photos; Zefa.